THE FOUR STAGES OF RABBINIC JUDAISM

Defined as the Judaism built on the story of God's revelation to Moses of the Torah at Sinai, Rabbinic Judaism is a book-religion. In this volume, Jacob Neusner outlines and examines the four stages in which the initial period of the historical development of Rabbinic Judaism divides, beginning with the Pentateuch and ending with its definitive and normative statement in the Talmud of Babylonia. He traces the development of Rabbinic Judaism by exploring the relationships between and among the cognate writings which embody its formative history.

This concise yet comprehensive volume provides a lucid introduction to the genesis and development of Rabbinic Judaism.

Jacob Neusner is Distinguished Research Professor of Religious Studies at the University of South Florida and Professor of Religion at Bard College, New York. He is the author of numerous publications, the most recent being *The Intellectual Foundations of Christian and Jewish Discourse*.

THE FOUR STAGES OF RABBINIC JUDAISM

Jacob Neusner

London and New York

First published 1999
by Routledge
11 New Fetter Lane, London EC4P 4EE

Simultaneously published in the USA and Canada
by Routledge
29 West 35th Street, New York, NY 10001

Typeset in Garamond by Routledge
Printed and bound in Great Britain by Page Bros (Norwich) Ltd

British Library Cataloguing in Publication Data
A catalogue record for this book is available from the British Library

Library of Congress Cataloging in Publication Data
Neusner, Jacob
The four stages of rabbinic judaism/Jacob Neusner
Includes bibliographical references and data
1. Judaism–History–To 70 A.D.
2. Judaism–History–Talmudic period, 10–425.
3. Bible. O.T. Pentateuch–Theology.
Rabbinical literature–History and criticism.
I. Title
BM165.N38 199998-44400
296'.09'015–dc21

ISBN 0–415–19530–6 (hbk)
ISBN 0–415–19531–4 (pbk)

CONTENTS

PREFACE

If God makes himself known through a revelation recorded in words in a book, then the religion consequent upon that revelation will reach its principal statement in books. For that, by God's own word, is where the faithful meet God. Rabbinic Judaism is a book religion defined as the Judaism built on the story of God's revelation to Moses of the Torah at Sinai in two media – writing and oral formulation and oral transmission in memory. That Judaism meets God in the record of God's self-revelation in the Torah, or Teaching, given at Sinai through Moses to holy Israel.[1] In this book we follow the four stages in which the initial period of its historical development divides, beginning with the Pentateuch and ending with its definitive and normative statement in the Talmud of Babylonia a thousand years later.

We trace the stages of that development, appropriately, through relationships between and among the cognate writings embodying that formative history. What other medium could better – more fittingly – have served a religion than that which through writing in particular records, hands on, and recapitulates the encounter with God? If in this Judaism, the faithful meet God in the Torah, consider, in the same framework of monotheism the alternative to a book-religion. This particular Judaism does not come from the seal of prophecy and a unique prophet or messiah, as do Islam and Christianity, who record God's words spoken to the Prophet, in the case of Islam, and the deeds and teachings of Jesus Christ, in the case of Christianity. By contrast, Rabbinic Judaism represents itself as the record of revelation preserved and handed on by a chain of tradition of learning formed by men qualified by learning through discipleship. To underscore their subordination within the process of collective tradition – in our terms, book-making – sages always called themselves "disciples of sages." None celebrated himself. To contribute to the tradition required the completely anonymous acceptance of a particular sage's tradition or viewpoint. So too the holy books are represented as the written tradition formed by the consensus of the masters of ancient traditions and their interpretation and application: no single figure forms a counterpart to the Prophet or to Christ.

While Islam focused uniquely upon the teaching and recording of the verbatim revelation by God to the Prophet and Christianity focused upon narratives of Christ, God's son, Rabbinic Judaism produced and preserved neither the distinctive and singular record of a particular sage nor books ("Gospels") about named sages. It set forth, rather, the collective and coherent statement of the collegium of sages, who together spoke for the tradition, or Torah, of Sinai. And, instead of stories of God's revelation to the prophet or narratives of Jesus Christ as God's only begotten son, in the language of Christianity, predictably, the narratives of particular rabbis conventionally record how a given figure entered the chain of tradition. Each begins as a disciple of a master, then himself becomes a master to the next generation of disciples, in a long chain of learning. So the media of Rabbinic Judaism represent a book-religion, and it is reasonable, then, to trace the formation of that Judaism through the books, or completed documents, that constitute its authoritative records.

If the testimonies to that religion – the way we know about it – consist of the record of a chain of tradition preserved in books and books alone, what is to be said about its social forms? The institutions of that religion are its schools, its authorities and its teachers. The holy man is a living book, and the master of tradition or of reasoning in tradition is highly valued. Material culture does not contribute much to our knowledge. Archaeology, now well advanced in the study of the Jews of the Land of Israel in the period at hand, has yet to turn up characteristic buildings of this Judaism – school houses, for example. The numerous synagogues that have emerged from the dirt rarely give evidence of conformity with the decorative and artistic norms that we find in the rabbis' writings. True, there is evidence of rabbis' burial places – but not their study halls or domestic establishments. Outside observers, whether pagan or Christian, writing about Judaism, rarely show detailed and systematic knowledge of the teachings of the rabbis. Were we to depend upon even their engaged critics and enemies among the Church Fathers, for example, we should find the reconstruction of the rabbis' principal beliefs and indicative practises difficult. So Rabbinic Judaism is a religion that we know from its own books alone, and so far as we wish to know how it took shape, the writings provide whatever history we shall have.

Paganism, for its part, forms the opposite of a religion known only through its writings. It presents us with a vast religious world attested not only through literary but also through archaeological evidence, inscriptions and even graffiti for example. We meet paganism not only in the arcane writings of its own virtuosi but also in the observations of outsiders, on the one side, and the reflections of the faithful who were not religious specialists, on the other. We know Judaism through words but paganism through pictures, sculpture, the detritus of a vital material culture. The great historian of pagan and Christian religion in late antiquity, Ramsay MacMullen, writes of paganism:

> This religion had no single center, spokesman, director, or definition of itself; therefore no one point of vulnerability. Everyone was free to choose his own credo; anyone who wished could consult a priest or ignore a priest, about how best to appeal to the divine. Appeal found expression in a great variety of words, acts, and arts, which...had been woven into the deepest levels of daily life and culture, the secular included....Not only motifs but people circulated everywhere – meaning worshipers with their religious ideas. Over the course of many hundreds of years of peaceful stirring about, the mix became constantly more complex and intimate, at least in urban settings. Variety itself became a characteristic binding together the whole fabric of religion into one whole, across space, as on the other hand, the long peace of the pax Romana had bound communities also to their past.[2]

MacMullen underscores "the variety of words, acts, and arts." Imagine, then, the layers upon layers of historically valuable information paganism affords, the diversity of evidence and viewpoints represented by that evidence, the institutional diffusion, the variety of media of religious encounter and expression, by contrast to the singular corpus of evidence that represents Rabbinic Judaism in its formative age. But the reason should not be lost: Rabbinic Judaism offered the encounter with God through the Torah, and from that indicative conviction all else followed.

MacMullen makes another point that affords perspective on our subject. He argues with great effect that paganism survived many centuries of the Christian challenge because it had no one point of vulnerability. And so did Judaism. The tenacity of paganism gives us a standpoint from which to see Rabbinic Judaism, which, long after its formative age, would retain the active and stubborn loyalty of the greater part of the Jewish people, and which even today defines the character of Judaism for the vast majority of Jews who practice that religion in any form. But the basis for Rabbinic Judaism's power to resist the Christian and later Islamic challenge is not that it had no one point of vulnerability, but the intangible, if not at all inchoate, character of its sustaining power, its generative conviction. For if we ask, did Rabbinic Judaism in its formative age possess a single center, spokesman, director, or definition of itself? The answer is self-evident: of course it did. But it was not a locative center: take that, and all else falls. It was utopian. And it was not a center formed by an institution. Destroy that, and all else is lost. Its center was its books, Scripture, and the oral tradition sages themselves received from Sinai and handed on to their disciples. That is where, if asked to point us to their center, the sages of any time and place would direct our attention. That too explains why, in medieval times, Christianity time and again burned the Talmud. True, Judaism had as its spokesman Moses (called "our rabbi") and looked for its definition to his writings in Scripture and the traditions held to commence with him for its definition. But Moses is represented as the starting point, the inner dynamics of the Torah's logic governing the articulation of the Torah. And, as history would show, Rabbinic Judaism exhibited no one point of vulnerability. It had many foci, strong points of the faithful, so to wipe out that Judaism, devastating a single center, silencing a single spokesman, would never accomplish the work. And that is so, even in our own day and even in the face of its singular disaster.

But unlike latitudinarian and tolerant paganism, Rabbinic Judaism, by its nature as the monotheist book-religion, found a ready definition of itself. No one was free to choose his own credo or ignore the sage's mediation in approaching the divine. A particular set of words, acts, and arts certainly did define that Judaism, excluding a broad range of the other words, acts, and arts, that Jews beyond the limits of the circle of the master and disciple valued. While in centuries to come, these artifacts of religious culture would pervade the everyday life of all Israel — of Jews wherever they lived — in the formative age, the sources show, tension between sages and ordinary folk attested to the particularity of Rabbinic

Judaism to its circles of masters and disciples. Its faith did not represent a common consensus, its practises, ordinary behavior. The way of life was learned, and the world-view the product of particular knowledge and distinctive modes of thinking about and analyzing that knowledge. That is why, from the perspective of the sages and their disciples, no one was free to choose his own credo, and none could imagine ignoring the master of the Torah and his ruling. The books that portray this Judaism do not present a portrait of variety but of coherence, harmonies of rationality and uniformities of conduct in actuality.

That explains why the four stages of Judaism become concrete in four periods in the unfolding of cognate writings, each represented as continuous with its predecessor. To follow the history of Rabbinic Judaism to the conclusion of its initial statement by the Talmud of Babylonia in the sixth century CE, we trace the four stages that mark the formation of the Judaism put forth by the rabbis of the first six centuries of the Common Era. Three of these four stages are marked by distinct, coherent pieces of writing. One, a long and critical moment, has to be reconstructed by our own logical analysis. That analysis focuses upon where matters stood at the outset, and where at the next known point, in the unfolding of what is a continuous sequence of cognate writings, we find ourselves.

The first of the four stages of Rabbinic Judaism (Chapter 1) finds its complete statement in the Pentateuch, which came to closure, it is commonly supposed, in circa 450 BCE.[3]

The second stage (Chapter 2) comprises the long period of oral tradition following the closure of the Pentateuch and the statement of the Mishnah, more than six hundred years later. I characterize that stage by examining the relationship between two cognate religious documents, the Pentateuch and the corpus of halakhah – normative law – set forth by the Mishnah and related compilations.

That third stage (Chapter 3) came to realization in particular in the Mishnah, a philosophical law code of circa 200 CE, together with supplementary collections of laws ("the Tosefta") and of scriptural exegesis ("Midrash") with special reference to legal passages of Scripture.

To complete the documentary repertoire, fourth, we point (in Chapter 4) to the systematic clarification and amplification of the Mishnah by the two Talmuds, along with collections of exegeses of passages of Scripture important in synagogue life. These are the Talmud of the Land of Israel (in the Roman empire) at circa 400 CE, and the Talmud of Babylonia (in the Iranian empire) at circa 600

CE The second of the two Talmuds made the conclusive statement of Rabbinic Judaism and marks the reference-point from its closure to the present day. It follows that three of these four stages are demarcated by closed and completed writings: Scripture, Mishnah, Talmud, Midrash.

Clearly, the uncertain moment comes at the second stage, Chapter 2, that long period between the Pentateuch and the Mishnah. Here is an age in which whatever took place reached articulation in an orally preserved tradition, and which later on entered into the Mishnah at the deepest layer of premises and generative conceptions taken for granted by the earliest layers of the law as formulated by the Mishnah and related compilations of halakhah. From the period from circa 450 BCE to circa 200 CE, we have no literary evidence within the canon of Rabbinic Judaism to tell us how the cognate writings, the later ones always building upon and referring back to the earlier ones, find their links to their point of origin. That is why for that long period the chain of tradition has to come to reconstruction through the comparison and contrast of the links in the chain that we do have, that is to say, the Pentateuch and the Mishnah and associated compilations of law.

To describe the state of Rabbinic Judaism in that undocumented period we examine the relationship between two cognate religious documents, the Pentateuch and the corpus of law set forth by the Mishnah. My description rests on completed research, *Scripture and the Generative Premises of the Halakhah,* which itself draws upon my *The Halakhah of the Oral Torah. A Religious Commentary.* At stake is the characterization of the legal and theological process and program in the interim between – in literary categories – the closure of the Pentateuch and the formulation of the native categories of the law that organize the Mishnah and the Tosefta and the writings that build upon the Mishnah and related writings.

The fact that Scripture's and the Mishnah's laws were asymmetrical is not our discovery in modern times, nor does the disjuncture represent a theological polemic against the Torah framed out of the historicism of nineteenth century Reform Judaism. Sages themselves were well aware of the gap between the Pentateuch and the completed construction of categories, fully articulated through concrete rules, set forth in the Mishnah and related writings. This they expressed in the following language:

A. The absolution of vows hovers in the air, for it has nothing [in the Written Torah] upon which to depend.

B. The laws of the Sabbath, festal offerings, and sacrilege – lo, they are like mountains hanging by a string,

C. for they have little Scripture for many laws.

D. Laws concerning civil litigations, the sacrificial cult, things to be kept cultically clean, sources of cultic uncleanness, and prohibited consanguineous marriages have much on which to depend.

E. And both these and those [equally] are the essentials of the Torah.

Mishnah-tractate Hagigah 1:9

The doctrine of the dual Torah, oral and written, bridged the gap between the one class of law and the other. The point is, therefore, that some of the laws of the Mishnah and related writings build upon broad foundations in the Pentateuch, some rest on asymmetrical bases with the Pentateuch, and some have little or no basis in the Written Torah, though they constitute the entirely authoritative revelation of God to Moses at Sinai: Torah, if not Pentateuchal Torah. The critical link in the chain from the Pentateuch to the Mishnah, two Talmuds, and Midrash-compilations – the second in the four stages of Rabbinic Judaism – requires characterization through the comparison and contrast of the Pentateuchal with the Mishnaic law.

The third and fourth stages, covered in Chapters 3 to 4 and 5 to 6 , respectively, require us to turn to writing in order to characterize a period in the unfolding of a religion. Specifically, the Mishnah (along with some related documents and traditions) exhibits certain traits of mind that adumbrate the qualities of the culture that produced and valued the writing. At the same time, we deal with the substance of matters, not only the form. For that purpose, we compare the Pentateuch's and the Mishnah's treatment of an issue critical to both – the Sabbath. In the comparison and contrast we are able to discern the characteristic traits of the Mishnaic period in the history of Judaism. When we turn to the Talmuds – the one of the Land of Israel, the other of Babylonia – we undertake the same dual task: the traits of the age as revealed by the qualities of the writing; then the principal developments of doctrine that mark the fourth and climactic phase in the formation of Judaism. Through the four periods into which I have divided the formative history of Judaism, we are able to follow coherent themes and unfolding conceptions, and it is the story of the development of the principal ideas of Judaism that I narrate in these pages.

ACKNOWLEDGEMENTS

I thank the University of South Florida and Bard College for the scholarly opportunities afforded by my positions as Distinguished Research Professor of Religious Studies and Professor of Religion, respectively. I express appreciation to both centers of higher learning for the concomitant Research Funds that they provide. With Professor William S. Green I discussed the problems of my *The Halakhah of the Oral Torah. A Religious Commentary,* as well as *The Theology of the Halakhah* and the present work. I find his comments uniformly stimulating and rely on his sound judgment.

1

THE PENTATEUCHAL STAGE

Rabbinic Judaism privileges the Pentateuch as the verbatim record of part of God's revelation Moses at Sinai, the written part. To frame their statement the sages of that Judaism transformed the narrative and diverse case-rules of the Pentateuch into a systematic account of holy Israel's social norms. Then the whole Torah, written and oral, set forth the law and theology of the social order that God had in mind in revealing himself by giving the Torah to Moses for Israel. The priority accorded to the Pentateuch by Rabbinic Judaism in its formative age provides the definitive indicator of that Judaism, marking that off from all other Judaisms of the same time and place. Other, competing Judaisms privileged other portions of Scripture altogether and none of them built their normative structure upon the foundations of the Pentateuch in particular. Only Rabbinic Judaism did. By "the Pentateuchal stage," therefore, I mean, how do the Five Books of Moses, read as a continuous, unfolding story, shape the religious system that accords to those books a primary position?

I

To begin with, we have to take up what is logically the generative issue: What lessons are there to be learned from the Pentateuch when read as the principal part of God's revelation to Moses?

The first response is negative but carries its own positive charge as well: sages did not read the Pentateuch as a linear, historical account of one-off events arranged in exact chronological sequence, nor did they receive an uninterpreted Scripture from Sinai. They therefore did not come to Scripture anticipating an account of beginnings, middles, and endings, nor did they account for themselves by telling stories, nor did they turn to Scripture for historical facts bearing self-evident messages of a normative character. Were sages to instruct us

1

in how to describe the first stage in the formation of Judaism, they would not take the route we do, that is, the way of beginning with the earliest document, the Pentateuch and of asking how matters unfolded from that point forward through the Mishnah and the Talmuds. The premise of that approach, the one that describes a religion as the outcome of two cumulative historical layers, the one prior, the other posterior, leads us away from, and not toward, the heart of the sages' Judaic religious system in its fulness.

So much for the negative, what about the positive answer to the same question: what do we learn about Rabbinic Judaism from the Pentateuch by reason of the priority accorded to it? The answer is, in the Pentateuch we enter the world in which, so far as sages are concerned, Israel lives in timeless eternity, a world outside the boundaries of past, present, and future. Abraham exemplifies enduring truth, Jacob abiding virtue, and read properly, the Pentateuch describes the here and now of Israel, and also the uncharted future. That is why the laws of the Pentateuch, properly systematized, defined the law of the Israel that the rabbinic sages designed, and it is also to reason that the narratives of the Pentateuch, appropriately treated as exemplary of enduring social rules, explained Israel's present and future.

So far as sages were concerned, no boundary distinguished past from present; time was understood in a completely different way. Within the conception of time that formed consciousness and culture, the past formed a perpetual presence, the present took place on the plane of the past, and no lines of structure or order distinguished the one from the other. Sages found in Scripture not (supposedly) compelling facts of history but exemplary data forming an intelligible pattern or paradigm; for sense they appealed to paradigm that imposed meaning and order on things that happened. What linked the ages into a single uniform existence? First came shared rationality. Sages conducted their enterprise on a level plane, with a common logic and shared givens linking authorities past and present in a single undifferentiated discourse. This is expressed in a famous story about how Moses and the second century CE authority, Aqiba, intersected, with Aqiba saying what Moses was told at Sinai:

A. R. Judah said Rab, "At the time that Moses went up on high, he found the Holy One in session, affixing crowns to the letters [of the words of the Torah]. He said to him, 'Lord of the universe, who is stopping you [from regarding the document as perfect without these additional crowns on the letters]?'

B. He said to him, 'There is a man who is going to arrive at the end of many generations, and Aqiba b. Joseph is his name, who is going to interpret on the basis of each point of the crowns heaps and heaps of laws.'
C. "He said to him, 'Lord of the Universe, show him to me.'
D. "He said to him, 'Turn around.'
E. "He went and took a seat at the end of eight rows, but he could not grasp what the people were saying. He felt faint. But when the discourse reached a certain matter, and the disciples said, 'My lord, how do you know this?' and he answered, 'It is a law given to Moses from Sinai,' he regained his composure."

BAVLI MENAHOT 3:7 II.5/29B

Moses understood that Aqiba had penetrated into the very core of the Torah that Moses himself had received and handed on as tradition. But there is a second point of juncture between one age and the next, forming of them all a single time. Not only implicitly, but elsewhere, in so many words, sages declare that considerations of temporal priority and posteriority do not register in the Torah. An example of how they take that position suffices, with the key-language italicized:

A. "And the Lord spoke to Moses in the wilderness of Sinai in the first month of the second year after they had come out of the land of Egypt, saying, ['Let the people of Israel keep the passover at its appointed time. On the fourteenth day of this month, in the evening, you shall keep it at its appointed time; according to all its statutes and all its ordinances you shall keep it.']" (Num. 9:1–14):
B. Scripture teaches you that *considerations of temporal order do not apply to the sequence of scriptural stories.*
C. For at the beginning of the present book Scripture states, "The Lord spoke to Moses in the wilderness of Sinai in the tent of meeting on the first day of the *second* month in the second year after they had come out of the land of Egypt" (Num. 1:1).
D. And here Scripture refers to "the *first* month,"
E. so serving to teach you that *considerations of temporal order do not apply to the sequence of scriptural stories.*

SIFRÉ TO NUMBERS LXIV:I.1

Temporal order does not govern, because the narratives of Scripture represent exemplary rules, facts requiring a process of generalization

3

and systematization. Just as, for science, the particularities of when a given experiment takes place mean little, but the logic of the experiment and its outcome mean much, so for sages, the truths embodied in events and their outcome pertained to fixed verities are unbound to particular times or places. So why should temporal order make any difference, except within the limits of the case? Then, thinking through paradigms, with a conception of time that elides past and present and removes all barriers between them, in fact governs the reception of Scripture in the Judaism of the sages.

So to delineate the stages of Rabbinic Judaism, the sages would not have called upon the Pentateuch to provide the first stage. But, then, the sages would have analyzed their system using other categories altogether than the ordinal ones that govern here, stages being understood in historical sequence, and by "stage" they would have meant something else altogether. The sages knew full well that their part of the Torah was written down only much later in the Mishnah and other authoritative documents of late antiquity. Then where can we begin to understand how the sages made sense of their own indicative doctrine, the one that held the revelation of Sinai to comprise both written and oral components, and that further assigned a place in that same revelation of Sinai to the other part of the Torah of Sinai? It is only within that conception that the past formed a presence in today's world, and the present participated in the past as well.

The sages of the Mishnah, Midrash, and Talmuds read the one Torah in the light of the other, specifically the written in the light of the oral. They recast both components of the Torah into a system of theology and philosophy realized in the social norms of the law, treating the Pentateuch's rules as cases of general laws, events as examples of the moral givens of world order, and persons and transactions as exemplary of how things are or ought to be. All of these modes of thought and analysis represent other-than-historical approaches to the construction of a rational universe such as Rabbinic Judaism proposed. Now, contemplating the names of the authorities of their own tradition in the account of Sinai's Torah, they explained in other than historical language what they meant in maintaining, the writings of their own time and place, the Mishnah, Talmuds, and Midrash, found a place in Sinai's revelation. The language to which they resorted need not detain us. It suffices to say, it was not historical in its character.

In speaking of "the stages of Judaism," therefore, I introduce a mode of thought of a clearly-historical character into the interpretation of a religious structure and system that took an-other-than-historical path, one that, in contemporary terms, would be called the method of the constructive social sciences, with their homogenization of data and transformation of cases into examples and their translation of perceived patterns into rules for further testing. If, however, sages read the Hebrew Scriptures in an other-than-historical framework and found in Scripture's words paradigms of an enduring present, by which all things must take their measure, we are not bound by their model. And while they possessed no conception whatsoever of the pastness of the past, we find order and meaning in stories of beginnings, middles, and ends. We want to know the connections between first and second and third and last, and we find order and sense in knowing what came first and what followed. Hence working our way from the conclusive statement in the Talmud of Babylonia backward to the starting point, we emerge at the Pentateuch, which, in the whole of Israelite Scripture, the sages of Rabbinic Judaism uniquely deemed the primary, the important, part of Scripture.

II

But, for the reasons spelled out in the Preface, the stages of Judaism, a book-religion, find delineation in cognate books, their relationship and their coherent statement. A negative and a positive consequence follows. Since we deal with writings and not the world portrayed by them beyond their pages, to appeal to the Pentateuch for the starting point we address the document alone. Our task in describing the stages in the unfolding of the ideas of a canon therefore does not require us to situate the first stage of the four stages of the formation of Judaism in the actualities of society and politics of the sixth or fifth centuries BCE, when, many concur, the Pentateuch reached the form in which we now know it. The Pentateuch marks the first stage in the unfolding of an intellectual tradition, a mostly literary tradition. But it does not tell us where, when, or among what sort of people that tradition got underway. And concomitantly, the positive side of asking books to delineate the stages of a religious tradition is self-evident: the books tell us about their authors' viewpoint – of that alone we may be certain. But for the present purpose, that suffices.

We accordingly cannot claim that, in the workaday world of Ezra and Nehemiah, groups coalesced around the Pentateuch who formed, in a secular, this-worldly sense, that chain of tradition that would come to fruition in the Mishnah, Talmuds, and Midrash. We do not know when in social reality Rabbinic Judaism reached its earliest tangible formulation – groups of people distinguishing themselves from the rest of Israel, whether in the Land or abroad, by their conduct and deportment. So far as sages claim a history for themselves, it extends not to Ezra but to Sinai.[1] But since to them, Sinai meant, first and foremost, the Pentateuch of Moses, we have to ask, what lessons did they find there? Concentrating attention on the books of Genesis, Exodus, Leviticus, Numbers, and Deuteronomy yields an account of that with which sages worked. In due course, we shall follow what it is that sages did with that with which they worked. But first we ask ourselves, what is the message that the Pentateuch inculcates in the very telling of the tale?

Sages read the Pentateuch as the account of two successive and partly-parallel "histories," the first of Adam and Eve in Eden, the second of Israel in the Land of Israel. Adam came to Eden, Israel came to the Land. Eden was perfect when Adam got there, the Land when Israel crossed the Jordan. Adam lost Eden, and Israel lost the Land. But there the parallel histories come to a parting of the ways. Eden never regained Eden but remained in the realm of death. Israel bears within its power the possibility of regaining Eden, in eternal possession of life forever. The paradigm that joins Man and Israel is expressed in so many words in the following language:

A. R. Abbahu in the name of R. Yosé bar Haninah: "It is written, 'But they [Israel] are like a man [Adam], they have transgressed the covenant' (Hos. 6:7).

B. " 'They are like a man,' specifically, like the first man. [We shall now compare the story of the first man in Eden with the story of Israel in its land.]

C. " 'In the case of the first man, I brought him into the garden of Eden, I commanded him, he violated my commandment, I judged him to be sent away and driven out, but I mourned for him, saying "How..." '[which begins the book of Lamentations, hence stands for a lament, but which, as we just saw, also is written with the consonants that also yield, 'Where are you'].

D. " 'I brought him into the garden of Eden,' as it is written, 'And the Lord God took the man and put him into the garden of Eden' (Gen. 2:15).

E. " 'I commanded him,' as it is written, 'And the Lord God commanded...' (Gen. 2:16).

F. "'And he violated my commandment,' as it is written, 'Did you eat from the tree concerning which I commanded you' (Gen. 3:11).

G. "'I judged him to be sent away,' as it is written, "And the Lord God sent him from the garden of Eden' (Gen. 3:23).

H. "'And I judged him to be driven out.' 'And he drove out the man' (Gen. 3:24).

I. "'But I mourned for him, saying, "How...".' 'And he said to him, "Where are you"' (Gen. 3:9), and the word for 'where are you' is written, 'How....'

J. "'So too in the case of his descendants, [God continues to speak,] I brought them into the Land of Israel, I commanded them, they violated my commandment, I judged them to be sent out and driven away but I mourned for them, saying, "How...."'

K. "'I brought them into the Land of Israel.' 'And I brought you into the land of Carmel' (Jer. 2:7).

L. "'I commanded them.' 'And you, command the children of Israel' (Ex. 27:20). 'Command the children of Israel' (Lev. 24:2).

M. "'They violated my commandment.' 'And all Israel have violated your Torah' (Dan. 9:11).

N. "'I judged them to be sent out.' 'Send them away, out of my sight and let them go forth' (Jer 15:1).

O. "'....and driven away.' 'From my house I shall drive them' (Hos. 9:15).

P. "'But I mourned for them, saying, "How...."' 'How has the city sat solitary, that was full of people' (Lam. 1:1)."

Genesis Rabbah XIX:IX.2

Israel and Man suffered exile. But, from the perspective of the Pentateuch, Israel not only lost the Land but recovered it. Rabbinic Judaism recapitulates the Pentateuch's story of how Israel got the Land, lost it, but would recover and hold it by reason of adherence to the Torah. The original reading of the Israel's existence as exile and return derives from the Pentateuch, composed in the aftermath of the destruction of the Temple in 586 B.C. and in response to the exile to Babylonia and the return to Zion. So the experience selected as normative for Israel and addressed by the authorship of the document is that of exile and restoration. In our own day, we may well regard the priority assigned to exile and return as normal, not merely normative, in light of the fulfillment of Zionism and the creation of the State of Israel. But as now, so then, not everyone participated in the selected paradigm.

Diverse experiences have been sorted out, various persons have been chosen, and the whole has been worked into a system by those who selected history out of events, exemplary models out of inchoate masses of persons. I say "selected," because no Jews after 586 actually experienced what in the aggregate Scripture says happened. None of them both went into exile and then came back to Jerusalem. So, to begin with, Scripture does not record a particular person's experience – history in any conventional sense. More to the point, if it is not autobiographical, writing for society at large the personal insight of a singular figure, it also is not an account of the whole Israelite nation's story. The reason is that the original exile encompassed mainly the political classes of Jerusalem and some useful populations alongside. Many Jews in the Judea of 586 never left. And, as is well known, a great many of those who ended up in Babylonia stayed there. Only a minority went back to Jerusalem. Consequently, the story of exile and return to Zion encompasses what happened to only a few families, who identified themselves as the family of Abraham, Isaac, and Jacob, and their genealogy as the history of Israel. Had those families that stayed and those that never came back written the Torah they would have told an altogether different tale as normative and paradigmatic.

The experience of the few that formed the paradigm for Israel beyond the restoration taught the lessons of alienation as normative. Let me state the lessons people claimed to learn out of the events they had chosen for their history: the life of the group is uncertain, subject to conditions and stipulations. Nothing is set and given, all things a gift: land and life itself. But what actually did happen in that uncertain world – exile but then restoration – marked the group as special, different, select. There were other ways of seeing things, and the Pentateuchal picture was no more compelling than any other. Those Jews who did not go into exile, and those who did not "come home" had no reason to take the view of matters that characterized the authorship of the Pentateuch. The life of the group need not have appeared more uncertain, more subject to contingency and stipulation, than the life of any other group. The land did not require the vision that imparted to it the enchantment, the personality, that, in Scripture, it received: "The land will vomit you out as it did those who were here before you." And the adventitious circumstance of Iranian imperial policy – a political happenstance – did not have to be recast into a providential return. So nothing in the system of Scripture – exile for reason, return as redemption – followed necessarily and logically. Everything was invented: interpreted.

That experience of the uncertainty of the life of the group in the century or so from the destruction of the First Temple of Jerusalem by the Babylonians in 586 to the building of the Second Temple of Jerusalem by the Jews, with Persian permission and sponsorship returned from exile, formed the paradigm. With the promulgation of the "Torah of Moses" under the sponsorship of Ezra, the Persians' viceroy, at circa 450 BCE, all future Israels would then refer to that formative experience. They would contemplate that experience as it had been set down and preserved as the norm for Israel in the mythic terms of that "original" Israel, the Israel not of Genesis and Sinai and the end at the moment of entry into the promised land, but the "Israel" of the families that recorded as the rule and the norm the story of both the exile and the return. In that minority genealogy, that story of exile and return, alienation and remission, we discern the recurrent pattern. It is one that is imposed on the received stories of pre-exilic Israel and adumbrated time and again in the Five Books of Moses and addressed by the framers of that document in their work over all. In the Pentateuch, enjoying privileged status, we find that paradigmatic statement in which every Judaism, from then to now, found its structure and deep syntax of social existence, the grammar of its intelligible message.

To recapitulate then, what is the foundation laid by the Pentateuch for the Judaism put forth in the Mishnah and Talmuds by the sages? Beginning with the creation of the world, the Pentateuch records the making of man and woman, the fall of humanity through disobedience, the flood that wiped out nearly all of humanity except for Noah, progenitor of all humanity, and the decline of humanity from Noah to Abraham. But that is then the turning point: the rise of humanity through Abraham, Isaac, Jacob also called Israel, the twelve sons of Jacob, to exile in Egypt and ultimately, Sinai. There, the Scriptural narrative continues, God revealed the Torah to Moses, and that revelation contained the terms of the covenant that God then made with Israel, the family of Abraham, Isaac, and Jacob. The book of Genesis narrates the story of creation and then of the beginnings of the family that Israel would always constitute, the children of Abraham, Isaac, and Jacob. The book of Exodus presents the story of the slavery of the children of Israel in Egypt and how God redeemed them from Egyptian bondage and brought them to Sinai, there to make a covenant, or contract, with them by which they would accept the Torah and carry out its rules. The book of Leviticus portrayed the founding of the priests' service of God through the sacrifice of the produce of the holy land to which God would bring Israel, specifying the rules and regulations to govern the kingdom of priests and the holy people. The book of Numbers provided an account of the wandering in the wilderness. The book of Deuteronomy then presented a reprise of the story, a long sermon by Moses looking back on the history of Israel from the beginnings through the point of entry into the promised land, followed by a restatement of the rules of the covenant, or contract, between Israel and God. And, throughout, the narrative carries the warning: Israel can lose the Land, as Adam and Eve lost Eden, by disobedience to God's commandments.

From the perspective of 586, everyone who encountered the Pentateuch knew precisely what was at stake. Israel's history then formed the story of how, because of its conduct on the land, its disobedience to the Torah, its willful exercise of free will to rebel against God, rather than to "love the Lord your God with all your heart, your heart, soul, and might," Israel lost its land, first in the north, then in the south – and that despite the prophets' persistent warnings. From the exile in Babylonia, the authorship of the Torah recast Israel's history into the story of the conditional existence of the people, their existence measured in their possession of the land upon the stipulation of God's favor. Everything depended on carrying out a contract: do this, get that, do not do this, do not get that – and nothing formed a given, beyond all stipulation. Since the formative pattern imposed that perpetual, self-conscious uncertainty, treating the life of the group as conditional and discontinuous, sages responded to that question with the answer of the dual Torah. Theirs was by no means the sole Judaism to respond to the Pentateuch's message. Looking back on Scripture and its message, the framers of other Judaic religious systems have ordinarily treated as special, subject to conditions and therefore uncertain what (in their view) other groups enjoyed as unconditional and simply given. The reason the paradigm renewed itself is clear: this particular view of matters generated expectations that could not be met, hence created resentment. It then provided comfort and the hope that made it possible to cope with that resentment. Promising what could not be delivered, then providing solace for the consequent disappointment, the system precipitated in succeeding ages the very conditions necessary for its own replication.

III

In reading Scripture as the account of the governing paradigm of humanity, from Creation forward, and of Israel therein, the sages conformed to the character of Scripture, not only to its self-evident message. For in its original statement, the system of the Pentateuch did not merely describe things that had actually happened, normal events so to speak, but rendered them normative and mythic, turning an experience into a paradigm of experience. The paradigm began as a paradigm, not as a set of actual events transformed into a normative pattern. And the conclusions generated by the paradigm, it must follow, derived not from reflection on things that happened but from the inexorable logic of the paradigm alone. Not only that, but the same paradigm would create expectations that could not be met, so would renew the resentment captured by the myth of exile, while at the same time setting the conditions for the remission of resentment, so resolving the crisis of exile with the promise of return. This self-generating, self-renewing paradigm formed that self-fulfilling prophecy that all Judaisms have offered as the generative tension and critical symbolic structure of their systems. The paradigm that impressed its imprint on the history of the day did not emerge from and was not generated by, the events of the age. First came the system, its world-view and way of life formed whole we know not where or by whom. Then came the selection, by the system, of consequential events and their patterning into systemic propositions. And finally, at a third stage (of an indeterminate length of time) came the formation and composition of the canon that would express the logic of the system and state those "events" that the system would select or invent for its own expression.

The generative tension persisted, precipitated by the interpretation of the Jews' life as exile and return, that had formed the critical center of the Torah of Moses persisted. Therefore the urgent question answered by the Torah retained its original character and definition – and the self-evidently valid answer – read in the synagogue every Sabbath morning, and on Monday and Thursday as well – retained its relevance. Why did the Pentateuch's authoritative answer not lose its power to persist and to persuade? It was because that same resentment, the product of a memory of loss and restoration, renewed itself added to the recognition, in the here and now, of the danger of a further loss. Not only that, but the question answered by the Five Books of Moses occupied the center of the national life and remained chronic as well as urgent. The answer provided by the Pentateuch therefore retained its self-evident importance. The question persisted, to be sure, because Scripture kept reminding people to ask that question, to see the world as the world was described, in Scripture's mythic terms, out of the perception of the experience of exile and return. To those troubled by the question of exile and return, that is, the chronic allegation that Israel's group-life did not constitute a given but formed a gift accorded on conditions and stipulations, then, the answer enjoyed the status of (mere) fact. For a small, uncertain people, captured by a vision of distant horizons, behind and ahead, a mere speck on the crowded plain of humanity, such a message bore its powerful and immediate message as a map of meaning. Israel's death and resurrection – as the Torah portrayed matters – therefore left nothing as it had been and changed everything for all time.

The problems addressed and solved by the Judaism of the Five Books of Moses remained chronic long after the period of its formation; the Pentateuch states a powerful answer to a pressing and urgent question. The Torah encapsulates, as normative and recurrent, the experience of the loss and recovery of the land and of political sovereignty. Israel, because of its (in its mind) amazing experience, had attained a self-consciousness that continuous existence in a single place under a long-term government denied others. There was nothing given, nothing to be merely celebrated or just taken for granted, in the life of a nation that had ceased to be a nation on its own land and then once more had regained that (once-normal, now abnormal) condition. The experience of both losing the Land and then coming back then defined the condition of Israel in the context of the story of Adam. Adam lost Eden and never got it back, Israel lost the Land but then got it back. What separates Adam from Israel is the Torah. And the rest follows.

But the Pentateuch said more than that. It also described the life of Israel in concrete terms. In that account, the altar was the center of life, the conduit of life from heaven to earth and from earth to heaven. All things are to be arrayed in relationship to the altar. The movement of the heavens demarcated and celebrated at the cult marked out the divisions of time in relationship to the altar. The spatial dimension of the Land was likewise demarcated and celebrated in relationship to the altar. The natural life of Israel's fields and corrals, the social life of its hierarchical caste-system, the political life (this was not only in theory by any means) centered on the Temple as the locus of ongoing government – all things in order and in place expressed the single message. The natural order of the world corresponded to, reinforced, and was reinforced by, the social order of Israel. Both were fully realized in the cult, the nexus between those opposite and corresponding forces, the heavens and the earth. The lines of structure emanated from the altar. And it was these lines of structure which constituted high and impenetrable frontiers to separate Israel from the gentiles. Israel, which was holy, ate holy food, reproduced itself in accord with the laws of holiness, and conducted all of its affairs, both affairs of state and the business of the table and the bed, in accord with the demands of holiness. So the cult defined holiness. Holiness meant separateness. Separateness meant life. Why? Because outside the Land, the realm of the holy, lay the domain of death. The lands are unclean. The Land is holy. For the Scriptural vocabulary, one antonym for *holy* is *unclean*, and one opposite of unclean is holy. The synonym of holy is life. The principal force and symbol of uncleanness and its highest expression are death. So the Torah stood for life, the covenant with the Lord would guarantee life, and the way of life required sanctification in the here and now of the natural world. That is the message of the Pentateuch, and that is the key to the system of Rabbinic Judaism – or any Judaism that privileges the Pentateuch.

IV

Now how does Rabbinic Judaism respond to the Pentateuch? The dual Torah reads Scripture as the account of loss and restoration. It makes provision for the restoration of Eden by Man realized in the Land of Israel by Israel. In line with Scripture's plain message, the sages' Torah explores the requirements of the restoration within the social formation of Israel in the Land of Israel. It systematically transforms particular topics into occasions for profound reflection upon principles, most of them to do with the sanctification of life through adherence to God's will: "...who has sanctified us by his commandments and commanded us to...." That is to say, the Torah taught by Rabbinic Judaism brings about transformation of the here and now and occasion (place and time and event, mostly in nature) into the embodiment, the exemplification, of the abstract ground of being. Involved is relationship of realms of the sacred: the rules of engagement between and among God, Land, Israel, time, place, circumstance.

That Judaism sets forth a systematic and coherent response to the tragic situation of Man, a response that works itself out in the governance of practical matters of time, place, and circumstance. In the articulation of that response, Eden precipitates thought about the human condition but does not impose narrow limits on the amplification of that thought. Rabbinic Judaism begins with Eden but progresses to the realization of God's kingdom within holy

Israel's social order. Through the provision of norms of conduct and conviction such as Scripture itself sets forth or logically invites, the oral part of the Torah written down in the Mishnah, Talmuds, and Midrash lays out an account of how the entire social order may be constructed to realize Eden once more, this time under God's rule. That restoration comes about not in the end of days when the Messiah comes, but in the here-and-now of the workaday world. It is there that Israelite Man formed by the discipline of the Torah learns both to atone for, and to overcome, his natural propensity willfully to rebel against God. Within the social order of an enlandized Israel, moral man constructs a godly society. That reading of the Written Torah and translation of its law into the canons of ordinary life speaks in the acutely-present tense to portray for Man a worthy future well within Man's own capacities to realize: "the Torah was given only to purify the heart of man," and "God wants the heart," as the Talmud frames matters.

Responding to the Pentateuch, the sages' writings viewed whole and in detail form an exercise in the realization of Scripture's principal themes. "Eden" not only stands for a situation (the perfection of repose on the holy Sabbath) but a story (Adam's and Eve's sin), and, furthermore, the story captures a theme (the need for atonement) and embodies it in narrative. The law of the Oral Torah set forth in the Mishnah and its supplements takes up the story of the perfection of Eden, then addresses the situation implicit in that story of Man's disobedience, and finally takes up the theme of the here-and-now embodiment of God's kingdom, the encompassing theological motif embodied in that story. Rabbinic Judaism transforms the narrative of Man set forth in Genesis through Deuteronomy and its extension from Joshua through Kings into a systematic statement upon Man and his counterpart, Israel; Eden and its counterpart, the Land of Israel.

These themes are explored in the framework of the eternal contest between God's word and Man's exercise of his free will to disobey, God's justice and Man's requirement to atone and attain reconciliation, God's holiness and Man's obligation to be holy, like God, as Genesis declares and as Leviticus demands (Gen. 3:9, Lev. 19:3, respectively). Through the halakhah read here as a theological structure and cogent system, we shall see Judaism recapitulates Scripture and perfectly realizes, in the norms of Israel's social order, Scripture's full truth about the human condition.

Rabbinic Judaism responds to the Pentateuch by selecting as the key event Man's exercise of free will to rebel against God's commandment. Like the Apostle Paul's masterpiece, his Letter to the Romans, with its tragic vision ("...as sin came into the world through one man and death through sin...", reminiscent of Fourth Ezra's "Oh Adam, what hast thou done!"), like Augustine's *City of God*, like Michelangelo's Last Judgment in the Sistine Chapel, and like John Milton's *Paradise Lost*, – to name just four counterparts to the halakhic meditation on the story of Man that begins in Eden – the Torah of the sages addresses the central problem of Western civilization as defined by Scripture. To all the heirs of Scripture Genesis records the nature and destiny of Man and sets the issues for reflection. But among all scripturally-founded constructions out of the vision of Man's tragedy, the Oral Torah's stands quite by itself. That is because the Oral Torah in its legal provisions provides for the formation of an entire society in the image, after the likeness, of Scripture's account of how matters are supposed to be.

That unique response to Eden and its aftermath comes about because of the Oral Torah's immediacy and practicality. The sages chose as their principal medium of reconstruction the formulation of norms of practical conduct, called halakhah. The halakhah, set forth principally in the Mishnah and its supplement, the Tosefta, and in modest proportion also in the two Talmuds, embodies the unique mode of thought conducted by the great sages of Judaism in its formative age, its concrete practicality, its insistence upon deed as the medium of deliberation. The Judaic sages thought deeply but valued thought only by reason of its practical power to change Man: "study of the Torah takes priority, because study leads to concrete deed" (Bavli Qiddushin 22a), they decided. That is why the halakhah forms an account of how the very social fabric of Man may be formed of a tapestry of right deeds to yield Eden within the very material of the ordinary and the everyday.

For sages responding to the character of the Pentateuch deliberation alone did not suffice, though their account of deeds to be done in the quest for human regeneration rests indeed upon deep layers of profound reflection. Like Plato in the *Republic*, the sages conducted their thought through legislating the design of Israel's social order. Unlike Plato they actively aimed to realize in everyday affairs the principles of their theory of matters. Augustine told the story of the social order through history, Scripture's history. For their part the Judaic sages wrote their *City of God* in law. In contemplating issues strikingly congruent to those addressed in the salvific program of Paul in Romans, it was not through theoretical theological reflections but practical rulings on the construction of the holy society that they conducted their inquiry into the logic of Man's fate and what is required for his redemption. And, in the nature of their writings, sages produced few word-pictures, though their halakhic writings adhered to a remarkably powerful aesthetics, both in form and in intellectual elegance.

Note the contrast. The great tragic theologians of Christianity, Paul and Augustine, produced profound reflection upon the human condition of sin. The counterpart artists, Michelangelo and Milton, conveyed the Fall through art and poetry, through eye and ear and intellect responding to the tragic moment of Eden and its aftermath. But none but the Judaic sages conceived of responding to the generalities of the human condition by defining the particular character of an entire social order, its norms of conviction and conduct, its culture embodied in rules of behavior and belief – all for the sake of regeneration and renewal, leading to eternal life. In their mind, the very character of the community as constructed by concrete laws would form a commentary upon Man and the loss of Eden – a response to Eden but also a remedy for the rebellion that reduced Man to his present estrangement from God. Had they wished to argue that the salvation of Man from the condition of the sin that brought about the fall would come about through law – the laws of the Torah in particular – they could not have framed a more compelling, and, in their context, a more eloquent statement than they did through the logic and exegesis of the halakhah.

The dual Torah set forth in the halakhah coheres, in its main lines of structure and system, and its point of coherence commences with the aim of restoring the perfection of Eden through the regeneration of Man by means of the social realization of the Torah. The sages of the Mishnah and Talmuds formed a system for the practical conduct of holy Israel's social order. There they defined as the remedy for the human condition, revealed first at Eden, the practicalities of quotidian life of an entire community. In accepting God's rule Israel would embody the City of God. Israel would accomplish corporately for Mankind what one man is supposed to have done for Paul's Christianity. In the Torah, as they portrayed the Torah, the system of norms of behavior was meant to realize within the social order the norms of belief set forth by the sages of Judaism in response to the tragedy of the Fall – the starting point of the entire system – and the promise of restoration – the climax of its structure. This they did by defining the labor of social renewal, relating the rules of regeneration in the exact sense.

How, exactly, do sages set forth their account of the Fall and

Man's hope? Like their counterparts among all heirs of Scripture, the Judaic sages accounted for creation and and the condition of humankind, beginning to end, by appealing to the Torah's narrative of Man, from Genesis forward. How then does the sages' Judaism seek to restore Eden and to put Adam and Eve back into Paradise? It does this by treating Israel, the people, as surrogates for and continuators of Man but with the difference marked by the Torah. Israel will be formed by those who will love God and carry out his will – Adam and Eve did not possess the potential to restore Eden. This they can and should do by turning Israel, first of all the enlandized part in the Land of Israel, into Eden, now defined as the sector of humanity and the segment of the territory of humanity that are fully permeated by God's will in the Torah, as God's choice for the renewed Eden. That account of Israel as Adam's successor, the Land in the stead of Eden, carries us far from the mundane realities of contemporary politics and wars. The sages' Judaism set forth a system that treats the holy people Israel as counterpart but ultimately opposite to Adam.

Adam lived in Eden but rebelled against God and was driven out. Israel lived in the Land of Israel and for a brief moment, upon entry, Israel recapitulated Eden. But as the Torah says in writing in the authorized history from Genesis through Kings, Israel rebelled against God and was driven out. But what distinguishes Israel from Adam is that Israel possessed the Torah, which held the power to transform the heart of man and so turn man from rebellion to loving submission. And when the Israelite man, regenerate in the Torah, fully conformed to the Torah, then Israel would recover its Eden, the Land of Israel. That is made explicit in the formulation of Abbahu, already cited. And that is why Israel represents the new Adam, God's way of correcting the errors of the initial creation. The Land of Israel stands for the new Eden. Just as Adam entered a perfect world but lost it, so Israel was given a perfect world – in repose at the moment of Israel's entry – but sinning against God, he lost it. The difference, however, is that Israel has what Adam did not have, which is the Torah, a point that does not enter here except indirectly. The Torah's theory of who is man and what God wants of man leaves no uncertainty. That God craves is man's willing submission to God's will, made known in the Torah, beginning with the drama, for which the halakhah legislates, of the proclamation of God's unity: "Hear, Israel, the Lord our God is unique. And you shall love the Lord your God with all your heart, with all your soul, and with all your might" (Dt. 4:6ff.).

The restoration of Israel to the Land then forms the key chapter in the story of the redemption of all mankind. The last things are to be known from the first. In the just plan of creation man was meant to live in Eden, and his counterpart, Israel in the Land of Israel, in time without end. The restoration to the Land will bring about that long and tragically postponed perfection of the world order, sealing the demonstration of the justice of God's plan for creation. Risen from the dead, having atoned through death, man will be judged according to his deeds. Israel for its part, when it repents and conforms its will to God's, recovers its Eden. So the consequences of rebellion and sin having been overcome, the struggle of man's will and God's word having been resolved, God's original plan will be realized at the last. The simple, global logic of the system, with its focus on the world order of justice established by God but disrupted by man, leads inexorably to this eschatology of restoration, the restoration of balance, order, proportion – eternity. Holy Israel, the people defined theologically and not politically, then assembles at prayer and expresses the hope that, in the end of days, God will call all humanity to his worship, as, even now, he has called holy Israel. Then everyone will acknowledge the sovereignty of the one and only God and accept his dominion.

When we ask, when and how is this supposed to take place?, we find our way to the practical halakhah set forth by the sages of ancient Judaism. Given their view of time and history, we should not find surprising that the time is the present, the hour immediate. In accord with the Judaic sages' account of the consequence of building the social order in accord with the halakhah of the Torah, Man – Adam and Eve – thereby would find the counterpart in Israel, and Eden, in the Land of Israel. How then does the past figure? Like Man, Israel at the moment of its creation entered the Land and found perfection like Eden's: all things arrayed in perfect repose. But Israel, like Man, had sinned and had lost the Land, its Eden. So the story of Joshua and Judges matches the tale of Genesis 1–3. But the revelation of Sinai intervenes. That is why it follows that, through realizing the law of the Torah, Israel would regain its Paradise. For, granted what Man had missed, which is the Torah, and guided by the Torah, holy Israel would restore Eden. This it would do in the Land that God had given it for Eden but that had been lost to sin. And the Torah, setting forth the halakhah, the rules for the social order of restored Eden, would make of Israel, even sinful Israel, capable, as Adam was, of rebellion against God's will, a worthy occupant of the Eden that the Land was meant to be, had been for a brief moment, and would once again become.

The sages chose to show that, in the very context of the crisis of Man's fall, the Torah would bring about in the here and now of everyday life that very regeneration that, in Paul's system, faith was meant to accomplish. In light of the workaday world for which sages legislated, moreover, it was as if they had read the City of God and undertook to show the Bishop of Hippo how to accomplish in the visible and tangible world the realization of the promise of citizenship in an unseen city. And, were they to have spread forth before the poet the artful language that conveys the halakhah in the Mishnah, they might have said to him, "Here, here is Paradise recovered, these are its natural sounds, the Mishnah to be memorized like your poem" and to the artist, "Paint this – this picture of the world in repose, of Man regenerate, of Eden restored: 'Paint what Balaam found himself impelled to see: "For from the top of the mountain I see him, from the hills I behold him; lo, a people dwelling alone"'" (Num. 23:9). Paul, Augustine, Michelangelo, Milton worked in solitary splendor to frame a vision. Only the sages of Judaism undertook to render palpable and tangible Man's hope for his restoration in Eden in God's dominion.

V

Having privileged the Pentateuch, the sages derived therefrom and conveyed the picture of a world order based on God's justice and equity. The categorical structure of the Oral Torah encompasses the components, God and man; the Torah; Israel and the nations. The working-system of the Oral Torah finds its dynamic in the struggle between God's plan for creation – to create a perfect world of justice – and man's will. That dialectic embodies in a single paradigm the events contained in the sequences, rebellion, sin, punishment, repentance, and atonement; exile and return; or the disruption of world order and the restoration of world order. Sages then formed these into a logos – a sustained, rigorous, coherent argument, that can be set forth in narrative-sequential form. Let me then define the four principles of the theology of the Oral Torah that sages framed in response to the Written Torah, principles that cohere, form a cogent statement, and are fully exposed in the later authoritative documents of Rabbinic Judaism:[2]

1. God formed creation in accord with a plan, which the Torah reveals. World order can be shown by the facts of nature and society set forth in that plan to conform to a pattern of reason

based upon justice. Those who possess the Torah – Israel – know God and those who do not – the gentiles – reject him in favor of idols. What happens to each of the two sectors of humanity, respectively, responds to their relationship with God. Israel in the present age is subordinate to the nations, because God has designated the gentiles as the medium for penalizing Israel's rebellion, meaning through Israel's subordination and exile to provoke Israel to repent. Private life as much as the public order conforms to the principle that God rules justly in a creation of perfection and stasis.

2. The perfection of creation, realized in the rule of exact justice, is signified by the timelessness of the world of human affairs, their conformity to a few enduring paradigms that transcend change (theology of history). No present, past, or future marks time, but only the recapitulation of those patterns. Perfection is further embodied in the unchanging relationships of the social commonwealth (theology of political economy), which assure that scarce resources, once allocated, remain in stasis. A further indication of perfection lies in the complementarity of the components of creation, on the one side, and, finally, the correspondence between God and man, in God's image (theological anthropology), on the other.

3. Israel's condition, public and personal, marks flaws in creation. What disrupts perfection is the sole power capable of standing on its own against God's power, and that is man's will. What man controls and God cannot coerce is man's capacity to form intention and therefore choose either arrogantly to defy, or humbly to love, God. Because man defies God, the sin that results from man's rebellion flaws creation and disrupts world order. The paradigm of the rebellion of Adam in Eden governs, the act of arrogant rebellion leading to exile from Eden thus accounting for the condition of humanity. But, as in the original transaction of alienation and consequent exile, God retains the power to encourage repentance through punishing man's arrogance. In mercy, moreover, God exercises the power to respond to repentance with forgiveness, that is, a change of attitude evoking a counterpart change. Since, commanding his own will, man also has the power to initiate the process of reconciliation with God, through repentance, an act of humility, man may restore the perfection of that order that through arrogance he has marred.

4. God will ultimately restore that perfection that embodied his plan for creation. In the work of restoration death that comes

about by reason of sin will die, the dead will be raised and judged for their deeds in this life, and most of them, having been justified, will go on to eternal life in the world to come. In the paradigm of man restored to Eden, Israel's return to the Land of Israel is realized. In that world or age to come, however, that sector of humanity that through the Torah knows God will encompass all of humanity. Idolators will perish, and humanity that comprises Israel at the end will know the one, true God and spend eternity in his light.

Now, recorded in this way, the story told by the Oral Torah proves remarkably familiar, with its stress on God's justice (to which his mercy is integral), man's correspondence with God in his possession of the power of will, man's sin and God's response – that is to say, the Oral Torah recapitulates the message of the Written Torah comprised by the Pentateuch. Sages maintained from the very beginning in saying they possessed the Torah revealed by God to Moses at Mount Sinai ("Moses received Torah at Sinai and handed it on to Joshua, Joshua to elders, and elders to prophets, and prophets handed it on to the men of the great assembly"). So here, beginning with the integrating basics, encompassing the entire expanse of creation and humanity, from first to last things, are the ideas that impart structure and order to, and sustain, the whole. Starting with the doctrine of world order that is just and concluding with eternal life, here is the simple logic that animates all the parts and makes them cohere. The generative categories prove not only imperative and irreducible but also logically sequential. Each of the four parts of the theology of the Oral Torah – [1] the perfectly just character of world order, [2] indications of its perfection, [3] sources of its imperfection, [4] media for the restoration of world order and their results – belongs in its place and set in any other sequence the four units become incomprehensible.

VI

In presenting the Pentateuch as the first stage of the Judaism of the dual Torah, I recapitulate the sages' own claim. When the sages insist upon the absolute unity of the two media of revelation, the Written, the Memorized or Oral Torah, calling them "the one whole Torah of Moses, our rabbi," they express that claim in so many words. So it remains to ask, are they right? In a very specific sense, they are: their theology is not only linked to verses of Scripture that prove the sages' points, it is also concentric with principal components of Scripture, and in particular, the Pentateuch.

In light of the foregoing account of the Pentateuchal foundations of Judaism, let us then turn to the claim that what the sages say in the Mishnah, Talmuds, and Midrash that the Written Torah says is actually what the ancient Israelite Scriptures do say. The governing criterion is, Will those who put forth the books of Genesis through Kings as a sustained narrative and those who in that same context selected and organized the writings of the prophets, Isaiah, Jeremiah, Ezekiel, and the twelve, in the aggregate have concurred in the sages' structure and system? Certainly others who lay claim to these same Scriptures did and today surely would not concur. At the time the sages did their greatest theological work, in the fourth and fifth century CE, their Christian counterparts, in the Latin, Greek and Syriac speaking sectors of Christianity alike, not only read Scripture in a very different way but also accused the rabbis of falsifying the Torah. How would the sages have responded to the charge?

By their constant citation of Scripture, and especially, for norms of conduct, the Pentateuch, sages persistently allege that they are right about Scripture. That allegation is ubiquitous because for nearly every proposition they set forth, they adduce the support of Pentateuchal law whenever they can. Moreover, the main beams of the structure of faith they construct are all set securely and symmetrically upon the written Torah. Proof-texts constantly take the measure of the structure. That is why sages speak of the one whole Torah, in two media, correlative and complementary. Accordingly – that is now the sages' view – if we take up the Oral Torah and explore its theological structure and system, we meet Judaism, pure and simple. There we find its learning and its piety, what it knows about and hears from God, what it has to say to God. So much for the claim of theological apologetics.

The facts support it. Sages have not only history but – as I have shown in the foregoing sections of this chapter – also Scripture's own hermeneutics on their side. In their reading of the written Torah whole, in canonical context, as a record of life with God, they are right to say their story goes over the written Torah's story. Scripture's account is rehearsed in the Oral Torah, the whole of Scripture's picture, start to finish. That encompasses creation and the making of man in God's image and man's fall, through Sinai and the making of Israel through the Torah, now to the fall of Jerusalem, all things perceived in the light of the prophets' rebuke, consolation, and hope for restoration. All is in proportion and balance. Viewed as a systematic hermeneutics, the sages' theology accurately sets forth the principal possibility of the theology that is implicit in the written part of the Torah – to be sure, in a more systematic and cogent manner than does Scripture.[3]

It is not merely that, start to finish, the Oral Torah builds its structure out of a reading of the Written Torah. The probative fact is, sages read, and explicitly stated that they intended to read, from the Written Torah forward to the Oral Torah. That is not only attested by the superficial character of proof-texting, but by the profound congruence of the theology of the Oral Torah with the course of the Scriptural exposition just now spelled out. How else are we to read the story, start to finish as sages did? Any outline of Scripture's account begins with creation and tells about the passage from Eden via Sinai and Jerusalem to Babylon – and back. It speaks of the patriarchal founders of Israel, the Exodus, Sinai, the Torah, covenants, Israel, the people of God, the priesthood and the tabernacle, the possession of the Land, exile and restoration. And so too my brief outline of the Oral Torah's theology focused upon all of these same matters. True, sages proportion matters within their own logic, laying heaviest emphasis upon perfection, imperfection, and restoration of perfection to creation, focusing upon Israel, God's stake in humanity.

A few obvious facts suffice. Take the principal propositions of Scripture read in sequence and systematically, meaning, as exemplary, from Genesis through Kings. Consider the story of the exile from Eden and the counterpart exile of Israel from the Land. Sages did not invent that paradigm. Scripture's framers did. Translate into propositional form the prophetic messages of admonition, rebuke, and consolation, the promise that as punishment follows sin, so consolation will come in consequence of repentance. Sages did not fabricate those categories and make up the rules that govern the sequence of events. The prophets said them all. Sages only recapitulated the prophetic propositions with little variation except in formulation. All the sages did was to interpret within the received paradigm the exemplary events of their own day, the destruction of Jerusalem and Israel's subjugation in particular. But even at that they simply asked Scripture's question of events that conformed to Scripture's pattern. Identify as the dynamics of human history the engagement of God with man, especially through Israel, and what do you have, if not the heart of the sages' doctrine of the origins and destiny of man. Review what Scripture intimates about the meaning and end of time, and how much do you miss of the sages' eschatology of restoration? Details, amplifications, clarifications, an unsuccessful effort at systematization – these do not obscure the basic confluence of the sages' and Scripture's account of last things (even though the word "last" has its own meaning for sages).

Just now I referred to the ubiquitous proof-texting that characterizes the Talmuds and Midrash-compilations. This should not be dismissed as an empty formality. Constant citations of scriptural texts cited as authority serve merely to signal the presence of a profound identity of viewpoint. The cited verses are not solely pretexts or formal proof-texts. A hermeneutics governs, dictating the course of exegesis. In concrete terms, the theology I have outlined generates the exegesis, the results of which we encounter on nearly every page of this the principal Rabbinic documents, excluding only the Mishnah. Sages cite and interpret verses of Scripture to show where and how the written Torah guides the oral one, supplying the specificities of the process of recapitulation. And what sages say about those verses originates not in the small details of those verses (such as Aqiba was able to interpret to Moses's stupefaction) but in the large theological structure and system that sages framed.

That is why I insist that the hermeneutics defined the exegesis, the exegesis did not define the hermeneutics. Not only so, but in most of the Midrash-compilations of the Oral Torah it is the simple fact that sages read from the whole to the parts, from the Written part of the Torah outward to the Oral part. That explains why nothing arbitrary or merely occasional, nothing ad hoc or episodic or notional characterized sages reading of Scripture, but a theology, formed whole in response to the whole. That explains why the sages did not think they imputed to Scripture meanings not actually there, and this account of their theology proves that they are right. Sages read Scripture as a letter written that morning to them in particular about the world they encountered. That is because for them the past was forever integral to the present. So they looked into the Written part of the Torah to construct the picture of reality that is explained by world-view set forth in the Oral part of the Torah.

They found their questions in Scripture; they identified the answers to those questions in Scripture; and they then organized and interpreted the contemporary situation of holy Israel in light of those questions and answers. To that process the narrow focus of atomistic exegesis proves simply incongruous. It is not what sages did, because it is not what they could have done. For the very category, proof-text, reduces that elegant theology of the here and now to the trivialities of grammar or spelling or other nonsense-details. It demeans sages' intellectual honesty, as is affirmed and attested by the very character of discourse on every page of the Talmud of Babylonia among many documents. And it misses the fact that Scripture's corpus of facts, like nature's, was deemed to transcend the bonds of time. That explains why sages found in Scripture the main lines of structure and system that formed the architecture of their theology.

And that same conviction accounts for the fact that, in the heavenly academy to which corner of Eden imagination carried them, the great sages could amiably conduct arguments with God and with Moses. Not only so, but they engage in on-going dialogue with the prophets and psalmists and the other saints of the written Torah as well as with those of their masters and teachers in the oral tradition who reached Eden earlier (much as entire legions of participants in the Oral Torah in recent centuries aspire to spend an afternoon in Eden with Moses Maimonides). A common language joined them all, for in their entire engagement with the written part of the Torah, sages mastered every line, every word, every letter, sorting matters of the day out in response to what they learned in the written tradition. That explains why we may justifiably say that on every page of the writings of the Oral Torah we encounter the sages' encompassing judgment of, response to, the heritage of ancient Israel's Scripture. There they met God, there they found God's plan for the world of perfect justice, the flawless, eternal world in stasis, and there in detail they learned what became of that teaching in ancient times and in their own day, everything seen in the same way. The result is spread out in the pages of this book: the sages' account of the Torah revealed by God to Moses at Sinai and handed on in tradition through the ages.

So if we ask, what if, in the timeless world of the Torah studied in the same heavenly academy, Moses and the prophets, sages, and scribes of Scripture were to take up the results of oral tradition produced by their heirs and successors in the oral part of the Torah? the answer is clear. They would have found themselves hearing familiar words, their own words, used by honest, faithful men, in familiar, wholly legitimate ways. When, for example, Moses heard in the tradition of the Oral Torah that a given law was a law revealed by God to Moses at Sinai, he may have kept his peace, though puzzled, or he may have remembered that, indeed, that is how it was, just so. In very concrete, explicit language the sages themselves laid their claim to possess the Torah of Moses. We recall how impressed Moses is by Aqiba, when he observed, from the rear of the study hall, how Aqiba was able to interpret on the basis of each point of the crowns heaps and heaps of laws. But he could not follow the debate and felt faint until he heard the later master declare, "It is a law given to Moses from Sinai," and then he regained his composure (Bavli tractate Menahot 3:7 II.5/29, cited above).

So to return to our question, are the rabbis of the Oral Torah right in maintaining that they have provided the originally-oral part of the one whole Torah of Moses our rabbi? To answer that question in the affirmative, sages would have only to point to their theology in the setting of Scripture's as they grasped it. The theology of the dual Torah, written and oral, put forth by the Rabbinic sages, tells a simple, sublime story.

[1] God created a perfect, just world and in it made man in his image, equal to God in the power of will.

[2] Man in his arrogance sinned and was expelled from the perfect world and given over to death. God gave man the Torah to purify his heart of sin.

[3] Man educated by the Torah in humility can repent, accepting God's will of his own free will. When he does, man will be restored to Eden and eternal life.

In our terms, we should call it a story with a beginning, middle, and end. In sages' framework, we realize, the story embodies an enduring and timeless paradigm of humanity in the encounter with God: man's powerful will, God's powerful word, in conflict, and the resolution thereof.

But if about the written Torah I claim sages were right, then what about the hermeneutics of others? If the sages claimed fully to spell out the message of the written Torah, as they do explicitly in nearly every document and on nearly every page of the Oral Torah, so too did others. And those others, who, like the sages, added to the received Scripture other writings of a (to them) authoritative character, set forth not only the story of the fall from grace that occupied sages but, in addition, different stories from those the sages told. They drew different consequences from the heritage of ancient Israel. Sages' critics will find their account not implausible but incomplete, a truncated reading of Scripture. They will wonder about leaving out nearly the entire apocalyptic tradition.[4] But, in the balance, sages' critics err. For no one can reasonably doubt that sages' reading of Scripture recovers, in proportion and accurate stress and balance, the main lines of Scripture's principal story, the one about creation, the fall of man and God's salvation of man through Israel and the Torah.

In familiar, though somewhat gauche, language, let me state the matter simply: from the first stage, represented by the Pentateuch, forward, "Judaism" (in context, Rabbinic Judaism in its classical statement and in its modern continuations) really is what common opinion thinks it is, which is, "the religion of the Old Testament." If, as the great Scripture-scholar, Brevard Childs, states, "The evangelists read from the New [Testament] backward to the Old,"[5] we may say very simply, and, when I say, the sages were right, I mean: *the sages read from the written Torah forward to the oral one.* That is the sense in which I claim, "sages are right:" they have not only privileged the Pentateuch, they have penetrated into its deepest structure. Now to show that that is so as we move on to the second stage of Judaism.

2

FROM SCRIPTURE TO THE MISHNAH

Between the closure of Scripture and the commencement of the earliest layers of articulated thought in the Mishnah, a vast labor of reflection yielded propositions of fundamental and enduring consequence. These form the second stage in the formation of Judaism. But concerning that next stage no direct evidence in documentary form – no compilations that reached closure and that was formulated and handed on in the line of tradition from Scripture to the Mishnah – informs us. We have not a single piece of writing to tell us where, when, and by whom such reflection was undertaken. For their part, the sages of Rabbinic Judaism accord no recognition to any document from the Pentateuch and the Scripture of which it is part to the Mishnah, though from that point on, that Judaism treats many compilations as authoritative. No public statement framed into a systematic reconstitution the rules and cases of Scripture. The category-formation of a vast and coherent legal system, itself embod-ying and realizing a counterpart theological structure took shape at this stage and constitutes the organizing construction of the law of Judaism. But all we know is, when the work on the Mishnah as we know it got under way, that structure had taken shape in its principal components.[1]

What, then, do we in fact know about that interval of eight hundred years? What we do have is the starting point, Scripture, and the end point, the halakhah set forth by the Mishnah and the Tosefta. Through the study of the relationship between those two cognate religious documents, the Pentateuch and the corpus of halakhah set forth by the Mishnah-Tosefta-Yerushalmi-Bavli, we are able to outline the principal lines of thought that took place during the long spell between documents. What we do is work backward from the generative premises of the halakhah of the Mishnah and the Tosefta to Scripture, to see whether and how, as I have proposed at the end of Chapter 1, the rabbinical sages worked forward from Scripture to the Mishnah.

That is how we know the main lines of the second stage of Judaism. The law of Judaism, beginning in the Pentateuch and elaborated in the Mishnah, Tosefta, halakhic exegetical works, and two Talmuds, systematically translates the theology set forth in the dual story – Adam's, then Israel's – of the Pentateuch. The work was done through law, and much of the system and structure had come to realization at just this time in that law. Called in its native category "halakhah," the law in significant measure focused upon the lessons of the parallel stories in succession. These lessons were then translated by sages into the norms of conduct that would define the society of holy Israel, that is, the people that accepted the Torah and God's dominion at Sinai. Israel would then reconstruct Eden – a realm freely choosing to obey God's will and live in God's kingdom – in the Land of Israel and so enter into that eternal life that Adam and Eve enjoyed before sin brought death.

Accordingly, Rabbinic Judaism responded to the Pentateuch by translating it into an account of a systematic social structure of the laws and stories of the Hebrew Scriptures of ancient Israel. Here – sages allege – is the message of Sinai, translated into the norms of an entire society. The sages' claim is sustained by the documents that sages set forth to define those norms. The halakhah of the Mishnah and related documents, embodies in rules of conduct specific responses to Scripture's account of Man – Adam and Eve – and their fall from Eden, on the one side, and Scripture's portrait of Israel and its loss of the Land of Israel, on the other.

The fact is, the generative premises of principal components of the halakhah – its organizing categories, its building blocks – are presupposed by the Mishnah at the primary levels of its unfolding. The Mishnah attributes laws to authorities who flourished from the early first through the late second century. We are able to assess whether or not the order of attributions – early, then late – corresponds to the logical progression of what is attributed – elementary, then secondary. And as we work our way back from the latest and best developed and articulated rulings to the premise on which all else rests, we identify the principles and conceptions that form the foundations for everything else. Now, as we follow the unfolding of opinion and the secondary and tertiary developments of the halakhah set forth in the Mishnah and the Tosefta – the principal media of the halakhah of formative Judaism – we find a simple fact. Prior to the elaboration of any category of the halakhah come principles that the law everywhere takes for granted but nowhere articulates. These form the generative premises of the halakhah and dictate primary category-formations and their character.[2]

Here is our point of entry into the description of the stage of Judaism between the Pentateuch and the Mishnah. When we ask, whence those generative premises, the answer at critical points is, the Pentateuch. When we further inquire, how specifically do those premises translate into social policy the lessons of the Pentateuchal account of Man and Israel, the evidence comes from the match between the message of the halakhah and Scripture's own clear meaning and intent. The undocumented period comes to us in the signals of premises taken for granted by the law of the Mishnah and related compilations but not incorporated, or only partially incorporated, by the norms of the Pentateuch itself. These represent that second stage. Here we encounter the development of what is implicit in the Pentateuchal story and its tensions and the translation of the implications of the narrative into the normative foundations of Israel's social order.

I

Since we deal with the relationship of cognate documents of the same canon, documents that cite one another constantly, last to first, the approach to the description of the period from the Pentateuch to the Mishnah is natural to the evidence itself. Not only so, but the sages themselves recognized the phenomena we address. They realized and stated that important components of the halakhah rested squarely on the foundations of Scripture, others, asymmetrically, and still others, not at all. This they expressed with their usual gift for poetry:

A. The absolution of vows hovers in the air, for it has nothing [in the Torah] upon which to depend.
B. The laws of the Sabbath, festal offerings, and sacrilege – lo, they are like mountains hanging by a string,
C. for they have little Scripture for many laws.
D. Laws concerning civil litigations, the sacrificial cult, things to be kept cultically clean, sources of cultic uncleanness, and prohibited consanguineous marriages have much on which to depend.
E. And both these and those [equally] are the essentials of the Torah.

Mishnah-tractate Hagigah 1:9

The Tosefta cites and glosses the Mishnah's formulation in this way; as usual, its clarifications amply open up the way to understanding the Mishnah's point:

A. *The absolution of vows hovers in the air, for it has nothing upon which to depend in the Torah* [M. Hag. 1:8A].

B. But a sage loosens a vow in accord with his wisdom.

C. *The laws of the Sabbath, festal-offerings, and sacrilege are like mountains hanging by a string, for they have little Scripture for many laws* [M. Hag. 1 :8B].

D. They have nothing upon which to depend.

F. *Laws concerning civil litigations, the sacrificial cult, things to be kept cultically clean, sources of cultic uncleanness, and prohibited consanguineous marriages* [M. Hag. 1:8D],

G. and added to them are laws concerning valuations, things declared *herem,* and things declared sacred –

H. for them there is abundant Scripture, exegesis, and many laws.

I. *They have much on which to depend* [M. Hag. 1:8D].

J. Abba Yosé b. Hanan says, "These eight topics of the Torah constitute *the essentials of the laws* [thereof] [T. Er. 8:24]" [M. Hag. 1:8D-E].

Tosefta Hagigah 1:9

Now what concerns us is clear, and that is, how the halakhah that does build – wholly or in part – upon Scripture reads Scripture and responds to its lessons. But so broad a question does not serve. It would carry us far afield to attempt a systematic and comprehensive characterization of the contribution to the formation of the halakhah of authorities who flourished (in temporal, historical terms) after the closure of the Pentateuch but before the commencement of the Mishnah-Tosefta-Yerushalmi-Bavli.[3] Within the layers of thought, the premises that sustained later inquiry, between Moses and the Mishnah we seek only one element, and that is, the halakhic response to the narrative of Eden – starting with creation and its climax, the Sabbath day.

II

Thus the heavens and the earth were finished and all the host of them. And on the seventh day God finished his work that he had done, and he rested on the seventh day from all his

31

work that he had done. So God blessed the seventh day and sanctified it, because on it God rested from all his work that he had done in creation.

Genesis 2:1–3

The Pentateuch explicitly treats the Sabbath as the occasion for the celebration of Eden, a response to its perfection by an act of perfect repose, and the Pentateuch further accords to the Land of Israel the right to Sabbath rest in the sabbatical year. Those two facts intersect to lead us to the starting point of any picture of how the halakhah at its foundations responds to the Pentateuchal law and lore. By Eden, Scripture means that place whole and at rest that God sanctified, creation in perfect repose. In the halakhah Eden then stands for not a particular place but nature in a defined condition, at a particular moment: creation in Sabbath repose, sanctified. Then a place in repose at the climax of creation, at sunset at the start of the seventh day, whole and at rest, embodies, realizes Eden.

How does the halakhah localize that place? Eden is the place to the perfection of which God responded in the act of sanctification at the advent of the seventh day. Where is that place? Here as elsewhere, the halakhah accommodates itself to both the enlandized and the utopian condition of Israel, the people. So, on the one hand, that place is the Land of Israel. The halakhah of the Oral Torah finds in Scripture ample basis for identifying with the Land of Israel that place perfected on the Sabbath. It is the Land that claims the right to repose on the seventh day and in the seventh year of the septennial cycle. But it is the location of Israel wherever that may be. We begin with enlandized Israel, that is, the Land of Israel, at the moment at which, then and there, Eden was made real: when Israel entered into the Land at the moment of perfection. That moment recovered, Eden is restored – the correct starting point, therefore, for an account of how at its foundations the halakhah rests on the theology found in Scripture by the sages who flourished between Scripture and the initial statement of the halakhah in the Mishnah and the Tosefta.

That view of the Land of Israel forms the explicit position of the halakhah of Shebi'it, the prohibitions of the Seventh Year, the halakhah in the Mishnah that elaborates the Written Torah's commandment:

When you enter the land that I am giving you, the land shall observe a Sabbath of the Lord. Six years you may sow your field and six years you may prune your vineyard and gather in the yield. But in the seventh year the land shall have a

Sabbath of complete rest, a Sabbath of the Lord; you shall not sow your field or prune your vineyard. You shall not reap the aftergrowth of your harvest or gather the grapes of your untrimmed vines; it shall be a year of complete rest for the land. But you may eat whatever the land during its Sabbath will produce – you, your male and female slaves, the hired-hand and bound laborers who live with you, and your cattle and the beasts in your land may eat all its yield.

Leviticus 25:1–8

Sages thus find in Scripture the explicit correlation of the advent of the Sabbath and the condition of the Land, meaning, "the land that I am giving you," which is to say, the Land of Israel. After six years of creation, the Land is owed a Sabbath, as much as is Man. A second, correlative commandment, at Dt. 15:1–3, is treated as well: "Every seventh year you shall practice remission of debts. This shall be the nature of the remission: every creditor shall remit the due that he claims from his neighbor; he shall not dun his neighbor or kinsman, for the remission proclaimed is of the Lord. You may dun the foreigner, but you must remit whatever is due you from your kinsmen."

The Torah represents God as the sole master of creation, the Sabbath as testimony to God's pleasure with the perfection, and therefore sanctification, of creation. The halakhah of Shebi'it sets forth the law that in relationship to the Land of Israel embodies that conviction. The law set forth in the Mishnah, Tosefta, and Talmud of the Land of Israel systematically works through Scripture's rules, treating [1] the prohibition of farming the land during the seventh year; [2] the use of the produce in the seventh year solely for eating, that is to say, its purpose and function by its very nature; and [3] the remission of debts. During the Sabbatical year, Israel relinquishes its ownership of the Land of Israel. So the Sabbath involves giving up ownership, a point to which we shall return later in this chapter. At that time Israelites in farming may do nothing that in secular years effects the assertion of ownership over the land (Avery-Peck, *Yerushalmi Shebi'it,* p. 2). Just as one may not utilize land one does not own, in the Sabbatical year, the farmer gives up ownership of the land that he does own.

What links the Sabbatical Year to Eden's restoration? The reason is clear: the Sabbatical Year recovers that perfect time of Eden when the world was at rest, all things in place. Before the rebellion, man did not have to labor on the land; he picked and ate his meals freely. And, in the nature of things, everything belonged to everybody; private ownership in response to individual labor did not exist, because man did not have to work anyhow. These then represent the halakhah's provisions for the Seventh Year. The Pentateuch goes still further when it treats the violation of the Sabbatical rules as the cause of Israel's exile: "And I will devastate the land...and I will scatter you among the nations...And your land shall be a desolation. Then the land shall enjoy its Sabbaths, as long as it lies desolate, while you are in your enemies' land, then the land shall rest and enjoy the Sabbaths. As long as it lies desolate it shall have rest, the rest that it had not in your Sabbaths when you dwelt upon it" (Lev. 26:32–35).

But what if Israel does accord to the Land its Sabbaths? Reverting to that perfect time, the Torah maintains that the land will provide adequate food for everyone, including the flocks and herds, even – or especially – if people do not work the land. But that is on condition that all claim of ownership lapses; the food is left in the fields, to be picked by anyone who wishes, but it may not be hoarded by the landowner in particular. Avery-Peck states this matter as follows:

> Scripture thus understands the Sabbatical year to represent a return to a perfected order of reality, in which all share equally in the bounty of a holy land that yields its food without human labor. The Sabbatical year provides a model through which, once every seven years, Israelites living in the here-and-now may enjoy the perfected order in which God always intended the world to exist and toward which, in the Israelite world view, history indeed is moving...The release of debts accomplishes for Israelites' economic relationships just what the agricultural Sabbatical accomplishes for the relationship between the people and the land. Eradicating debt allows the Israelite economy to return to the state of equilibrium that existed at the time of creation, when all shared equally in the bounty of the Land.
>
> (Avery-Peck, *Yerushalmi Shebi'it,* p. 3)

The Priestly Code expresses that same concept when it arranges for the return of inherited property at the Jubilee Year to the original family-ownership:

> You shall count off seven weeks of years, so that the period of seven weeks of years gives you a total of forty-nine years... You shall proclaim release throughout the land for all its inhabitants. It shall be a jubilee for you; each of you shall

return to his holding and each of you shall return to his family.

Leviticus 25:8–10

The Jubilee year is observed as is the Sabbatical year, meaning that for two successive years the land is not to be worked. The halakhah we shall examine in due course will establish that when land is sold, it is for the span of time remaining to the next jubilee year. That then marks the reordering of land-holding to its original pattern, when Israel inherited the land to begin with and commenced to enjoy its produce.

Just as the Sabbath commemorates the completion of creation, the perfection of world-order, so does the Sabbatical year. So too, the Jubilee year brings about the restoration of real property to the original division. In both instances, Israelites so act as to indicate they are not absolute owners of the Land, which belongs to God and which is divided in the manner that God arranged in perpetuity. Avery-Peck states the matter in the following way:

> On the Sabbath of creation, during the Sabbatical year, and in the Jubilee year, diverse aspects of Israelite life are to return to the way that they were at the time of creation. Israelites thus acknowledge that, in the beginning, God created a perfect world, and they assure that the world of the here-and-now does not overly shift from its perfect character. By providing opportunities for Israelites to model their contemporary existence upon a perfected order of things, these commemorations further prepare the people for messianic times, when, under God's rule, the world will permanently revert to the ideal character of the time of creation.
>
> (Avery-Peck, *Yerushalmi,* p. 4)

Here we find the halakhic counterpart to the restorationist theology that the Oral Torah sets forth in the aggadah. Israel matches Adam, the Land of Israel, Eden, and, we now see, the Sabbatical year commemorates the perfection of creation and replicates it. (Later in this chapter we shall see that the same conception of relinquishing ownership of one's real property operates to facilitate everyday activities on the Sabbath.)

The Sabbatical year takes effect at the moment of Israel's entry into the Land. That repeated point of insistence then treats the moment of the entry into the Land as the counterpart to the moment of repose, of perfection at rest, of Creation. Observing the commandments of the Sabbatical year marks Israel's effort at keeping the Land like Eden, six days of creation, one day of rest, and so too here:

Sifra CCXLV:I.2.

A. "When you come [into the land which I give you, the land shall keep a Sabbath to the Lord]":

B. Might one suppose that the sabbatical year was to take effect once they had reached Transjordan?

C. Scripture says, "into the land."

D. It is that particular land.

Now comes the key point: the Sabbatical year takes effect only when Israel enters the Land, which is to say, Israel's entry into the Land marks the counterpart to the beginning of the creation of Eden. But a further point will register in a moment. It is when Eden/the Land enters into stasis, the families receiving each its share in the Land, that the process of the formation of the new Eden comes to its climax; then each Israelite bears responsibility for his share of the Land. That is when the Land has reached that state of order and permanence that corresponds to Eden at sunset on the sixth day:

E. Might one suppose that the sabbatical year was to take effect once they had reached Ammon and Moab?

F. Scripture says, "which I give you,"

G. and not to Ammon and Moab.

H. And on what basis do you maintain that when they had conquered the land but not divided it, divided it among familiars but not among fathers' houses so that each individual does not yet recognize his share —

I. might one suppose that they should be responsible to observe the sabbatical year?

J. Scripture says, "[Six years you shall sow] your field,"

K. meaning, each one should recognize his own field.

L. "...your vineyard":

M. meaning, each one should recognize his own vineyard.

N. You turn out to rule:

O. Once the Israelites had crossed the Jordan, they incurred liability to separate dough-offering and to observe the prohibition against eating the fruit of fruit trees for the first three years after planting and the prohibition against eating produce of the new growing season prior to the waving of the sheaf of new grain [that is, on the fifteenth of Nisan].[4]

P. When the sixteenth of Nisan came, they incurred liability to wave the sheaf of new grain.

Q. With the passage of fifty days from then they incurred the liability to the offering of the Two Loaves.

R. At the fourteenth year they became liable for the separation of tithes.

The Sabbatical takes over only when the Israelite farmers have asserted their ownership of the land and its crops. Then the process of counting the years begins.

In relationship to God, the Land of Israel, as much as the People of Israel, emerges as a principal player. The Land is treated as a living entity, a participant in the cosmic drama, as well it should, being the scene of creation and its unfolding. If the perfection of creation is the well-ordered condition of the natural world, then the Land of Israel, counterpart to Eden, must be formed into the model of the initial perfection, restored to that initial condition. So the Sabbath takes over and enchants the Land of Israel as much as it transforms Israel itself. Newman expresses this view in the following language:

For the priestly writer of Leviticus, the seventh year, like the seventh day, is sanctified. Just as God rested from the work of creation on the seventh day and sanctified it as a day of rest, so too God has designated the seventh year for the land's rest. Implicit in this view is the notion that the Land of Israel has human qualities and needs. It must 'observe a Sabbath of the Lord' because, like the people of Israel and God, it too experiences fatigue and requires a period of repose.

> The Land of Israel, unlike all other countries, is enchanted, for it enjoys a unique relationship to God and to the people of Israel. That is to say, God sanctified this land by giving it to his chosen people as an exclusive possession. Israelites, in turn, are obligated to work the Land and to handle its produce in accordance with God's wishes.
>
> (Newman, *Shebi'it,* p. 15)

The counterpart in the matter of the remission of debts works out the conception that all Israelites by right share in the Land and its gifts, and if they have fallen into debt, they have been denied their share; that imbalance is righted every seven years.

The halakhah of the Mishnah then rests on the development of these premises. It outlines where and how man participates in establishing the sanctity of the Sabbatical year, expanding the span of the year to accommodate man's intentionality in working the land now for advantage then. It insists that man's perceptions of the facts, not the facts themselves, govern: what looks like a law violation *is* a law violation. In these and other ways the halakhah of Shebi'it works out the problematics of man's participation in the sanctification of the Land in the Sabbatical year. The topic of the law, restoring the perfection of creation, then joins with the generative problematics of the halakhah to make the point that Israel has in its power to restore the perfection of creation, the ordering of all things to accord with the condition that prevailed when God declared creation good. God, therefore sanctified creation and declared the Sabbath. The particular topic served as the obvious, indeed the ideal, medium to deliver in the context of that message of restoration the critical statement. It is that Israel by a fulfilled act of will bore within its power the capacity to attain the perfection of the world. That is because to begin with Israel's perception of matters – and its actions consequent upon those perceptions – made all the difference.

So the premise of the Mishnah's law, the testimony to the character of the long stage between the Pentateuch and the Mishnah, may be set forth in a few words. During that period of time, sages devoted deep thought to the matter of intentionality, on the one hand, and Eden, on the other. First, God pays the closest attention to Israel's attitudes and intentions. Otherwise there is no way to explain the priority accorded to Israelite perception of whether or not the law is kept, Israelite intention in cultivating the fields in the sixth year, and other critical components of the governing, generative problematic. Second, God furthermore identifies the Land of Israel as the archetype of Eden and model of the world to come. That is why God treats the Land in its perfection just as he treats Eden, by according to the Land the Sabbath rest. He deems the union of Israel and the Land of Israel to effect the sanctification of the Land in its ascending degrees corresponding to the length of the term of Israel's possession. And, finally, God insists, as the ultimate owner of the Land, that at regular intervals, the possession of the Land be relinquished, signalled as null, and that at those same intervals ownership of the produce of the Land at least in potentiality be equally shared among all its inhabitants. Some of these propositions may be deemed implicit in Scripture, some may be understood to require the making of connections between one point of Scripture and another, and some may be regarded as fresh. What is important, in the period under discussion, is that all of them coalesced into a coherent statement, on the foundation of which the law of the Mishnah erected its structure.

III

Now we proceed to another case, where we shall identify the same governing conceptions. Specifically we ask, How is the narrative of Eden and the fall, extending to the formation of Israel as the medium of mankind's regeneration, translated into a system for the governance of the social order? Within the metaphor of Eden and Adam, the Land stands for Eden, Israel the holy people for Adam. Then God relates to Israel through the Land and the arrangements that he imposes upon the Land, beginning with the point of intersection, rules governing the use of the fruit of the trees of the Land. We cannot come closer to the realization of the metaphor of Eden than that! In that context God relates to the Land in response to Israel's residence thereon. But God relates to the Land in a direct way, providing for the Land, as he provides for Israel, the sanctifying moment of the Sabbath. So a web of relationships, direct and indirect, hold together God, Land, and Israel. That is for the here-and-now, all the more so for the world to come. And if that is how God relates to Israel, Israel relates to God in one way above all, and that is, by exercising in ways that show love for God and acceptance of God's dominion the power of free will that God has given man. That brings us to a natural companion of the halakhah of Shebi'it, which is that of 'Orlah – the necessary second step in this exposition of how the halakhah effects the restoration of Eden.

Devoted to the prohibition of the use of the produce of a fruit tree for the first three years after its planting and the restriction as to the use of that same tree's produce in the fourth year after its planting, the halakhah of 'Orlah elaborates the Torah's commandment:

> 'When you come to the land and plant any kind of tree for food, you shall treat it as forbidden. For three years it shall be forbidden, it shall not be eaten. In the fourth year all its fruit shall be set aside for jubilation before the Lord, and only in the fifth year may you use its fruit, that its yield to you may be increased: I am the Lord your God.
>
> Leviticus 19:23–25

The produce of the fourth year after planting is brought to Jerusalem ("for jubilation before the Lord") and eaten there. But the main point of the halakhah centers upon the prohibition of the fruit for the first three years.

In the halakhah, the role of man in precipitating the effect of the prohibition takes priority. Man has a role in bringing about the prohibition of the law, but man cannot by his intentionality change the facts of the case. How does the Israelite farmer's intentionality govern? It is man's assessment of the use of the tree that classifies the tree as a fruit-tree or as a tree of some other category, e.g., one meant for lumber. If man deems the tree planted for fruit, then the prohibition applies. But man cannot declare as a fruit-tree, so subjecting the produce to the prohibition for three years from planting, one that does not bear fruit at all. Man's actions reveal his original intentionality for the tree, e.g., how the tree is planted.

Here is an explicit statement, in connection with the exegesis of the halakhah, that intentionality dictates whether or not a tree that can bear fruit is actually covered by the prohibition. Trees not used for fruit are not affected by the prohibition, so the farmer may use the lumber even in the first three years from planting; and parts of trees not intended for fruit are not subject to it either, so may be pruned off and used for fuel. But intention cannot classify what nature has already designated for one or another category. In the following, Simeon b. Gamaliel refines the law by insisting that man's intention conform to the facts of nature. That is to say, if one planted a tree for lumber or firewood but it is not appropriate for such a use, then his intentionality is null.

7. A. "…trees for food":
    B. this excludes the case of planting trees for fence posts or lumber or firewood.

C. R. Yosé says, "Even if he said, 'The side of the tree facing inward is to be used for food and the side outward is to be used as a fence, the side of the tree inward is liable to the laws of 'orlah, and the side of the tree facing outward is exempt" [M. Orlah 1:1A-D].

D. Said Rabban Simeon b. Gamaliel, "Under what circumstances? When he planted it as a fence for lumber or for firewood, a use appropriate for those trees. But when he planted it as a fence, for lumber, or for firewood in a case not appropriate for that species, the tree is liable to the laws of 'orlah" [T. Orl 1:1C-H].

E. How do we know the law given just now?

F. Scripture says, "all kinds of trees."

The matter of appropriateness will recur many times, since the intense interest of the halakhah in the correct classification of things comes to expression in an interesting notion. A thing has its inherent, intrinsic purpose, and when it serves that purpose, it is properly used; when it does not, it is improperly used. How does that make a difference? What is edible is food, and produce that may serve for food or for fuel, if it is of a sacred status, cannot be used for anything but food. So intentionality meets its limits in the purpose that a thing is supposed to serve, that is to say, intentionality is limited by teleology. That explains why, also, if the farmer planted the tree for firewood and changed his mind, then the change of his intentionality effects a change in the status of the tree:

G. If he planted it for firewood and then gave thought to use the tree for food, how do we know that it is liable?

H. Scripture says, "And you will plant every kind of fruit tree."

I. From what point do they count the years of the tree for purposes of determining liability to 'orlah?

J. From the time that it is planted [T. Orl. 1:1I-L].

The connection of the tree to the land dictates liability; a fruit-tree planted in an unperforated pot is exempt from the law. The law extends not only to the whole fruit but also to defective produce and parts of the fruit. And what is interesting, the time when the farmer initially plants the tree marks the starting point for reckoning the three years, not when he decides to use it for fruit rather than lumber. In that case, the actuality takes over, and sets aside the intentionality. The farmer's initial intent may classify the tree as other-than-a-fruit-tree, but the potentiality as a fruit-tree persists, so when the farmer's second thoughts take over the initial status of the tree, not the intervening one, is what counts, a very profound way of seeing the matter, rich in potential consequences that are not explored here.

The power of the metaphor of Eden emerges, we shall now see, in specificities of the law. These turn out to define with some precision a message on the relationship of Israel to the Land of Israel and to God. If we turn to Sifra, a systematic exegesis of the book of Leviticus in dialogue with the halakhah of the Mishnah, at Sifra CCII:I.1, our attention is drawn to a number of quite specific traits of the law of 'Orlah, and these make explicit matters of religious conviction that we might otherwise miss. The first is that the prohibition of 'orlah-fruit applies solely within the Land of Israel and not to the neighboring territories occupied by Israelites, which means that, once again, it is the union of Israel with the Land of Israel that invokes the prohibition:

Sifra CCII:I.1. A. "When you come [into the land and plant all kinds of trees for food, then you shall count their fruit as forbidden; three years it shall be forbidden to you, it must not be eaten. And in the fourth year all their fruit shall be holy, an offering of praise to the Lord. But in the fifth year you may eat of their fruit, that they may yield more richly for you: I am the Lord your God" (Lev. 19:23–25).]

B. Might one suppose that the law applied once they came to Transjordan?

C. Scripture says, "...into the land,"

D. the particular Land [of Israel].

What that means is that some trait deemed to inhere in the Land of Israel and no other territory must define the law, and a particular message ought to inhere in this law.

This same point registers once more: it is only trees that Israelites plant in the Land that are subject to the prohibition, not those that gentiles planted before the Israelites inherited the land:

Sifra CCII:I.2. A. "When you come into the land and plant":

B. excluding those that gentiles have planted prior to the Israelites' coming into the land.

C. Or should I then exclude those that gentiles

> planted even after the Israelites came into the
> land?
> D. Scripture says, "all kinds of trees."

A further point of special interest requires that the Israelite plant the tree as an act of deliberation; if the tree merely grows up on its own, it is not subject to the prohibition. So Israelite action joined to Israelite intention is required:

Sifra CCII:I.4. A. "...and plant...":
                  B. excluding one that grows up on its own.
                  C. "...and plant...":
                  D. excluding one that grows out of a grafting or sinking a root.

The several points on which Sifra's reading of the halakhah and the verses of Scripture that declare the halakhah alert us to a very specific religious principle embedded in the halakhah of 'orlah.

First, as with Shebi'it, the law takes effect only from the point at which Israel enters the land. That is to say, the point of Israel's entry into the Land marks the beginning of the Land's consequential fecundity. In simpler language, the fact that trees produce fruit matters only from Israel's entry onward. To see what is at stake, we recall that the entry of Israel into the Land marks the restoration of Eden. The Land bears fruit — I emphasize — *of which God takes cognizance* only when the counterpart-moment of creation has struck. The halakhah has no better way of saying, the entry of Israel into the Land compares with the moment at which the creation of Eden took place. In this way, moreover, the law of Shebi'it finds its counterpart. Shebi'it concerns telling time, marking off seven years to the Sabbath of creation, the one that affords rest to the Land. The halakhah of 'Orlah also means telling time. Specifically, 'Orlah-law marks the time of the creation of produce from the moment of Israel's entry into the land. Israel's entry into the Land marks a new beginning, comparable to the very creation of the world, just as the Land at the end matches Eden at the outset.

Second, Israelite intentionality is required to subject a tree to the 'orlah-rule. If an Israelite does not plant the tree with the plan of producing fruit, then the tree is not subject to the rule. If the tree grows up on its own, not by the act and precipitating intentionality of the Israelite, the 'orlah-rule does not apply. If an Israelite does not plant the tree to produce fruit, the 'orlah-rule does not apply. And given the character of creation, which marks the norm, the tree must be planted in the ordinary way; if grafted or sunk as a root, the law does not apply.

Third, the entire issue of the halakhah comes down to Israelite restraint in using the produce of the orchards. What is the counterpart to Israelite observance of the restraint of three years? And why should Israelite intentionality play so critical a role, since, Sifra itself notes, the 'orlah-rule applies to trees planted even by gentiles? The answer becomes obvious we ask another question: Can we think of any other commandments concerning fruit-trees in the Land that – sages say time and again – is Eden? Of course we can: "Of every tree of the garden you are free to eat; but as for the tree of knowledge of good and evil, you must not eat of it" (Gen. 2:16). But the halakhah of 'orlah imposes upon Israel a more demanding commandment. Of *no* fruit-tree in the new Eden may Israel eat for three years. That demands considerable restraint. Israel must exceed the humble requirement of obedience in regard to a fruit-tree that God assigned to Adam, the Land imposes obligations far in excess of those carried by Eden. And the issue devolves upon Israel's will or attitude, much as Eden turned tragic by reason of Man's rebellious will.

That is because Israel's own intentionality – not God's – imposes upon every fruit-bearing tree – and not only the one of Eden – the prohibition of three years. That is the point of the stress on the effects of Israel's desire for the fruit. So once Israel wants the fruit, it must show that it can restrain its desire and wait for three years. By Israel's act of will, Israel has imposed upon itself the requirement of restraint. Taking the entry-point as our guide, we may say that, from the entry into the Land and for the next three years, trees that Israelites value for their fruit and plant with the produce in mind must be left untouched. And, for all time thereafter, when Israelites plant fruit-trees, they must recapitulate that same exercise of self-restraint, that is, act as though, for the case at hand, they have just come into the Land.

To find the context in which these rules make their statement, we must ask that details, not only the main point, carry the message. So we ask, why three years in particular? A glance at the narrative of Creation provides the obvious answer. Fruit trees were created on the third day of creation. Then, when Israel by intention and action designates a tree – any tree – as fruit-bearing, Israel recapitulates the order of creation and so must wait for three years, as creation waited for three years. Then the planting of every tree imposes upon Israel the occasion to meet once more the temptation that the first Adam could not overcome. Israel now relives the temptation of Adam then, but Israel, the New Adam, possesses, and is possessed by, the Torah. By its own action and intention in planting fruit trees, Israel finds itself in a veritable orchard of trees like the tree of knowledge of good and evil. Permitted to eat all fruit but one, Adam ate the forbidden fruit, while Israel refrains for a specified span of time from fruit from all trees. The difference between Adam and Israel marks what has taken place through Israel, in the Land of Israel, which is the regeneration of humanity. The enlandizement of the halakhah bears that very special message, and I can imagine no other way of making that statement through law than in the explicit concern sages register for the fruit-trees of the Land of Israel. No wonder, then, that 'orlah-law finds its position, in the Priestly Code, in the rules of sanctification.

So when Israel enters the Land, in exactly the right detail Israel recapitulates the drama of Adam in Eden, but with this formidable difference. The outcome ought not to be the same. By its own act of will Israel addresses the temptation of Adam and overcomes the same temptation, not once but every day through time beyond measure. Adam could not wait out the week, but Israel waits for three years – the same length of time God waited in creating fruit trees. Adam picked and ate. But here too there is a detail not to be missed. Even after three years, Israel may not eat the fruit wherever it chooses. Rather, in the fourth year from planting, Israel will still show restraint, bringing the fruit only "for jubilation before the Lord" in Jerusalem. This signals that the once-forbidden fruit now eaten in public, not in secret, before the Lord, is a moment of celebration. That detail too recalls the Fall and makes its comment upon the horror of the fall. That is, when Adam ate the fruit, he shamefully hid from God for having eaten the fruit. But when Israel eats the fruit, it does so proudly, joyfully, above all, publicly before the Lord. The contrast is not to be missed, so too the message. Faithful Israel refrains when it is supposed to, and so it has every reason to cease to refrain and to eat "before the Lord." It has nothing to hide, and everything to show.

And there is more. In the fifth year Israel may eat on its own, the time of any restraint from enjoying the gifts of the Land having ended. That sequence provides fruit for the second Sabbath of creation, and so through time. How so? Placing Adam's sin on the first day after the first Sabbath, thus Sunday, then calculating the three forbidden years as Monday, Tuesday, and Wednesday of the second week of creation, reckoning on the jubilation of Thursday, we come to the Friday, eve of the second Sabbath of creation. So now, a year representing a day of the Sabbatical week, just as Leviticus says so many times in connection with the Sabbatical year, the three prohibited years allow Israel to show its true character, fully regenerate, wholly and humbly accepting God's commandment, the one Adam broke. And the rest follows.

Here, then, is the message of the 'orlah-halakhah, the statement that only through the details of the laws of 'orlah as laid out in both parts of the Torah, written and oral, the halakhah could hope to make. By its own act of restraint, the New Adam, Israel, in detailed action displays its repentance in respect to the very sin that the Old Adam committed, the sin of disobedience and rebellion. Facing the same opportunity to sin, Israel again and again over time refrains from the very sin that cost Adam Eden. So by its manner of cultivation of the Land and its orchards, Israel manifests what in the very condition of humanity has changed by the giving of the Torah: the advent of humanity's second chance, through Israel. Only in the Land that succeeds Eden can Israel, succeeding Adam, carry out the acts of regeneration that the Torah makes possible.

But, I hasten to add, the halakhah presents as the norms for a social system not only what happened in Eden, with its tragic consequences, but also what happened with Israel in the Land of Israel, producing equally weighty results. Israel corrupted the perfected Land, losing out on Eden, as the narrative from Joshua through Kings conveys. So the halakhah will have to, and does, accommodate not only the restoration of Eden in the Land by the New Adam that is Israel, but also the recapitulation of the tragedy of Eden by Israel in the Land, as Lev. 26 explicitly states. It is the principle of the priority of Israelite will, the consequentiality of Israelite intentionality, that we encounter time and again in the halakhic chapters of Eden and the Land.

IV

An enlandized relationship, then, identifies the encounter between Israel and God with not only the right time and the right person but also the right place: the Land God has chosen for the People whom he has chosen. When it comes to the details, the Written Torah defines the conditions in which Israel is to work that particular Land, deriving its sustenance from the Land and its exceptional gifts. These are the rules of interior relationship that govern when in God's presence and by his act, holy Israel and the Land are (re)joined together. These rules turn out to establish for the Land the order and system that characterize Eden: all things properly classified, species by species.

Here, again, the generative premises of the Mishnah's halakhah turn out to form the layer between the laconic statement of the Pentateuch and the elaborate articulation of the Mishnah itself – the layer and as before, the foundation of all to follow. The halakhah of Kilayim elaborates upon Leviticus:

> You shall not let your cattle mate with a different kind; you shall not sow your field with two kinds of seed; you shall not put on cloth from a mixture of two kinds of material.
>
> Leviticus 19:19

Further, Deuteronomy figures:

> You shall not sow your vineyard with a second kind of seed, otherwise the crop from the seed you have sown and the produce of the vineyard may not be used; you shall not plow with an ox and an ass together; you shall not wear cloth that combines wool and linen.
>
> Deuteronomy 22:9–11

Lev. 19:2 places into the context of the sanctification of Israel the considerations of meticulous division among classes or species of the animal and vegetable world that define the tractate's topic. Sanctification takes place in the context of Gen. 1:1–2:4, the orderly creation of the world, species by species. The act of sanctification of creation took place when all things were ordered, properly in place, each according to its kind. Creation takes place when chaos is brought under control and ordered, that is when the world is made perfect and ready for God's act of sanctification. Mandelbaum observes, "The point of the laws of the Priestly Code in Leviticus…is to prevent the confusion of those classes and categories that were established at the creation. P thus commands man to restore the world from its present condition of chaos to its original orderly state, and so to make the world ready once again for sanctification."[5]

From one viewpoint Kilayim takes God's perspective on the Land, imagining the landscape as seen from on high. God wants to see in the Land an orderly and regular landscape, each species in its proper place. He wants to see Israel clothed in garments that preserve the distinction between animal and vegetable. He wants to see animals ordered by their species, just as they were when Noah brought them into the ark (Gen. 7:14). What that means is that grapes and wheat are not to grow together, oxen and asses are not to be yoked together, and wool and linen – animal and vegetable fibers – are not to be worn in a single garment together.

But from another viewpoint, it is the perspective of not God but man, Israel in particular, that dictates matters. For who bears responsibility for restoring the perfection of creation? The Priestly Code wants the land to be returned to its condition of an unchanging perfection. But the Mishnah, Mandelbaum states, has a different view:

> The Mishnah underlines man's power to impose order upon the world, a capacity unaffected by historical events. In spite of the occurrence of catastrophes and disasters, man retains the ability to affect the world around him through such ordinary activities as sowing a field. While the Priestly Code thus has man confront confusion by reconstructing the ideal order of creation, the Mishnah regards man as imposing his own order upon a world in a state of chaos, and, so, in effect, as participating in the process of creation.[6]

Man has the power to do in the Land of Israel what God did in creating the world at Eden, that is, establish order, overcome chaos, perfect the world for the occasion of sanctification. The law thus embodies in the topic at hand the view prevailing throughout the halakhah, as formulated at M. Kel. 17:11: "Everything is according to the measure of the man." The halakhah that elaborates the commandments on the present topic set forth in Scripture makes man God's partner in overcoming chaos and establishing order. It is man's perspective that governs, man's discernment that identifies chaos or affirms order.

Now if we ask ourselves, how in a religious system that deems man created in God's image, after God's likeness, do we account for the law's stress on man's view, an answer immediately presents itself. Man's perspective governs, how man sees the Land determines whether or not the law is obeyed, for two reasons. The first is that, with man created "in our image, after our likeness," man's and God's perspectives are the same. If man discerns the confusion of species, so would God, and if man does not, then neither would God. But when the halakhah leaves matters relative to appearance to man, the actualities of mixed seeds no longer matter, or matter so much as appearances. And that requires a second reason as well. For if God cares that "you shall not sow your field with two kinds of seed and that you shall not sow your vineyard with a second kind of seed," surely the actuality, not the appearance, ought to prevail – unless another consideration registers. That consideration comes into play when we ask, how, through the shared engagement with the Land, do God and Israel collaborate, and to what end?

The answer to that question exposes the second, and I think, principal, explanation for the emphasis of the halakhah upon how man sees things, Israelite man being the subject throughout. Israel is in charge of the Land. Israel not only bears responsibility for what happens in the land, but also bears the blame and the penalty when matters are not right. Israel relates to God through Israel's trusteeship of the Land. The tractates that deal with the enlandizement of the relationship of Israel to God, Kilayim and the others, present Israel as the trustee of the Land and, as we see in the present tractate, assign to Israel the task of cultivating the Land in a manner appropriate to the perfection of creation at the outset. No wonder, then, that Israel's view of matters must prevail, for Israel bears full responsibility on the spot for how things will appear to Heaven.

That fact – Israel's responsibility to farm the Land in accord with the orderly rule of Eden – makes Israel not only the custodian of the Land but also partner in that vast labor of reform that, in the end, will bring about the restoration of Adam to Eden. Adam did not have to labor – for a harvest he needed only to reach up and pick the fruit. His only responsibility was not to eat the produce of one particular tree. Israel for its part had to work the Land and bore responsibility for the appearance of the whole of it. For, we recall, it is God's plan at the end to bring to life all Israel and in the world or age to come to restore all Israel to the Land of Israel, completing the return to Eden but with the difference made by the Torah: Israel back to the Land of Israel compares to Adam in Eden in all but one aspect. Armed with the Torah, Israel will not rebel as Adam did. That is why, the restorationist teleology maintains, the world to come will endure: chaos overcome, order will prevail. How Israel cultivates the Holy Land entrusted to it then makes all the difference, field by field in its correct configuration.

The restoration of Adam to Eden takes place, at the end, in and through the restoration, to the Land of Israel, of Israel, the particular embodiment of that part of Adam, or humanity, that knows God through the Torah. So all matters cohere. In assigning to Israel the task of farming the country in a manner appropriate to the principles of creation, therefore, the halakhah asks Israel to do its concrete part in restorationist teleology: to make the end like the beginning, Eden recovered. Once God has assigned the Land to Israel and instructed

Israel on how to attain and preserve its condition of perfection as at creation, then Israel's perspective, not God's, must govern, because, for Israel, the stakes are very high: the resurrection of the dead to life, the restoration of Israel to the Land. But the halakhah concerns the here and now, and that brings us to the Sabbath of creation, which Israel celebrates, in the Land and otherwise, every seventh day.

V

The key to the entire system of interaction between God and Israel through the Land and its gifts emerges in the halakhah of Ma'aserot and its companions, which deal – along the lines of Shebi'it and 'Erubin (treated in Chapter Three, in the context of the Mishnah's own stage) – with the difference between possession and ownership. We shall now see that it is in the interim between the Pentateuch and the earliest phases of the Mishnah's halakhah that that distinction is worked out and established.

It takes the following form. God owns the world, which he made. But God has accorded to man the right of possession of the earth and its produce. This he did twice, once to Man in Eden, the second time to Israel in the Land of Israel. And to learn the lesson that Adam did not master, that possession is not ownership but custody and stewardship, Israel has to acknowledge the claims of the creator to the glory of all creation, which is the Land. This Israel does by giving back God's share of the produce of the Land at the time, and in the manner, that God defines. The enlandized components of the halakhah therefore form a single, cogent statement of matters.

If there is a single obstacle to obedience to God's will, it is man's natural inclination to take possession for ownership. For it is the attitude expressed in the claim of entire right of ownership – "my power and the might of my hand have gotten me this abundance" (Dt. 8:17) – that conveys the arrogance motivating rebellion such as took place to begin with in Eden. Man made his own the fruit of the tree, an act of ownership declaring, my will alone governs the disposition of this fruit. Someone who can do anything that he wants with a given object or person or property owns that object, person, or property. Someone whose will therefore is limited by the will of Another does not. Hence, for its part, the antidote to rebellion and sin, which is the Torah, would impose upon ownership of the Land the supererogatory obligation to acknowledge a divided right of ownership and possession, that is to say, a partner's claim. And for Israel in the Land, the partner is God. And at stake is Israel's demonstration that, this time around, Man acts with correct intentionality, responding to God's will with obedience, not rebellion.

Ma'aserot, the tractate concerning generic "tithes," discusses the entire set of agricultural dues, viewed generically: what the Israelite owes God out of the produce of the Land (and not in particular the tenth of the crop paid to this party, or the tenth of that tenth paid to that). The rules set forth here pertain to all the agricultural tithes and offerings and dictate the procedures – liability, timing, special problems – that pertain to them in general. The point of the halakhah, permeating all categories, is that when Israel asserts its rights of possession, God's interest in that same crop is provoked, and he lays claim to his share in the crop of Land that ownership of which is held in partnership between God and the Israelite farmer. Then the rest follows, a vast exercise in how the will of God and the will of the Israelite meet in concord, Israel obeying God's laws about the disposition of the abundance of the Land. The link to Eden is firm: Israel obeys laws concerning the disposition of the fruit of the Land in the way in which Adam did not obey those concerning the fruit of Eden.

The basic halakhic principle concerns not only Israel's relationship with God but also Israel's correspondence to God. In concrete terms the halakhah realizes the theological position of the Pentateuchal account, which makes explicit that God and Israel relate through the Land. That is where the conflict of wills – the free will of Israelite man, the commanding voice of the God who created all things – works itself out. And the point of conflict focuses upon the conduct of Israel in the Land. The halakhah accords to Israel possession, but not ownership of the Land, which God alone retains. God asserts his ownership when Israel proposes to exercise its rights of usufruct: when the tenant takes his share of the crop, he must also hand over to the Landowner (and to those designated by him to receive his share) the portion of the crop that is owing. And until the tenant, in possession of the Land, does pay his rent, he may not utilize the crop as owners may freely do.

In his commentary to Mishnah-Tosefta Ma'aserot Jaffee states the religious principle in this language:

> A supernatural claim to the tithes is made upon produce grown by Israelites at the precise moment at which they wish to use it...The farmer's appropriation of the produce offers an opportunity to explore issues involving the nature of ownership and the effects of human intentions in bringing out ownership. These reflections on the tension between the

farmer's right to his produce and his duty to satisfy super-natural claims upon it before he eats it comprise the bulk of the tractate.

(Jaffee, *Mishnah*, p. 13)

The obligation to tithe represents God's limitation on rights of ownership of the Land. Israel possesses the Land, but God is the owner, in that God can evict Israel from the Land and has done so in the past, just as God evicted prior occupants.

It follows that the halakhah rests upon the principle that, while Israel possesses it, God owns the Land, and the agricultural offerings that Israel sets aside for those designated by God as his scheduled castes – the priest, the poor, the support of Jerusalem, for example – represent God's share of the crops. God and man lay claim to the produce of the Land. Only when the produce is shown by the actions of the farmer to be valuable to the farmer does God's claim emerge: "Only after produce has ripened may we expect the farmer to use it in his own meals or sell it for others for use in theirs. Thus God's claim to it is first provoked…from that point onward" (Jaffee, *Mishnah*, p. 4). That principle is expressed in the law that produce that is ownerless is not liable to tithing, e.g., produce of the Seventh Year and the like. In this connection Jaffee further states:

Produce is liable to the removal of tithes either at the time it is intended for use as a meal or at the time it is claimed as private property, whichever happens to come first.…In both instances a human being has appropriated for his personal benefit produce against which God has a claim. God's claim is violated…whenever an Israelite farmer or householder prepares to use untithed produce as if he had full rights regarding its disposition. Whether he prepares it for a meal out in the field or brings raw food into his home for the use of his family, he has claimed rights of ownership that in fact are still God's. Accordingly, the Israelite must give to God his due before exercising his own property rights.

(Jaffee, *Mishnah*, p. 3)

The farmer may use the produce as his own only when he has acknowledged God's claim, not eating the produce as if it were his own, but only after setting aside God's share. If the farmer prepares to make a meal of the produce in the field or claims to be sole owner, he loses his right to eat the food until he tithes (Jaffee, p. 4). Meeting God's claim, the farmer may then use the produce.

The system of obligatory tithing then gets underway when the Israelite proposes to exercise his will over his domain and its produce. But at that point, it is not only God's will that comes into play. Every other party to the system then responds to the intentionality of the farmer. As Jaffee points out, priests cannot claim their dues whenever they choose, and God does not take an active role in determining when the produce must be tithed (Jaffee, p. 4). Human actions that reveal human intentions provoke God: when the farmer indicates that he plans to dispose of the fruit, God wants his share. Jaffee expresses this matter in the following language:

> The fundamental theological datum of Maaserot...is that God acts and wills in response to human intentions. God's invisible action can be discerned by carefully studying the actions of human beings....the halakhah of Maaserot locates the play of God's power...in an invisible realm immune from the hazards of history...the realm of human appetite and intention...God...acts and wills...only in reaction to the action and intention of his Israelite partner on the Land....Those who impose upon themselves the task of reconstructing the human and social fabric of Israelite life make effective the holiness of the Land and make real the claims of its God.
>
> (Jaffee, *Mishnah*, p. 5)

As we see, the halakhah spins out the implications of the distinction between possession and ownership. How do I claim that the present halakhic construction bears the burden of Eden? Just as, in connection with Shebi'it and 'Erubin, the halakhah underscores the ambiguous character of Israel's possession of its own domain, in the one case asserting God's ownership, in the other insisting upon the householder's relinquishing his control of his domain, so here too the same transaction characterizes Israel's relationship with God. Israel holds with open arms what God has given, thus the distinction between possession and ownership.

But the connection not only recapitulates what is already familiar. It also yields a further and fresh, if related, consideration. In the account of Eden, God's will comes into conflict with Man's, showing God and Man to be emotionally consubstantial, so here too, God and Man respond in the same way to the same facts. How is it that Israel and God relate in so concrete and specific a situation as is defined by the course of nature, the ripening of the crops? It is because, the halakhah takes for granted, God and Israel bear the same attitudes, feel the same emotions, form corresponding intentions. God and man are alike not only in intellect – the same rules of reasoning applying to both – but also, and especially, in attitude and emotion, in virtue in the classic sense. God commands Israel to love him, therefore God values and prizes the emotion of love. Man is commanded to love God. But that is not the only emotion shared by man and God. In the biblical biography of God, the tragic hero, God, will despair, love, hope, feel disappointment or exultation. The biblical record of God's feelings and God's will concerning the feelings of humanity – wanting human love, for example – leaves no room for doubt. In this matter, the Rabbinic literature is explicit when it says, "the merciful God wants the heart." God commands that humanity love God with full heart, soul, mind and might, because God feels and values that same emotion. God's heart, not only his rationality, corresponds to man's. In that context we take up the halakhic position outlined in Ma'aserot. When the farmer wants the crop, so too does God. When the householder takes the view that the crop is worthwhile, God responds by forming the same opinion. The theological anthropology that brings God and the householder into the same continuum prepares the way for understanding what makes the entire Mishnaic system work.

The agricultural dues to which Ma'aserot in general makes reference are assigned to God's dependents, specifically the sacerdotal castes, priests and Levites, and the poor; and they are further used to support the holy city, Jerusalem, by securing an enhanced supply of food and an increased flow of funds to the city. In addition, obligatory and votive offerings for the Temple, both in specie (Temple coin) and the produce of nature (animals, wine, and grain), support the Temple buildings and the cycle of regular offerings that are maintained in the city. The upshot is, Israel in the holy Land, God's partners in the possession of the country and its abundance, give back to Heaven through designated castes, locations, and activities, God's share in the whole, and this the holy people do both in obedience to God's commandments and also on their own initiative.

VI

From tithes read generically, we proceed to the priestly rations ("heave-offering") and how these are represented, first in Scripture, then in the Mishnah – but principally in the space in-between. What we shall now see is profound reflection on the interplay between Israel's will and the actualities of the natural world, a generative premise emerging that is entirely familiar up to this point, but explicitly present in the Pentateuch in no specific way I can discern, though perhaps implicitly in many contexts. What Scripture has to say is very simple. The pertinent verses of Scripture are in Numbers:

> Then the Lord said to Aaron, "Behold, I have given to you whatever is kept of the offerings made to me, all the consecrated things of the people of Israel; I have given them to you as a perpetual due. This shall be yours of the Most Holy Things reserved from the fire: every offering of theirs, every cereal offering of theirs and every sin offering of theirs and every guilt offering of theirs, which they render to me, shall be most holy to you and to your sons. In a Most Holy Place you shall eat of it; it is holy to you. This also is yours: the offering of their gift, all the wave offerings of the people of Israel; I have given them to you and to your sons and daughters with you, as a perpetual due; every one who is clean in your house may eat of it. All the best of the oil and all the best of the wine and of the grain, the first of them, which they give to the Lord, I give to you. The first ripe fruits of all that is in their land, which they bring to the Lord, shall be yours; every one who is clean in your house may eat of it."
>
> Numbers 18:8–13

Accordingly, the heave-offering is holy and belongs to the priests, to be eaten in a state of cultic cleanness by the priest and his household.

The halakhah of Terumot constitutes a vast exegesis of a single religious principle: the Israelite has the power by an act of will confirmed (where required) by a concrete deed to sanctify what is common. The Israelite then is accorded by God the remarkable power to designate as holy, by reason of the Israelite's own uncoerced will, what is otherwise ordinary and not sacred. Not the only category of the halakhah to embody in concrete actions that considerable proposition, the halakhah of Terumot nonetheless forms a remarkably apt medium for delivering that message. That is because of the stress in the halakhah at hand on considerations of particularity: the householder's act of sanctification pertains to a very specific batch of produce, the consequence of sanctification invokes a very particular teleology inherent in the type of produce that has been sanctified.

The upshot is, Israel's and God's purposes and power intersect. And, to revert to what we have learned in the halakhah of Ma'aserot, here possession shades over, if not to ownership, then to responsibility: for that which is subject to one's will, one is responsible, and that means, specifically, one must conform to God's will that which is subject to one's own will.

A critical component of the Israelite's relationship to God is his responsibility for preserving the sanctification of what belongs to God and is designated for God's clients. It is the thought, confirmed by deed, of the Israelite that what is secular is made sacred. Avery-Peck expressed that principle in the following language: "It is the common Israelite, the non-priest, who, while forbidden to eat holy produce, has the power to cause produce to be deemed holy." The active player in the designation and disposition of the portion of the crops to serve as heave-offering for the priest therefore is the Israelite householder or farmer, not the priest, and not God (except through the working of chance). Once God's interest in the crop has made the crop liable to the separation of the various tithes and offerings, it is the householder who takes over, and by an act of deliberation and intentionality, imparts the status of holiness to the portion of the crop he designates for the priesthood. And he bears full responsibility, also, for what happens to the designated produce until it is handed over to the priest. Avery-Peck frames the matter in this way:

> The common Israelite is central in the process of sanctification. The holy heave-offering comes into being only if man properly formulates the intention to sanctify part of his produce and indicates that intention through corresponding words and actions.
>
> (Avery-Peck, *Mishnah*, p. 3)

All else flows from that basic principle. The Israelite householder has the power to initiate the entire process of sanctification, to transform the classification of produce and to subject that produce to the logic that inheres in its very character: its own teleology. The householder then restores to God his share in the crop and imposes upon God's share the discipline required by the logical character of that particular crop.

A productive corollary insists that the intentionality of the Israelite pertain to a very specific, differentiated corpus of produce. While holiness does not inhere in a given batch, so that the heave-offering of one batch may serve for several, nonetheless batches must be formed of like produce. That means that one's intentionality pertains to the species, not to the genus: olive oil, not olives in general, and so throughout. The particularity of the focus of intentionality cannot be overstated; the halakhah stresses the matter in a wide range of cases, e.g., they may not separate oil as heave-offering for olives which have been crushed, nor wine as heave-offering for grapes which have been trampled but the processing of which has not yet been completed.

On the other hand, when it comes to the actual identification of the portion of the crop to serve as heave-offering and so to be sanctified, the householder cannot act deliberately, choosing this part and not that, but must act in such a way that chance produces the selection. One cannot measure, weigh, or count out the produce that is to be sanctified; rather, God indicates his choice through the workings of chance. That chance constitutes the expression of God's will is made explicit in various aggadic passages, and here the halakhah makes exactly the same statement. So man's intentionality arouses God's participation in the transaction, but God's role in making the selection then excludes man's participation in that chapter of the matter.

This brings us back to the correlative considerations, the specificity of intentionality, the teleology of that to which intentionality pertains. To state the matter in concrete terms: man's intentionality to sanctify an object must pertain to the particular object in mind, and God's intentionality for the sanctified object must be deemed equally specific. Man must sanctify a specific thing. God in creating that same specific thing did so for a particular purpose, and whoever gains the thing that man has sanctified must use that same thing in the manner that God has intended. The prerequisite of the act of sanctification – specificity – then finds its match in the teleology of that which is sanctified, man's intent, God's plan, matching for what is holy. What matches is the priority of an actor's plan.

Man's intent for a given object accordingly bears the power to classify as sacred that particular object. God's intent in making that same object controls the legitimate use of the object that is sanctified. So the plan or attitude or program of each party to the transaction – the householder's, God's – governs. But that takes place for each party in his own way. Man's intentionality dictates the classification of the object as God's (that is, as sanctified) and then, God's, the disposition, of the object now subjected to his ownership. That is where the teleology of things enters in. We may then say, once man has assigned ownership to God (through God's surrogates), God's plan in making an object, the teleology that inheres in that object, takes over. No wonder, then, that the halakhah so emphasizes the specificity of the transaction: this particular object (batch of produce), serving the natural purpose that inheres in this particular object, forming the transaction at which man and God intersect.

That somewhat complicated calculus yields a quite simple and now obvious proposition. In assigning to the status of sanctification a portion of the crop, the householder gives up his possession of, thus his right to subject to his own will, a batch of produce and assigns that which he gives up to God's domain, therefore making the produce subject to God's will. God's will then extends to Israel in its way, to nature in its context. Stated in this way, the transaction in heave-offering represents an act of submission by man's to God's will that is very specific and concrete. The importance of the specificity of intentionality, on the one side, and the particularity of the teleology that governs the use of heave-offering, on the other hand, now merges. Israel and nature relate to God in accord with the same rules, in the same way, but in quite different dimensions.

Two distinct categories of the halakhah turn out to work together to make a single, quite remarkable statement, the one through the rules of sanctification through an act of will, the other through the disposition of that which has been sanctified in accord with the teleology that inheres therein. The message is the same: all things conform to the intention of the One who made them, each in its context and for its purpose. The obedience is not only the householder to the will of the senior partner, the Land-owner; it is also the conformity of the utilization of what has been sanctified to the purpose and intent of that same Actor. The householder conforms his will to God's. The produce likewise accords, in how it is legitimately utilized, to God's purpose. Designating produce as heave-offering and then utilizing it in an appropriate manner then form a drama in which the actor and the acted upon – that is, the component of nature that is classified, sanctified – come together. Israel and nature, each in its way, carry out God's purpose, the one by the act of will, the other by the very character of its being. Israel by an act of will realizes God's will, nature, acted upon, bears witness to God by teleology's forming the criterion of legitimate utilization, that alone.

So the halakhah of Terumot returns us by a direct and smooth route to the issues of creation, once more realizing in concrete words and gestures the dynamics of the relationship between God and man – now: Israelite man, the householder – in creation. God has created the realm of nature, Eden and the Land (to invoke the principal locative categories of the aggadic-halakhic system, respectively). He did so with a purpose, and in each component of creation the Creator's plan for that thing is inherent. And, we may now say, [1] when, through man's initiative, a component of creation is declared sacred, that particular thing, subject to the intentionality of man, must then realize the distinct and specific plan or purpose that defines the attitude of man. When then [2] man assigns to God a portion of the crop, that act of sanctification places that portion of the crop under God's plan and purpose in carrying out the act of creation. The rules that dictate the disposition of heave-offering therefore bring about a transaction in which wills work together, [2] God's and [1] man's, now to realize God's purpose in creation, on the one hand, and demonstrate man's accord with that purpose, on the other.

By an act of will, Man assigns to God his share in the produce of the Land, at which point that batch of produce becomes subject to God's will – meaning, the particular teleology of that produce, by species, not only genus. The act of sanctification then takes place when man by his act of will concerning what is subject to his possession declares subject to God's will that which, once made subject to God's will, must be utilized as God intended. Man then by the act of sanctification declares nature subject to God's initial purpose. In the setting of Terumot, which the system finds particularly appropriate for a statement of this character, Israelite man by an act of will declares subject to God's plan and program the produce of the Land that is God's share – a perfectly simple, rational, and right transaction reaffirming the order of nature. And that is a conception that the halakhah of Ma'aserot has not set forth, but for which that halakhah has prepared us. Israel in the Land has its role to play in restoring nature to its original perfection.

VII

The fields yield their offering, the household its portion too. When the householder takes possession of his share of the crops, he also designates God's share. Within the household itself, the householder does the same, but not for the same reason. I refer to dough-offering. The Hallah- or dough-offering is given to the priest, so Scripture states:

> The Lord said to Moses, "Say to the people of Israel: when you come into the Land to which I bring you, and when you eat of the food of the land, you shall present an offering to the Lord. Of the first of your coarse meal you shall present a

cake as an offering, as an offering from the threshing floor, so shall you present it. Of the first of your coarse meal you shall give to the Lord an offering throughout your generations."

Numbers 15:17–21

Sages understand the verses to require the separation of a portion from the bread; it is to be coarse meal, taken to mean unbaked bread-dough. It is comparable to the offering of the threshing flood, which sages call heave-offering. Since, as we know, heave-offering is given to the priest, so sages assume dough-offering is assigned to the priest as well. Havivi comments (p. 150), "Scripture describes the dough-offering as an offering of bread. The tractates authorities wish to provide a definition of bread, so that it is possible to judge with precision which types of dough are liable to the offering and which are not. Mishnah-tractate Hallah also explores two matters on which Scripture is silent: first, the precise point in the processing of the dough at which the dough becomes liable to the offering; and, second, the amount that one must separate." The halakhah emerges at the end of a long process of profound thought on the nature of life-processes in nourishing Israel in the Land of Israel.

At issue is God's share of the bread, but to understand what is at stake here and why God claims a portion – dough-offering – we must identify the exact point at which the obligation to separate God's share actually is incurred. For, in the model of our analysis of the halakhah of Maʿaserot, when we know *when* God's interest is provoked, we also know *why* – that is to say, what man does that elicits God's participation. Three principal considerations intersect: what constitutes bread that is liable to dough-offering, when liability takes effect, and where is the offering required? When we know the answers to these three questions, we may identify the religious conceptions that inhere in the halakhah. We start with the definition of bread: it is a baked food produce that is made of flour that rises upon being moistened and kneaded and fermented. What derives from flour that does not leaven is not liable to dough-offering and not classified as bread for purposes of Passover either.

Two criteria of liability coexist, one marking the beginning, the other the end, of the spell. First, people snack on dough without giving dough offering until the dough is made into a ball or is rolled out in a solid mass. But formal liability takes effect when a crust forms, which is to say, when the enzyme that brings about leavening dies.[7] These points of demarcation – when the liability commences, when the liability must be met – correspond to the points at which the crop in the field *may* be tithed, at the outset, and *must* be tithed, at the end of the harvesting-process. So the spell of liability commences with the mixture of flour and water and the working of the two into a mass, and it is fixed with the conclusion of the same process. The upshot is, the span of susceptibility coincides with the process of fermentation: the activation of the enzyme, at the outset, then the cultivation of the fermentation process, and finally the realization of the goal of that process in the forming of a crust, the conclusion of fermentation. And, to address the third question briefly, dough-offering must be presented out of dough made from grain that is eaten by Israel in the Land of Israel.[8] The Mishnah insists that the priests will not accept dough-offering from bread prepared overseas.

We may say that the critical criterion is [1] dough that has incurred liability within the Land of Israel and [2] that is consumed by Israelites [3] in the Land. So there is a very specific point of intersection that dictates which dough is liable to dough-offering: [1] dough prepared from wheat and comparable flour, which, when mixed with yeast and water, has the power to ferment; [2] dough at the point at which the fermentation-process has realized its goal. The upshot is that the derivation of the grain by itself bears no consequence. But the processing of the flour produced by the grain, and the location of the Israelites who consume the bread form the critical criteria.

Dough that has formed a crust within the Land of Israel is liable, whatever the origin of the flour. In the priests' view dough-offering may not be brought from outside of the Land of Israel, but that is not because considerations of cultic cleanness pertain, which would exclude the produce of foreign lands, unclean as they are by definition. That is an explicit issue at M. Hallah 2:3, even though one may designate an unclean portion as dough-offering (Aqiba): just as he may designate dough-offering for a clean portion of dough, so he may designate dough-offering for an unclean portion of dough. This is then burned. So why the priests should reject dough-offering brought by Israelites from abroad is clear: it is when Israelites in the Land of Israel prepare dough that liability takes effect. Then the actuality of Israel dwelling on the Land, not the origin of the grain, determines: Israelites living in the Land of Israel separate dough-offering from the bread that they are going to eat, from the point at which the bread begins to ferment, and they are obligated to do so from the point at which the bread has ceased to ferment.

That the whole forms an exercise in thinking about the fermentation process is demonstrated, moreover, by the explicit insistence that just as flour produces dough subject to dough-offering only if a fermentation process is possible, so flour produces unleavened bread valid for Passover only if a fermentation process is possible but is thwarted. So the bread that the Israelites in the Land of Israel eat to which God establishes his claim is comparable in its traits to the bread that the Israelites leaving Egypt, or commemorating their Exodus from Egypt, are required to eat – and that bread too is liable to dough-offering, as a matter of fact. At stake, then, is the fermentation-process itself: *Then God takes notice.* The process need not take place, but it must bear the potential to take place. So it may not affect the bread of the Exodus – which is liable to dough-offering – but it must affect the bread of Israel in the Land of Israel – also liable.

Having come this far, we may readily perceive the broad outlines of a simple message: bread in which God takes an interest is bread subject to living processes of nature: the life of the enzyme (as we should express matters). Leavening then is the key to the definition of bread. Taken as a natural process, leavening is animate, or is perceived as animate. It comes about "through the action of gas bubbles developed naturally or folded in from the atmosphere. Leavening may result from yeast or bacterial fermentation, from chemical reactions or from the distribution in the batter of atmospheric or injected gases."[9] Fermentation, required for wine or beer as much as for bread involves a process of frothing brought about by micro-organisms growing in the absence of air.

How then to draw conclusions from natural processes of fermentation, perceived as the animation of the food? The calculus then is readily discerned: Israel's life in the Land of Israel is nourished through the transformation of grain into bread, that is, through the life-process that takes grain and makes it edible and life-sustaining. Then and there God lays his claim to a share: when Israel renews its life, meal by meal, its action in invoking the life-process of fermentation, start to finish, provokes God's reaction. That is because God too has a share in the transaction by which life is maintained – but (as the priests clearly maintained) only in the transaction that takes place between Israel and the Land of Israel.

Does Israel have a say in the inauguration of the fermentation process and the engagement of God therein? To this exchange, this transfer and renewal of Israel's life in engagement with the living processes of nature, Israel's intentionality plays no role; the processes go forward willy-nilly. Then what about intentionality, e.g., that of the baker? In fact, that point is raised explicitly, in connection with M. Hallah 1:5. There the question is raised on whether a third party imposes upon grain the status of that which has been fully processed and is liable to be tithed. One authority maintains that he has imposed liability, even though the owner of the pile of grain does not know and approve of his action, the other denies it. That is in line with M. Hallah 1:7: As regards women who gave dough to the baker to make it into leaven for them – if the dough of each woman comprises less than the prescribed minimum volume subject to dough-offering, the dough is exempt from dough-offering. If the volume of all the women all together does meet the requisite amount to impose liability to dough-offering, the dough will be exempt, because it was the baker, not the woman, who owned the dough, who imposed liability. But contrary opinion registers as well.

Israel becomes responsible for the cultic cleanness of the produce only by an act of intentionality, but Israel becomes liable to hand over God's share of the produce willy-nilly. So it is with life. Let me explain, beginning with the question of why intentionality plays no role in the liability of the dough to dough-offering. The reason becomes clear when we recall the critical role human intentionality plays in the halakhah of Lev. 11:34, 37, worked out in tractate Makhshirin, the counterpart and opposite of the halakhah of Hallah. That halakhic category maintains that produce that is dry is insusceptible to uncleanness, that which is wet is susceptible; but the wetting down, to prove affective, must take place by intention. Thus, while what is deliberately wet down is subject to uncleanness, what is accidentally wet down is not. Here, by contrast, the mixing of the flour, salt, yeast, and water inaugurates a process through which, at the end, liability to the offering is incurred – whether the process came about deliberately or accidentally. A simple formulation involves a concrete case. A householder takes flour, which is dry and has not been deliberately wet down. Why not? Because once wet down, the flour moulders. The householder further takes yeast. And, putting the two together, the householder adds water. At that moment, when the process of kneading dough to bake bread commences (in contemporary language: with the irrigation of the yeast and the dough, the moment at which the dough congeals and the yeast buds and ferments, producing its sugar, its carbon dioxide, and its ethanol) – at that exact moment, the instant of animation, at which the bread begins to live, the householder goes on the alert for dangers to the bread – and so throughout the process.

That explains why the householder goes on the alert at the point at which he or she intentionally puts water on the dough. Then the flour, now dough, is susceptible to uncleanness. So in a cuisine based on bread (not potatoes, not rice, for example) what is at stake in "wetting down seed," based on the analogy of adding water to dry flour and yeast, is the point at which vegetation begins the process by which it becomes maximally edible and useful to the householder. Then – life bubbling away in the process of fermentation, deliberately inaugurated – the state of sanctification comes under threat from the source of uncleanness, such as corpse-uncleanness and its analogues, that the Torah has identified.

The moment of wetting grain down defines the hour of conflict between life and death, yielding sanctification or uncleanness – and this in concrete ways. Then, at the very time, the act done with deliberation precipitates the conflict. But that is only if the householder cares. If the householder does not intend the dough to congeal and the yeast to rise, in regard to susceptibility to uncleanness nothing of consequence happens. It is the Israelite's will and intention and the act that realizes them that endow with consequence what by nature happens willy-nilly. But so far as the process itself, it does not depend upon the householder's intentionality. The fermentation process that animates the flour and produces bread goes forward whether or not the householder intended it to. Nothing he does can stop it once it has started, and no call upon his alertness to prevent uncleanness is issued. That is why God's claim on the dough, for the dough-offering for the priesthood, does not depend upon man's intentionality – irrelevant to the process of animation, of bringing life to the inert flour – but upon God's own reason for engagement. That has to do with the maintenance of the processes of life, man's and nature's.

If I had to identify where the everyday meets the Eternal, I should choose the here and now of petty obsessions with tiny events and their intangible, animated histories, down to the moment of adding water to the yeast and dough when making bread: when life renews itself through the life-precipitating touch of water to the flour and the yeast. Here considerations of uncleanness and those of sanctification intersect. That is the point that precipitates concern with the forces of death, prime source of cultic uncleanness. Then, to preserve purity, Israel goes on the alert for the danger of pollution: at the moment when yeast, flour, and water ignite the processes of animation. So too for all of their counterparts: "if water be put on the seed," take care. Now we see the other half of the story. Unclean or otherwise, the dough congeals, the yeast ferments and yields gas, and so, life-processes have commenced, though death and its surrogates threaten. Then the householder goes on the alert – if he cares, if by an act of deliberation he has made life happen. And there too, by sharing the outcome of the fermentation with God, the householder acknowledges the opposite of death, which is life, embodied in the living processes by which the bread comes into being, and resulting in the presence, within the dough, of a portion subject to sanctification: donation to the priest in the present instance.

The particularity of dough-offering should now register. It is paid from bread made from grain from which the heave-offering has already been removed. So the critical point of differentiation – an offering from the mixture of flour, yeast, and water, taken from when fermentation starts to when it ends – takes on still greater consequence. Wine and beer ferment, but no counterpart offering from wine, over and above the heave-offering and tithes to which all produce is liable, is demanded, nor from beer. In the wine-olive-oil-wheat-culture of the Land of Israel, it is only wheat, in the course of its later processing, that becomes subject to a further offering of the present kind, one linked to its life-cycle. And that is because – so it seems to me – bread stands for life, consumed to be sure with oil and wine. Therefore it is the processing of flour into bread to sustain life where fermentation represents life that particularly registers. That marks the occasion for the affirmation of God's presence in all life-forms and processes: God lays his claim to his share, because God's claim upon the Israelite householder extends to the outer limits of vitality. Enough has been said to render redundant the observation: without these generative premises, we have no halakhah for either Ma'aserot or Terumot. Sometime after the closure of Scripture but before the beginning of work on the Mishnah, sages reached the conclusions concerning Eden and its meaning that come to expression in the later statement of the halakhah.

VIII

Thus far we have seen how the theme of Eden and the Land plays itself out in the formation of halakhic category-formations and in their articulation. But to characterize the work of the nameless ages of the Oral Tradition who, between Scripture and the Mishnah, identified the generative premises of the Pentateuch and build upon them, we have to broaden the range of our survey. For Eden supplies them with not only a myth but a theme, as we have now seen many times, the theme of intentionality, a considerable presence in other Israelite thought – beyond the circles from the Pentateuch to the commencement of the Mishnah – in Second Temple times, as we see in Fourth Ezra's reflection on what Adam has done, in Paul's Letter to the Romans in his plaintive observation about "the good that I would, that I do not," among other writings.

So sages are not alone when in their judgment they determined that it is the conflict of wills that Eden portrays. However, that conflict reaches us in abstract form in the introduction of man's will in areas of the halakhah of the Mishnah and the Tosefta that do not intersect in any obvious way with the story of Eden. And it is the recurrent introduction of the priority of intentionality that, as a matter of fact, constitutes the principal, the definitive trait of the period between the Pentateuch and the Mishnah. To see how that theme of Eden that transcends the story of Eden works its way into aspects of Pentateuchal law in which, in the statement of Pentateuch itself, it is lacking, we turn to the halakhah of purifying corpse-uncleanness that is set forth at Numbers 19 and in Mishnah- and Tosefta-tractate Parah, on the burning of the red cow and the preparation of purification-water out of its ashes.

First we consider the Pentateuchal statement on the matter, then survey the halakhah and identify that premise of the halakhah that is everywhere taken for granted and nowhere subjected to dispute. In the disjuncture between the Pentateuchal framing of matters and the Mishnah's presupposition on the governing considerations we enter into the thought-world of the intervening spell between the conclusion of the one and the commencement of the development of the other.

Scripture defines a distinctive process of purification from corpse-uncleanness in particular. This it does by providing for the preparation of purification-water, a mixture of the ashes of a red cow and water, and for the application of that water upon a person or object that has suffered corpse-uncleanness. The mixture is applied on the third and seventh days after contamination, and on the seventh day the unclean person immerses and regains cleanness with the sunset. The pertinent verses of Scripture are as follows:

> Now the Lord said to Moses and to Aaron, "This is the statute of the law which the Lord has commanded: tell the people of Israel to bring you a red heifer without defect, in which there is no blemish, and upon which a yoke has never come. And you shall give her to Eleazar the priest, and she shall be taken outside the camp and slaughtered before him; and Eleazar the priest shall take some of her blood with his finger, and sprinkle some of her blood toward the front of the tent of meeting seven times. And the heifer shall be

burned in his sight; her skin, her flesh, and her blood, with her dung, shall be burned; and the priest shall take cedar wood and hyssop and scarlet stuff and cast them into the midst of the burning of the heifer. Then the priest shall wash his clothes and bathe his body in water, and afterwards he shall come into the camp and the priest shall be unclean until evening. He who burns the heifer shall wash his clothes in water and bathe his body in water, and shall be unclean until evening. And a man who is clean shall gather up the ashes of the heifer and deposit them outside the camp in a clean place; and they shall be kept for the congregation of the people of Israel for the water for impurity, for the removal of sin. And he who gathers the ashes of the heifer shall wash his clothes and be unclean until evening. And this shall be to the people of Israel and to the stranger who sojourns among them a perpetual statute. He who touches the dead body of any person shall be unclean seven days; he shall cleanse himself with the water on the third day and on the seventh day and so be clean; but if he does not cleanse himself on the third day and on the seventh day, he will not become clean. Whoever touches a dead person, the body of any man who has died, and does not cleanse himself, defiles the tabernacle of the Lord, and that person shall be cut off from Israel, because the water for impurity was not thrown upon him, he shall be unclean; his uncleanness is still on him. This is the law when a man dies in a tent: every one who comes into the tent, and every one who is in the tent, shall be unclean seven days. And every open vessel, which has no cover fastened upon it, is unclean. Whoever in the open field touches one who is slain with a sword or a dead body or a bone of a man or a grave shall be unclean seven days. For the unclean they shall take some ashes of the burnt sin offering, and running water shall be added in a vessel. Then a clean person shall take hyssop and dip it in the water and sprinkle it on the tent and upon all the furnishings and upon the persons who were there, and upon him who touches the bone or the slain or the dead or the grave; and the clean person shall sprinkle on the unclean on the third day and on the seventh day; thus on the seventh day he shall cleanse him, and he shall wash his clothes and bathe himself in water, and at evening he shall be clean. But the man who is unclean and does not cleanse himself, that person shall be put off from the midst of the assembly; since he has defiled the sanctuary of the Lord, because the water for impurity has not been thrown upon him, he is unclean. And it shall be a perpetual statute for them. He who sprinkles the water for impurity shall wash his clothes; and he who touches the water for impurity shall be unclean until evening. And whatever the unclean person touches shall be unclean; and anyone who touches it shall be unclean until evening."

Numbers 19:1–22

The halakhah recapitulates the Written Torah's account of the purification rite, just as is the case in Negaim. But Scripture says little, and the halakhah much, about the collection and mixing of water and ash, the protection of both from uncleanness, the role of intentionality in the procedure, and the like. Moreover, Scripture's rules leave open the generative question that the halakhah takes as the center of its program: how does a rite conducted outside of the Temple courtyard ("the camp") relate to the rules governing rites conducted inside? And, at a still deeper level, the problem awaits attention: how can the mixture of ash and water that purifies derive from a rite that contaminates all of its participants, and how can that same purification-water both purify the person that is made unclean by a corpse and also contaminate the person that applies the water? It should be noted that the condition of uncleanness that the rite and the utilization of its results brings about is not corpse-uncleanness, but an uncleanness that can be removed through immersion and sunset, that is, an uncleanness in the first remove from the Father of uncleanness that contamination by the corpse – the Father of Fathers of uncleanness – imparts.

Now to compare the halakhah of the Mishnah and the Tosefta with that of Scripture, we turn to the details of the law by their principal categories, asking whence they come. The units of halakhic exposition and amplification begin by treating facts provided by Scripture, then proceed to issues that the topic as set forth by Scripture does not encompass. We are able to differentiate between halakhah that clearly amplifies Scripture's own rules and that that builds upon premises not supplied by, or even implicit in, Scripture. The latter are the ones that concern us here. Here the details make all the difference, so let us survey the laws that comprise the category.

The cow acceptable for the purification-ash The cow must be unblemished; it must never have been used, e.g., for labor, for bearing burdens, or for mating. It may never have been ridden or leaned upon, it may never have carried weight or been used even for crossing a river or holding a cloak. It must be born naturally, it may never have served in commerce (e.g., in exchange for personal services). Ambiguous actions, e.g., tying it up to a rope, are classified by intent: if they are done for the sake of the cow, they do not invalidate it; if for the convenience of the owner, they do. If one brought it in to the threshing team to suck, and it accidentally threshed with its mother, it is fit.

Conditions of slaughtering the cow and burning the carcass   The rite enjoys distinctions comparable to those distinguishing the offerings on the Day of Atonement. It is performed by the high priest, wearing white garments, with feet and hands sanctified. But we take account of the location of the rite, outside the holy place. Having prepared the priest and the water and transported them in such a way as to avoid corpse-uncleanness, we want the priest to be in a diminished condition of cleanness, as a tebul yom; that status accords recognition to the location of the rite, conducted with remarkable punctiliousness to the requirements of cleanness, but at the same time differentiated, as to cleanness, from rites conducted in the Temple itself.

The priest who performs the rite is to be free of all uncleanness, so he is subjected to a seven-day purification-rite to remove the corpse-uncleanness that may have affected him. The water is collected by youngsters who have been born and raised in a condition of cultic cleanness, that is, in rock cells, immune to corpse-uncleanness that may be buried in the ground. They fill stone cups, being carried on doors borne by oxen, which interpose against buried uncleanness. So the officiating priest and the required assistants are protected from corpse-uncleanness that may be buried in the depths and unknown. The priest, the cow, and all assistants cross from the Temple Mount to the Mount of Olives on a causeway over arches, once more to protect against graves in the depths. The upshot is, the conditions of cultic cleanness pertaining in the Temple courtyard are replicated outside of the Temple, so far as this is possible, for transport to, and labor on, the Mount of Olives opposite the Temple mount. But then, on the mount of Olives, the officiating priest would be rendered unclean by the hands of others, and he would then immerse. He would slaughter the beast in the status of one unclean as a Tebul Yom. Thus the rite in the world outside of the cult was carried on by a person in the condition of uncleanness.

The wood for burning the cow was laid out so that its fore-side faced westward, that is to say, the Temple. The head of the beast was

faced toward the Temple, that is, to the west. The priest slaughtered
the beast facing the Temple. The blood is tossed toward the door of
the Holy of Holies. The priest slaughtered with the right hand and
received the blood in his left hand, as he would in the Temple. Judah
has him receive the blood in the right hand and put it into the left
hand, a mirror image of what he would do in the Temple: He would
slaughter with his right hand and then put the knife down before
him or give it to this one who stands at his side, and he receives the
blood with the palm of his right hand, and puts it into his left hand,
and sprinkles with his right finger. So the issue is clear: having
created a realm of reduced uncleanness, do we conduct the rite
exactly as we would in the Temple or, facing the Temple, in the opposite way?

The character of the water   The water for mixing with the ash of the
red cow must be spring, or living-water. Only flowing water serves to
remove corpse-uncleanness and the other types of uncleanness of the
same classification, that is, *Zob*-uncleanness and *nega'*-uncleanness.
This is made explicit, also, at M. Miq. 1:8: "Above them: Living water
– in which take place immersion for Zabim, and sprinkling for
lepers; and which is suitable to mix the purification water." It must
derive from a source that flows reliably and that is pure and clear, not
turbid. Water from rivers is unfit for mixing the purification-water.
It may come from a distance, so long as it is watched over the length
of its flow. The water must be drawn only by a utensil, not by human
intervention in any other wise. If one splashed water with his hand
and with his feet and with the clay sherds, not with a trough a utensil
– it is unsuitable, because the water was not drawn with a utensil.
But if the jar broke and one splashed it out with his hands, feet, and
clay sherds, not with a trough, it is suitable, because it was originally
drawn with a utensil.

Conditions of gathering the water and mixing the water and the ashes
Here we proceed to matters not introduced by Scripture's presentation of the topic. But the principles we now examine form the
bed-rock of the halakhah; no named authority claims credit for them,
nor does anyone ever challenge them. The halakhah in its details can
have commenced its articulation only when these matters were fully
worked out. I say so because the very category itself, the shape and
structure of the formation that dictates the character of the details of
the law, depends upon the premise everywhere operative but nowhere
articulated in the halakhah of the Mishnah and the Tosefta.

We take up, specifically, the halakhic category that dictates the attitude of the participants in the rite. The water must be collected by sentient man, and it must be constantly subject to the intentionality of man that it serve for the specified purpose (once more the concretization of teleology!). It must be collected in valid utensils recognized by man as useful for that purpose. The water and ashes must be mixed in valid utensils. All utensils serve, of whatever material they are made. But the utensils must be made subject to human will and purpose. They cannot take shape by nature, e.g., a trough hewn from a rock cannot be used for drawing water or mixing ashes with the water and so on. If it was originally movable and then attached to a rock, it may be used. Broken utensils cannot be used, but if they are planed and repaired and made useful, they can. The water must be drawn deliberately, for the specific composite of ash alone. One must be constantly occupied with the mixing. There can be no extraneous act of labor along with the drawing or mixing. But an act of labor connected with the drawing or mixing does not invalidate the rite. An individual who drew five jars of water to mix a single mixture he would take each one out and pour – even though he closed the door behind him, it is fit, because he is occupied with the mixing. And if after he took out the last, he closed the door behind him, it all is unfit, because he did extraneous work with it along with the rite.

Now we moved into completely original territory. In connection with mixing the ash and the water, one may not perform an extrinsic act of labor. Every action that he takes must involve the requirements of the mixing process. One's intentionality plays a role here. If he cuts off olive leaves, if so that the ash will enter the reed, it is fit. If he does so so that it will hold a large quantity of ash, it is unfit. The performance of extrinsic work spoils the drawn water, whether it is for him or for someone else. One must complete his own needs before attending to those of the purification rite. He who draws water for his own use and for the purification-rite draws his own first and ties it to the carrying yoke, and afterward he draws the water of the purification-rite. If he was drawing water to drink, and it was not possible to have arranged them other than both on a single yoke whether he drew his own first and afterward drew that of the purification-rite, or whether he drew the water of the purification-rite first and afterward drew his own, he places his own behind him and the purification-water before him. And if he placed the water of the purification-rite behind him, it is unfit. The water is invalidated by someone who, while carrying it, teaches a lesson, shows others the way, kills a snake, or the like.

Uncleanness and the purification-rite   Scripture never suggests that the rite involves a high order of cultic cleanness; on the contrary, all those who participate are made unclean thereby. And why should anyone suppose otherwise, when the rite of burning the cow and mixing the water takes place outside the walls of the Temple. But here a different premise governs: we can and must establish a realm of cleanness even outside of the Temple walls, and we do so by imposing the most stringent rules of cleanness that we are able to invent. So we assume that the rite can, and therefore should, be conducted as though it were in the Temple, and that means we take for granted cultic cleanness can be attained in the realm beyond the sanctuary. That drains the rite of the paradox of cleanness coming about through uncleanness. We assume that because the rite involves the Temple, even though it is performed outside of the Temple, the entire population observes the cleanness rules in connection with the preparation of purification-ash and water. Everyone, even lay folk, is assumed to take precautions to preserve the cleanness of the rite, including all utensils to be used in the rite. The utensils that are to be used are constantly watched as they are fired. If people do not ordinarily keep the laws of cultic cleanness outside of the Temple, they nonetheless are assumed to do so for this rite, and people who do keep those laws take for granted that utensils kept pure by outsiders for the purification-rite are valid also for use in connection with priestly rations. But the outsider is not assumed to observe the same rules when it comes to utensils for use with priestly rations alone.

Those involved in the work of burning the cow – e.g., carrying the water – impart uncleanness to their clothing or other utensils that they touch at the time of the rite. They do not contaminate persons or clay utensils. While the activity imparts uncleanness, the cow itself does not. The clothing cannot be made unclean by the activity, but it is made unclean by the made who has engaged therein. If the rite is unfit, then the persons involved to not render clothing unclean.

To protect the purification water, the highest standard of alertness for preserving cultic cleanness is required. A higher standard of cleanness applies to preserve the purity of purification-water and ash as these are prepared and mixed than even to the preservation of the cleanness of Holy Things. That is expressed at Mishnah-tractate Hagigah 2:5, 7, as follows:

A.   For purposes of cultic purification, it is sufficient if they wash the hands for eating unconsecrated food, tithe, and heave offering;

B. and for eating food in the status of Holy Things it is sufficient only if they immerse;

C. and as to the preparation of purification water through the burning of the red cow, if one's hands are made unclean, his entire body is deemed to be unclean as well.

Mishnah-tractate Hagigah 2:5

A. The clothing of ordinary folk is in the status of midras uncleanness for abstainers who eat unconsecrated food in a state of cultic cleanness.

B. The clothing of abstainers is in the status of midras uncleanness for those priests who eat heave offering.

C. The clothing of those who eat heave offering is in the status of midras uncleanness for those officiating priests who eat Holy Things.

D. The clothing of those who eat Holy Things is in the status of midras uncleanness for those engaged in the preparation of purification water.

Mishnah-tractate Hagigah 2:7

Not only so, but in connection with preparation of the mixture, anything that is susceptible to midras-uncleanness, e.g., chairs and beds, is deemed actually unclean with maddaf-uncleanness, and that is without regard to the facts of the matter. The same considerations govern in connection with corpse-uncleanness. The distinction between the hands and the body, important in Yadayim, does not pertain.

The upshot is, those involved in preparing the water cannot relax in any way; they cannot touch chairs or beds; they must assume that everything that forms a receptacle is unclean with maddaf-uncleanness. In cases of doubt, any matter of a suspended decision in respect to heave offering – in regard to the purification water rite, the water is poured out. A person who requires immersion, whether by the rules of the Torah or of the scribes, imparts uncleanness in the context of the purification-rite. One who is clean for the purification-rite, the hands of whom were made unclean – his body is made unclean. He makes his fellow unclean, and his fellow, his fellow. And as to the outer part of a pitcher: A pitcher of purification-water, the outer side of which is made unclean – its inside is made unclean. It renders its fellow unclean, and its fellow, its fellow, and also the one who sprinkles. Removes of uncleanness do not pertain – even to a hundred removes. They do not say in connection with the purifica-tion-rite, "This is first and this is last." But they are all in the first

73

remove of uncleanness. For they do not count removes of uncleanness with reference to sprinkling the purification-water. A piece of dough which is prepared in connection with the purification-rite, and the dead creeping thing touched one of them even if they are a hundred, they are all first. For they do not count removes of uncleanness with reference to the purification-rite. The rite, conducted outside of the Temple, is walled in by these restrictions; high walls of alertness substitute for the boundaries of the Temple courtyard in establishing a realm of cultic cleanness beyond the Temple limits.

The role of intentionality   The rules of uncleanness guarantee the highest level of alertness beginning to end, and that means, an intense focus of intentionality to prepare the purification-water in a proper manner must define the entire process, start to finish. So far as assessing whether or not an act of labor has been done with the cow, we differentiate the intention that has brought about the action. If the owner utilized the cow for his own convenience, it is invalidated; if for the cow's own benefit, it remains valid. So intentionality forms the criterion. One's intention in slaughtering the beast, receiving and sprinkling the blood, and the like, must focus on the purification-rite in particular. That is to say, the beast having been designated for the purification-rite, the priest must offer the beast for that purpose and for no other purpose, and so with the other activities connected to the sacrifice. Improper intentionality invalidates the rite, just as it does the sin- and guilt-offering; the animal must be used for the purpose for which it was originally designated. It is improper to form the intention to drink purification-water, but the water is rendered unfit not by mere intent but only by an action confirming the intentionality.

The rite as set forth in Scripture and amplified in the halakhah of the Oral Torah encompasses two paradoxes, involving the creation of cleanness out of uncleanness, and uncleanness out of cleanness. The first paradox is that it is possible to create a realm of cultic cleanness in the unclean world that lies outside the boundaries of the Temple – the world of death. This is expressed in the proposition that the cow is burned outside of the camp, that is to say, outside of the Temple, in an unclean place. Its blood is tossed not on the altar but in the direction of the altar, toward the front of the tent of meeting. Then the cow is burned outside of the Temple, the ashes are gathered and mixed with water, and the purification-water is then prepared. So the halakhah underscores that, in the condition of uncleanness, media for achieving cleanness from the most virulent source of uncleanness, the corpse, are to be brought into being. And the halakhah is explicit in identifying the threat as that of corpse-uncleanness.

So in the very realm of death, media for overcoming the contamination of death come into being. The lesson for Israel contained within that paradox will come to our attention presently. Here it suffices to note that the highest level of cleanness is required – higher than that demanded even for eating Holy Things off the Lord's altar in the Temple itself – from all those who are engaged in the rite. The most perfect sentience is demanded from them. Everything they see that can become unclean is deemed (for the present purpose) to be unclean. It would be difficult to state more eloquently the simple proposition that faced with the most extreme challenges to attaining uncleanness, Israel can become cultically clean. Nor does the implicit lesson require articulation: what Israel must do to overcome death is self-evident.

The second paradox is that, even encompassing those who have gained the highest level of purification, uncleanness envelops the world, for all persons everywhere death is ever-present. Thus those who have attained and maintained the extraordinary level of consciousness required to participate in the rite of burning the cow, collecting the ashes, gathering and transporting water, and mixing the ash and the water, as well as those who propose to utilize the purification-water so brought into being – all by virtue of their very activity in creating media of purification are deemed unclean. They have defied death in the realm of death and overcome – but have contracted uncleanness nonetheless, indeed a paradox. They are decreed to be unclean in the remove that suffices for affecting their clothing as well, therefore requiring immersion and the setting of the sun to return to the ordinary condition of cleanness that they (presumably) enjoyed prior to entering into the work of the rite itself. So it is not corpse-uncleanness that they suffer, but uncleanness nonetheless. That is Scripture's decree, and it sets forth the paradox that out of cleanness comes the cause of uncleanness. So the upshot is, the high priest, who performs the rite involving the cow, is unclean, so too the one who burns the cow. A clean man (a priest is not specified) gathers the ashes and keeps them in a clean place outside of the Temple; he too is made unclean by participation in the rite.

So, paradoxically, out of a contaminating rite comes water for purification, and, still, the one who sprinkles the purification-water also becomes unclean. Now sages explore the requirements of an offering conducted in a condition of uncleanness, in a place that is unclean by definition, by priests who contract uncleanness (but not corpse-uncleanness) by participating in the rite. Does that mean we impose more stringent purification-rules, to create a circle of cleanness in the unclean world? Or do we impose diminished rules, taking account of the givens of the circumstance? Along these same lines, do we perform the rite exactly as we should in the Temple at the altar, or do we perform the rite in exactly the opposite way, that is, as a mirror-image of how it would be done in the Temple? These parallel questions provoked by the twin-paradoxes of Scripture's and the halakhah's rules for the rite, respectively, define the problem addressed by the halakhah, which contains the Oral Torah's deepest thinking upon the meaning of sanctifying the secular, ordinary world.

The halakhah decisively answers the generative question: the highest level of alertness, the keenest exercise of caution against uncleanness – these alone will create that circle of cleanness in the world beyond the Temple courtyard that, by definition, is unclean. That accounts for the bizarre arrangements for transporting the youngsters with the stone cups from the Temple, where they have been born and brought up, to the Siloam pool and thence to the Mount of Olives – all to avoid corpse-matter buried at great depths. And still more to the point, the halakhah suspends the strict purity-rules protecting from contamination not only common food or priestly rations but even Holy Things and imposes much more stringent ones.

This it does in a variety of ways, three of which represent the rest. First, while hand-washing suffices for eating in a state of cleanness food in the familiar classifications, to purify oneself for participating in preparing the purification-water, total immersion is required; the familiar distinction between hands and body falls away. Second and more decisive, purification-water contracts uncleanness (and so is rendered useless) at any number of removes from the original source of uncleanness, even one hundred; that is to say, we do not count removes. Everything is unclean by reason of its history – a history of which we may well be ignorant. Third, persons involved in preparing the mixture – collecting the ashes, gathering the water, mixing the two – must remain not only constantly alert but perpetually active. From the beginning to the end of their work, they may do only what concerns the task. If they sit down on a chair or lie down on a bed, they automatically contract uncleanness, for what can contract uncleanness is deemed unclean for them. And intentionality enters in at critical points in the classification of actions, e.g., whether or not they are extrinsic to the rite. We need hardly review the details of the law to reach the halakhah's obvious proposition: perfect concentration on the task, uninterrupted by any extrinsic action or even consideration, alone suffices. So the halakhah declares to the participants: "Do not stand still, do not sit down anywhere on any bench, do not stop, do only the job, the job alone, until the job is done – and then go immerse from the uncleanness that under ordinary circumstances you cannot have contracted."

We find no difficulty in understanding the extreme character of the rules governing the activity and intentionality of those involved in the rite. These rules form the paradigm of what it means, of what is required, to attain cultic cleanness: the most intense, best focused, concentration on the matter at hand. But what lessons does the halakhah of the Oral Torah set forth in its context through those rules? The key to the entire construction, so remarkably cogent as it is, presents itself in the paradox noted just now. Scripture is clear that those who participate in preparing the water or in using it in a purification-process later on contract uncleanness through their activity. So, as the medieval commentaries to Numbers 19 underscore, we have the paradox of uncleanness produced by what is clean, matching that of cleanness produced from a rite involving uncleanness.

It follows that cultic cleanness beyond the cult is possible only through the exercise of enormous resources of will and concentration. But however devotedly Israel undertakes the work, the perpetual prevalence of uncleanness persists: the person who has attained an astonishing level of cleanness to participate in the rite and who has concentrated all his energies and attention upon the rite and succeeded – that person, Scripture itself decrees, emerges unclean from his labor in perfect cleanness to prepare purification-water. The one proposition – to participate, the highest, most extraordinary level of cleanness is required – requires the other – one emerges unclean from the labor. Thus cultic cleanness beyond the cult is possible, but the world beyond the Temple remains what it is – no matter what. Having created the instruments for removing corpse-uncleanness, the parties to the rite immerse just as they ordinarily would, wait for sunset, and only then eat their evening meal in the condition of cultic purity that the halakhah makes possible: the ordinary immersion-pool, the quotidian sunset suffice, but only provisionally. Tomorrow is another day, and it has already begun, if in the state of cleanness that is, or ought to be, the norm for Israel.

To the formulation of that message, Scripture has contributed facts. The halakhah has provided the insight and the dynamics to translate the insight into detailed norms. And that process, instantiated in the present case, represents the work of the silent sages of the age from the conclusion of the Pentateuch to the category-formation out of which the Mishnah, and therefore the halakhah, ultimately took shape. Building on these foundations, the Mishnah would articulate the halakhah of the Oral Torah – finding its own voice to do so.

3

THE MISHNAH ON ITS OWN

The initial statement

The advent of the Mishnah marks the fruition of the third stage in the unfolding of Judaism. Commencing at its earliest layers of thought in Scripture itself and coming to closure at circa 200, the Mishnah stands beyond Scripture as the only free-standing document of Judaism and, after Scripture, the authoritative one. Itself the subject of commentaries – the Tosefta, circa 300, a collection of complementary and supplementary rules, and the two Talmuds, circa 400 and 600 respectively, to begin with – the Mishnah does not organize its ideas as a commentary to Scripture. In form a law code possessed of autonomy, in essence an exercise in applied reason and practical logic in the service of a philosophical system, the Mishnah marks the critical turning point. From the Mishnah, the lines of order and structure emerge. To the Mishnah, all later writings refer directly or implicitly.

Before proceeding, let me specify the contents of the document, parallel to the Pentateuch's divisions, Genesis, Exodus, Leviticus, Numbers, and Deuteronomy. Later on, we shall return to the substance of matters. To begin with, it is necessary to know that the Mishnah is divided into six large divisions, and each division is subdivided into topical expositions called tractates, sixty-two in all, most of them topically organized, spelling out the law on a given subject, as follows:

1. Agriculture (Zera'im): Berakhot (Blessings); Peah (the corner of the field); Demai (doubtfully tithed produce); Kilayim (mixed seeds); Shebi'it (the seventh year); Terumot (heave offering or priestly rations); Ma'aserot (tithes); Ma'aser Sheni (second tithe); Hallah (dough offering); Orlah (produce of trees in the first three years after planting, which is prohibited); and Bikkurim (first fruits).
2. Appointed times (Mo'ed): Shabbat (the Sabbath); 'Erubin (the fictive fusion meal or boundary); Pesahim (Passover); Sheqalim

(the Temple tax); Yoma (the Day of Atonement); Sukkah (the festival of Tabernacles); Besah (the preparation of food on the festivals and Sabbath); Rosh Hashanah (the New Year); Taanit (fast days); Megillah (Purim); Mo'ed Qatan (the intermediate days of the festivals of Passover and Tabernacles); Hagigah (the festal offering).

3. Women (Nashim): Yebamot (the levirate widow); Ketubot (the marriage contract); Nedarim (vows); Nazir (the special vow of the Nazirite); Sotah (the wife accused of adultery); Gittin (writs of divorce); Qiddushin (betrothal).

4. Damages or civil law (Neziqin): Baba Qamma, Baba Mesia, Baba Batra (civil law, covering damages and torts, then correct conduct of business, labor, and real estate transactions); Sanhedrin (institutions of government; criminal penalties); Makkot (flogging); Shabuot (oaths); Eduyyot (a collection arranged on other than topical lines); Horayot (rules governing improper conduct of civil authorities);

5. Holy things (Qodoshim): Zebahim (every day animal offerings); Menahot (meal offerings); Hullin (animals slaughtered for secular purposes); Bekhorot (firstlings); Arakhin (vows of valuation); Temurah (vows of exchange of a beast for an already consecrated beast); Keritot (penalty of extirpation or premature death); Me'ilah (sacrilege); Tamid (the daily whole offering); Middot (the layout of the Temple building); Qinnim (how to deal with bird offerings designated for a given purpose and then mixed up);

6. Purity (Tohorot): Kelim (susceptibility of utensils to uncleanness); Ohalot (transmission of corpse-uncleanness in the tent of a corpse; Negaim (the uncleanness described at Lev. 13–14); Parah the preparation of purification-water); Tohorot (problems of doubt in connection with matters of cleanness); Miqvaot (immersion-pools); Niddah (menstrual uncleanness); Makhsirin (rendering susceptible to uncleanness produce that is dry and so not susceptible); Zabim (the uncleanness covered at Lev. 15); Tebul-Yom (the uncleanness of one who has immersed on that self-same day and awaits sunset for completion of the purification rites); Yadayim (the uncleanness of hands); Uqsin (the uncleanness transmitted through what is connected to unclean produce).

In volume, the sixth division covers approximately a quarter of the entire document. Topics of interest to the priesthood and the Temple, such as priestly fees, conduct of the cult on holy days, conduct of the cult on ordinary days and management and upkeep of the Temple, and the rules of cultic cleanness, furthermore predominate in the first, second, fifth, and sixth divisions. Rules governing the social order – family, civil law – form the bulk of the third and fourth. Of these tractates, only Eduyyot is organized along other than topical lines, rather collecting sayings on diverse subjects attributed to particular authorities. The Mishnah as printed today always includes Abot (sayings of the sages), but that compilations reached closure about a generation later than the Mishnah. While it serves as the Mishnah's initial apologetic, it does not conform to the formal, rhetorical, or logical traits characteristic of the Mishnah overall.

I

Three definitive traits mark the autonomy of the Mishnah from Scripture. First and most important, the Mishnah ignores the entire category-formation of Scripture in favor of its own. Were we to outline the topical categories of Scripture, we should produce a large number of diverse formations, exhibiting no clear principles of order or agglutination. Take the huge corpus of law – we cannot really call it a code – set forth in Dt. 12–26. At any point, we find a few rules on this, a few on that, but no large-scale and well-organized thematic expositions. Where, on the other hand, Scripture does present a well-crafted composition, such as at Lev. 1–15 – an account of offerings in the Temple and their classifications, the consecration of the priesthood to the task of the cult, and the uncleanness-rules to be observed to protect the Temple from cultic contamination, we have a well-crafted topical exposition but no large-scale coverage of Israel's social order. The fragmentary and unsystematic character of the counterpart legal presentations in Exodus and in Numbers need not detain us; many of them provide cogent expositions of single subjects, none a logical and fully-exposed formulation of an entire legal system.[1]

But the Mishnah is organized within the logic of a topical presentation, six large divisions on principal topics of the social order and its regulation. These then are topically subdivided, and most of the subdivisions or tractates themselves follow the logic required by the exposition of their themes and the proposition sages wish to set forth through the presentation of those themes. Each can be outlined, and the outline will show why one problem is set forth prior to some other, a logically-fundamental question must be answered before a secondary and derivative question can be addressed.

Is that to say that the Mishnah takes up subjects that Scripture ignores, and omits reference to subjects on which Scripture dwells?

Not at all. Of the fifty-nine topical tractates (omitting 'Eduyyot, Qinnim, and Middot) of the Mishnah, only eight, Berakhot, Demai, Ketubot, Qiddushin, Taanit, Tamid, Tohorot, and Uqsin, are organized around categories in no way adumbrated by Scripture. Even these, e.g., Berakhot, Taanit, Tamid, address subjects that occur in Scripture, if not articulated as law. Then does the Mishnah simply recapitulate in a different form and its own particular language (as I shall explain in a moment) precisely what Scripture says, in Scripture's own way? Of the fifty-one remaining topical tractates of the Mishnah, only seven, Horayot, Negaim, Pesahim, Shebuot, Sotah, Sukkah, Yoma, simply repeat in the Mishnah's own way the propositions on their subjects that Scripture dictates and contain nothing new. The remaining forty-four tractates take up topics introduced by Scripture and in an original and purposive way recast those topics to explore issues not introduced by, or demonstrably implicit in, the Pentateuchal presentation of those same topics. So the Pentateuch contributes fifty-two of the Mishnah's sixty principal category formations. Of the other eight, none introduces a subject utterly alien to the Pentateuchal program.

So when I say that the Mishnah innovates in category-formation, I mean, the Mishnah reorganizes the entire program of Scripture, treating as weighty some topics that Scripture disposes of in one of two ways. It either ignores them (exemplified by Ketubot, marriage-contracts, Uqsin, secondary connections pertaining to produce in connection with the reception and transmission of uncleanness), or it treats them quite en passant (for instance, Qiddushin, betrothals, among many). But, more to the point, not only recasting, reorganizing, and reproportioning, the Mishnah brings a whole, distinctive program to a vast range of subjects that the Pentateuch discusses as well. Given a topic fully exposed in the Pentateuch, we cannot predict, on the basis of what Scripture says about that topic, the shape and direction of the Mishnah's reading of the same topic. And that is a remarkable fact, evidence of the independence of intellect characteristic of the Mishnaic stage in the formation of Judaism.

Now let me review the category-formation of the Mishnah in somewhat greater depth. That formation is important beyond its appearance, because for the next thousand years, until Maimonides's Mishneh-Torah, the Mishnah's category-formation would dictate the organization of nearly all halakhic discourse. That began as a commentary to the Mishnah, therefore within the Mishnah's categories, in the Tosefta (more than a commentary to be sure, but totally dependent on the Mishnah's category-formation), and continued its development in the two Talmuds, also organized as Mishnah-commentary and in significant proportion exactly that.

To understand the complete system set forth by the Mishnah, we review the topical program of the six divisions as they were finally spelled out.

The division of agriculture treats two topics, first, producing crops in accord with the scriptural rules on the subject, second, paying the required offerings and tithes to the priests, Levites, and poor. The principal point of the Division is that the Land is holy, because God has a claim both on it and upon what it produces. God's claim must be honored by setting aside a portion of the produce for those for whom God has designated it. God's ownership must be acknowledged by observing the rules God has laid down for use of the Land. In the temporal context in which the Mishnah was produced, some generations after the disastrous defeat by the Romans of Bar Kokhba and the permanent closure of Jerusalem to access by Jews, the stress of the division brought assurance that those aspects of the sanctification of Israel – land of Israel, Israel itself and its social order, the holy cycle of time – that survived also remained holy and subject to the rules of Heaven.

The division of appointed times carried forward the same emphasis upon sanctification, now of the high points of the lunar-solar calendar of Israel. The second division forms a system in which the advent of a holy day, like the Sabbath of creation, sanctifies the life of the Israelite village through imposing on the village rules on the model of those of the Temple. The purpose of the system, therefore, is to bring into alignment the moment of sanctification of the village and the life of the home with the moment of sanctification of the Temple on those same occasions of appointed times. The underlying and generative logic of the system comes to expression in a concrete way here. We recall the rule of like and opposite, comparison and contrast. What is not like something follows the rule opposite to that pertaining to that something. Here, therefore, since the village is the mirror image of the Temple, the upshot is dictated by the analogical-contrastive logic of the system as a whole. If things are done in one way in the Temple, they will be done in the opposite way in the village. Together the village and the Temple on the occasion of the holy day therefore form a single continuum, a completed creation, thus awaiting sanctification. The village is made like the Temple in that on appointed times one may not freely cross the lines distinguishing the village from the rest of the world, just as one may not freely cross the lines distinguishing the Temple from the world. But the village is a mirror image of the Temple. The boundary lines prevent free entry into the Temple, so they restrict free egress from the village. On the holy day what one may do in the Temple is precisely what one may not do in the village.

So the advent of the holy day affects the village by bringing it into sacred symmetry in such wise as to effect a system of opposites; each is holy, in a way precisely the opposite of the other. Because of the underlying conception of perfection attained through the union of opposites, the village is not represented as conforming to the model of the cult, but of constituting its antithesis. The world thus regains perfection when on the holy day heaven and earth are united, the whole completed and done: the heaven, the earth, and all their hosts. This moment of perfection renders the events of ordinary time, of "history," essentially irrelevant. For what really matters in time is that moment in which sacred time intervenes and effects the perfection formed of the union of heaven and earth, of Temple, in the model of the former, and Israel, its complement. It is not a return to a perfect time but a recovery of perfect being, a fulfillment of creation, which explains the essentially ahistorical character of the Mishnah's Division on Appointed Times. Sanctification constitutes an ontological category and is effected by the creator.

This explains why the division in its rich detail is composed of two quite distinct sets of materials. First, it addresses what one does in the sacred space of the Temple on the occasion of sacred time, as distinct from what one does in that same sacred space on ordinary, undifferentiated days, which is a subject worked out in Holy Things. Second, the Division defines how for the occasion of the holy day one creates a corresponding space in one's own circumstance, and what one does, within that space, during sacred time. The division as a whole holds together through a shared, generative metaphor. It is, as I said, the comparison, in the context of sacred time, of the spatial life of the Temple to the spatial life of the village, with activities and restrictions to be specified for each, upon the common occasion of the Sabbath or festival. The Mishnah's purpose therefore is to correlate the sanctity of the Temple, as defined by the holy day, with the restrictions of space and of action which make the life of the village different and holy, as defined by the holy day.

The division of women defines the women in the social economy of Israel's supernatural and natural reality. Women acquire definition wholly in relationship to men, who impart form to the Israelite social economy. The status of women is effected through both supernatural and natural, this-worldly action. Women formed a critical systemic component, because the proper regulation of women – subject to the father, then the husband – was deemed a central concern of Heaven, so that a betrothal would be subject to Heaven's supervision (Qiddushin, sanctification, being the pertinent tractate); documents, such as the marriage-contract or the writ of divorce, drawn up on earth, stand also for Heaven's concern with the sanctity of women in their marital relationship; so too, Heaven may through levirate marriage dictate whom a woman marries. What man and woman do on earth accordingly provokes a response in heaven, and the correspondences are perfect. So women are defined and secured both in heaven and here on earth, and that position is always and invariably relative to men.

The principal interest for the Mishnah is interstitial, just as, in general, sanctification comes into play at interstitial relationships, those that require decisive classification. Here it is the point at which a woman becomes, and ceases to be, holy to a particular man, that is, enters and leaves the marital union. These transfers of women are the dangerous and disorderly points in the relationship of woman to man, therefore, the Mishnah states, to society as well. The division's systemic statement stresses the preservation of order in transactions involving women and (other) property. Within this orderly world of documentary and procedural concerns a place is made for the disorderly conception of the marriage not formed by human volition but decreed in heaven, the levirate connection. Mishnah-tractate *Yebamot* states that supernature sanctifies a woman to a man (under the conditions of the levirate connection). What it says by indirection is that man sanctifies too: man, like God, can sanctify that relationship between a man and a woman, and can also effect the cessation of the sanctity of that same relationship.

Five of the seven tractates of the Division of Women are devoted to the formation and dissolution of the marital bond. Of them, three treat what is done by man here on earth, that is, formation of a marital bond through betrothal and marriage contract and dissolution through divorce and its consequences. The Division and its system therefore delineate the natural and supernatural character of the woman's role in the social economy framed by man: the beginning, end, and middle of the relationship. The whole constitutes a significant part of the Mishnah's encompassing system of sanctification, for the reason that heaven confirms what men do on earth. A correctly prepared writ of divorce on earth changes the status of the woman to whom it is given, so that in heaven she is available for sanctification to some other man, while, without that same writ, in heaven's view, should she go to some other man, she would be liable to be put to death. The earthly deed and the heavenly perspective correlate. That is indeed very much part of a larger system, which says the same thing over and over again.

The division of damages comprises two subsystems, which fit together in a logical way. One part presents rules for the normal conduct of civil society. These cover commerce, trade, real estate, and other matters of everyday intercourse, as well as mishaps, such as damages by chattels and persons, fraud, overcharge, interest, and the like, in that same context of everyday social life. The other part describes the institutions governing the normal conduct of civil society, that is, courts of administration, and the penalties at the disposal of the government for the enforcement of the law. The two subjects form a single tight and systematic dissertation on the nature of Israelite society and its economic, social, and political relationships, as the Mishnah envisages them. The main point of the first of the two parts of the Division is that the task of society is to maintain perfect stasis, to preserve the prevailing situation, and to secure the stability of all relationships. To this end, in the interchanges of buying and selling, giving and taking, borrowing and lending, it is important that there be an essential equality of interchange. No party in the end should have more than what he had at the outset, and none should be the victim of a sizable shift in fortune and circumstance. All parties' rights to, and in, this stable and unchanging economy of society are to be preserved. When the condition of a person is violated, so far as possible the law will secure the restoration of the antecedent status.

The goal of the system of civil law is the recovery of the prevailing order and balance, the preservation of the established wholeness of the social economy. This idea is powerfully expressed in the organization of the three tractates that comprise the civil law, which treat first abnormal and then normal transactions. The framers deal with damages done by chattels and by human beings, thefts and other sorts of malfeasance against the property of others. The civil law in both aspects pays closest attention to how the property and person of the injured party so far as possible are restored to their prior condition, that is, a state of normality. So attention to torts focuses upon penalties paid by the malefactor to the victim, rather than upon penalties inflicted by the court on the malefactor for what he has done. When speaking of damages, the Mishnah thus takes as its principal concern the restoration of the fortune of victims of assault or robbery. Then the framers take up the complementary and corresponding set of topics, the regulation of normal transactions. When we rapidly survey the kinds of transactions of special interest, we see from the topics selected for discussion what we have already uncovered in the deepest structure of organization and articulation of the basic theme.

The other half of this same unit of three tractates presents laws governing normal and routine transactions, many of them of the same sort as those dealt with in the first half. At issue are deposits of goods or possessions that one person leaves in safe-keeping with another. Called bailments, for example, cases of such transactions occur in both wings of the triple tractate, first, bailments subjected to misappropriation, or accusation thereof, by the bailiff, then, bailments transacted under normal circumstances. Under the rubric of routine transactions are those of workers and householders, that is, the purchase and sale of labor; rentals and bailments; real estate transactions; and inheritances and estates. Of the lot, the one involving real estate transactions is the most fully articulated and covers the widest range of problems and topics. The three tractates of the civil law all together thus provide a complete account of the orderly governance of balanced transactions and unchanging civil relationships within Israelite society under ordinary conditions.

The character and interests of the Division of Damages present probative evidence of the larger program of the philosophers of the Mishnah. Their intention is to create nothing less than a full-scale Israelite government, subject to the administration of sages. This government is fully supplied with a constitution and bylaws. It makes provision for a court system and procedures, as well as a full set of laws governing civil society and criminal justice. This government, moreover, mediates between its own community and the outside ("pagan") world. Through its system of laws it expresses its judgment of the others and at the same time defines, protects, and defends its own society and social frontiers. It even makes provision for procedures of remission, to expiate its own errors. The (then non-existent) Israelite government imagined by the second-century philosophers centers upon the (then non-existent) Temple, and the (then forbidden) city, Jerusalem. For the Temple is one principal focus. There the highest court is in session; there the high priest reigns.

The penalties for law infringement are of three kinds, one of which involves sacrifice in the Temple. (The others are compensation, physical punishment, and death.) The basic conception of punishment, moreover, is that unintentional infringement of the rules of society, whether "religious" or otherwise, is not penalized but rather expiated through an offering in the Temple. If a member of the people of Israel intentionally infringes against the law, to be sure, that one must be removed from society and is put to death. And if there is a claim of one member of the people against another, that must be righted, so that the prior, prevailing status may be restored. So offerings in the Temple are given up to appease heaven and restore a whole bond between heaven and Israel, specifically on those occasions on which without malice or ill will an Israelite has disturbed the relationship. Israelite civil society without a Temple is not stable or normal, and not to be imagined. And the Mishnah is above all an act of imagination in defiance of reality.

The plan for the government involves a clear-cut philosophy of society, a philosophy that defines the purpose of the government and ensures that its task is not merely to perpetuate its own power. What the Israelite government, within the Mishnaic fantasy, is supposed to do is to preserve a perfect, steady-state society. That state of perfection which, within the same fantasy, the society to begin with everywhere attains and expresses forms the goal of the system throughout: no change anywhere from a perfect balance, proportion, and arrangement of the social order, its goods and services, responsibilities and benefits. This is in at least five aspects, as follows.

First of all, one of the ongoing principles of the law, expressed in one tractate after another, is that people are to follow and maintain the prevailing practice of their locale. Second, the purpose of civil penalties, as we have noted, is to restore the injured party to his prior condition, so far as this is possible, rather than merely to penalize the aggressor. Third, there is the conception of true value, meaning that a given object has an intrinsic worth, which, in the course of a transaction, must be paid. In this way the seller does not leave the transaction any richer than when he entered it, or the buyer any poorer (parallel to penalties for damages). Fourth, there can be no usury, a biblical prohibition adopted and vastly enriched in the Mishnaic thought, for money ("coins") is what it is. Any pretense that it has become more than what it was violates, in its way, the conception of true value. Fifth, when real estate is divided, it must be done with full attention to the rights of all concerned, so that, once more, one party does not gain at the expense of the other.

In these and many other aspects the law expresses its obsession with the perfect stasis of Israelite society. Its paramount purpose is in preserving and ensuring that that perfection of the division of this world is kept inviolate or restored to its true status when violated.

The division of holy things   presents a system of sacrifice and sanctuary. The division centers upon the everyday and rules always applicable to the cult: the daily whole offering, the sin offering and guilt-offering which one may bring any time under ordinary circumstances; the right sequence of diverse offerings; the way in which the rites of the whole-, sin-, and guilt-offerings are carried out; what sorts of animals are acceptable; the accompanying cereal offerings; the support and provision of animals for the cult and of meat for the priesthood; the support and material maintenance of the cult and its building. We have a system before us: the system of the cult of the Jerusalem Temple, seen as an ordinary and everyday affair, a continuing and routine operation. That is why special rules for the cult, both in respect to the altar and in regard to the maintenance of the buildings, personnel, and even the whole city, will be elsewhere – in Appointed Times and Agriculture. But from the perspective of Holy Things, those divisions intersect by supplying special rules and raising extraordinary (Agriculture: land-bound; Appointed Times: time-bound) considerations for that theme which Holy Things claims to set forth in its most general and unexceptional way: the cult as something permanent and everyday.

The division of purities   presents a very simple system of three principal parts: sources of uncleanness, objects and substances susceptible to uncleanness, and modes of purification from uncleanness. So it tells the story of what makes a given sort of object unclean and what makes it clean. Viewed as a whole, the Division of Purities treats the interplay of persons, food, and liquids. Dry inanimate objects or food are not susceptible to uncleanness. What is wet is susceptible. So liquids activate the system. What is unclean, moreover, emerges from uncleanness through the operation of liquids, specifically, through immersion in fit water of requisite volume and in natural condition. Liquids thus deactivate the system. Thus, water in its natural condition is what concludes the process by removing uncleanness. Water in its unnatural condition, that is, deliberately affected by human agency, is what imparts susceptibility to uncleanness to begin with. The uncleanness of persons, furthermore, is signified by body liquids or flux in the case of the menstruating woman and the *zab* (the person suffering from the form of uncleanness described at Lev. 15:1ff.). Corpse uncleanness is conceived to be a kind of effluent, a viscous gas, which flows like liquid. Utensils for their part receive uncleanness when they form receptacles able to contain liquid.

In sum, we have a system in which the invisible flow of fluid-like substances or powers serve to put food, drink, and receptacles into the status of uncleanness and to remove those things from that status. Whether or not we call the system "metaphysical," it certainly has no material base but is conditioned upon highly abstract notions. Thus in material terms, the effect of liquid is upon food, drink, utensils, and man. The consequence has to do with who may eat and drink what food and liquid, and what food and drink may be consumed in which pots and pans. These loci are specified by tractates on utensils and on food and drink.

The human being is ambivalent. Persons fall in the middle, between sources and loci of uncleanness, because they are both. They serve as sources of uncleanness. They also become unclean. The *zab*, suffering the uncleanness described in Leviticus Chapter 15, the menstruating woman, the woman after childbirth, and the person afflicted with the skin ailment described in Leviticus Chapters 13 and 14 – all are sources of uncleanness. But being unclean, they fall within the system's loci, its program of consequences. So they make other things unclean and are subject to penalties because they are unclean. Unambiguous sources of uncleanness never also constitute loci affected by uncleanness. They always are unclean and never can become clean: the corpse, the dead creeping thing, and things like them. Inanimate sources of uncleanness and inanimate objects convey uncleanness *ex opere operato*; their status of being unclean never changes; they present no ambiguity. Systemically unique, man and liquids have the capacity to inaugurate the processes of uncleanness (as sources) and also are subject to those same processes (as objects of uncleanness).

Omitted divisions   When we listen to the silences of the system of the Mishnah, as much as to its points of stress, we hear a single message concerning consequential events. No division, no tractate, scarcely a single chapter, takes up the analysis of history and its meaning. Through its silences, the Mishnah sets forth a message of a system that answered a single encompassing question, and the question formed a stunning counterpart to that of the sixth century BC. The Pentateuchal system addressed one reading of the events of the sixth century, highlighted by the destruction of the Jerusalem Temple in 586 BC. At stake was how Israel as defined by that system related to its land, represented by its Temple, and the message may be simply stated: what appears to be the given is in fact a gift, subject to stipulations. The precipitating event for the Mishnaic system was the destruction of the Jerusalem Temple in A.D. 70, the question turned obsession with the defeat of Bar Kokhba and the closure of Jerusalem to Jews. The urgent issue taken up by the Mishnah was, specifically, what, in the aftermath of the destruction of the holy place and holy cult, remained of the sanctity of the holy caste, the priesthood, the holy land, and, above all, the holy people and its holy way of life? The answer was that sanctity persists, indelibly, in Israel, the people, in its way of life, in its land, in its priesthood, in its food, in its mode of sustaining life, in its manner of procreating and so sustaining the nation.

The Mishnah's system therefore focused upon the holiness of the life of Israel, the people, a holiness that had formerly centered on the Temple. The logically consequent question was, what is the meaning of sanctity, and how shall Israel attain, or give evidence of, sanctification? The answer to the question derived from the original creation, the end of the Temple directing attention to the beginning of the natural world that the Temple had embodied. For the meaning of sanctity the framers therefore turned to that first act of sanctification, the one in creation. It came about when, all things in array, in place, each with its proper names, God blessed and sanctified the seventh day on the eve of the first Sabbath. Creation was made ready for the blessing and the sanctification when all things were very good, that is to say, in their rightful order, called by their rightful name. An orderly nature was a sanctified and blessed nature, so dictated Scripture in the name of the Supernatural. So to receive the blessing and to be made holy, all things in nature and society were to be set in right array.

Given the condition of Israel, the people, in its land, in the aftermath of the catastrophic war against Rome led by Bar Kokhba in 132–135, putting things in order was no easy task. But that is why, after all, the question pressed, the answer proving inexorable and obvious. The condition of society corresponded to the critical question that obsessed the system-builders. So much for the relationship of the Mishnah's program to that of the Pentateuch: partly symmetrical, partly asymmetrical, partly altogether out of phase. So to conclude the exposition, the Mishnah marks a distinct stage in the unfolding of Judaism, because it does not replicate the Pentateuch's modes of category-formation or, consequently, of organizing and ordering the categories. But that is only the first important distinguishing trait of the document and the stage for which it stands. The second involves language.

II

Second, the framers of the Mishnah use a form of Hebrew markedly different in morphology, syntax, and even vocabulary, from Scripture's. They do not imitate biblical Hebrew and its literary genres, as the writers of the documents found at the Dead Sea do, with their psalms and their imitative law passages, for example. Their heirs, moreover, were acutely aware that there were differences between "the language of sages and the language of Scripture and the language of ordinary folk," as the following excerpt from a longer story shows dramatically:

A. There was a man from Nehardea who went into a butcher shop in Pumbedita. He said to them, "Give me meat."

B. They said to him, "Wait until the servant of R. Judah bar Ezekiel gets his, and then we'll give to you."

C. He said, "So who is this Judah bar Sheviskel who comes before me to get served before me?"

D. They went and told R. Judah.

E. He excommunicated him.

F. They said, "He is in the habit of calling people slaves."

G. He proclaimed concerning him, "He is a slave."

H. The other party went and sued him in court before R. Nahman.

I. When the summons came, R. Judah went to R. Huna, he said to him, "Should I go, or shouldn't I go?"

J. He said to him, "In point of fact, you really don't have to go, because you are an eminent authority. But on account of the honor owing to the household of the patriarch [of the Babylonian Jews], get up and go."

K. He came. He found him making a parapet.

L. He said to him, "Doesn't the master concur with what R. Huna bar Idi said Samuel said, 'Once a man is appointed administrator of the community, it is forbidden for him to do servile labor before three persons'?"

M. He said to him, "I'm just making a little piece of the balustrade."

N. He said to him, "So what's so bad about the word, 'parapet,' that the Torah uses, or the word 'partition,' that rabbis use?"

O. He said to him, "Will the master sit down on a seat?"

P. He said to him, "So what's so bad about 'chair,' which rabbis use, or the word 'stool,' which people generally use?"

Q. He said to him, "Will the master eat a piece of citron-fruit?"

R. He said to him, "This is what Samuel said, 'Whoever uses the word "citron-fruit" is a third puffed up with pride.' It should be called either etrog, as the rabbis do, or 'lemony-thing,' as people do."

S. He said to him, "Would the master like to drink a goblet of wine?"

T. He said to him, "So what's so bad about the word 'wineglass,' as rabbis say, or 'a drink,' as people say?"

B. Qiddushin 4:1–2 V.5/70A–B

The Mishnah in time comes first, and in function forms the foundation, of the language of sages, distinct from the language of Scripture. And, as the story indicates, these differences counted for much. What the Mishnah offers is a new language for a new statement.[2]

III

Third and most important, the Mishnah's modes of thought, its intellectual foundations take their leave from Scripture in every fundamental way. So the document derives from, and brings about the formation of, a world of thought utterly distinct from Scriptures. Scripture has God dictate the Torah to Moses, validating statements with the mythic language, "The Lord spoke to Moses saying, Speak to the children and say to them." The organization of data, the formulation of category-formations, the presentation of propositions – all refer back to God's unilateral declaration of how things are. And it follows, Scripture never represents more than a single opinion, more than one possibility among propositions. And, finally, Scripture presents no proposition along with evidence and an argument, in favor of one view and against another, but only the naked truth, divinely declared. The Mishnah never invokes God's name as source of truth, and only occasionally even cites proof-texts of Scripture's law. That is so not only when the Mishnah addresses topics ignored by Scripture or those introduced by Scripture but treated in an original manner in the Mishnah. It is also the case when the Mishnah goes over topics treated by the Pentateuch and does little more than recapitulate the Pentateuch's presentation of those same topics!

If the Mishnah appeals – mostly or entirely – to a different source of truth from revelation, and if it sets forth two or more conflicting opinions on a given subject, unlike the Pentateuch, which gives only the ruling of Moses in God's authority, then what is the foundation for the Mishnah's independence of mind. Let us take up first the Mishnah's own logic, specifically, how the Mishnah's framers set forth category-formations, both defining them and analyzing their traits, and then the meaning of the Mishnah's constant presentation of conflicting views on most propositions, small and large, that the document sets forth.

The Mishnah's sole logic of coherent discourse is philosophical, indeed, most commonly syllogistic. It is a logic that rests on the coherence yielded by the classification of things by their intrinsic traits and the formulation of the rule governing things of a given class; one classification is then compared and contrasted to others of a like character, with the object of setting forth the hierarchy of the classifications. This method of scientific inquiry is called *Listenwissenschaft,* that is, natural history: classification of things in accord with their intrinsic taxonomic traits, and (concomitantly) the hierarchization of the classes of things, that is, species of the same genus.

How this logic of coherent discourse forms quantities of facts into coherent propositions is illustrated by Mishnah-tractate Sanhedrin 2:2–3, where the authorship wishes to say that Israel has two heads, one of state, the other of cult, the king and the high priest, respectively, and that these two offices are nearly wholly congruent with one another, with a few differences based on the particular traits of each. Broadly speaking, therefore, our exercise is one of setting forth the genus and the species. The genus is head of holy Israel. The species are king and high priest. Here are the traits in common and those not shared, and the exercise is fully exposed for what it is, an inquiry into the rules that govern, the points of regularity and order, in this minor matter, of political structure. My outline, imposed in bold-face type, makes the point important in this setting.

MISHNAH-TRACTATE SANHEDRIN CHAPTER TWO

1. **The rules of the high priest: subject to the law, marital rites, conduct in bereavement**

MISHNAH-TRACTATE SANHEDRIN 2:1

A. A high priest judges, and [others] judge him;

B. gives testimony, and [others] give testimony about him;

C. performs the rite of removing the shoe [Deut. 25:7–9], and [others] perform the rite of removing the shoe with his wife.

D. [Others] enter levirate marriage with his wife, but he does not enter into levirate marriage,

E. because he is prohibited to marry a widow.

F. [If] he suffers a death [in his family], he does not follow the bier.
G. "But when [the bearers of the bier] are not visible, he is visible; when they are visible, he is not.
H. "And he goes with them to the city gate," the words of R. Meir.
I. R. Judah says, "He never leaves the sanctuary,
J. "since it says, 'Nor shall he go out of the sanctuary' (Lev. 21:12)."
K. And when he gives comfort to others
L. the accepted practice is for all the people to pass one after another, and the appointed [prefect of the priests] stands between him and the people.
M. And when he receives consolation from others,
N. all the people say to him, "Let us be your atonement."
O. And he says to them, "May you be blessed by Heaven."
P. And when they provide him with the funeral meal,
Q. all the people sit on the ground, while he sits on a stool.

2. **The rules of the king: not subject to the law, marital rites, conduct in bereavement**

MISHNAH-TRACTATE SANHEDRIN 2:2

A. The king does not judge, and [others] do not judge him;
B. does not give testimony, and [others] do not give testimony about him;
C. does not perform the rite of removing the shoe, and others do not perform the rite of removing the shoe with his wife;
D   does not enter into levirate marriage, nor [do his brothers] enter levirate marriage with his wife.
E. R. Judah says, "If he wanted to perform the rite of removing the shoe or to enter into levirate marriage, his memory is a blessing."
F. They said to him, "They pay no attention to him [if he expressed the wish to do so]."
G. [Others] do not marry his widow.
H. R. Judah says, "A king may marry the widow of a king.
I. "For so we find in the case of David, that he married the widow of Saul,
J. "For it is said, 'And I gave you your master's house and your master's wives into your embrace' (2 Sam. 12:8)."

95

MISHNAH-TRACTATE SANHEDRIN 2:3

A. [If] [the king] suffers a death in his family, he does not leave the gate of his palace.

B. R. Judah says, "If he wants to go out after the bier, he goes out,

C. "for thus we find in the case of David, that he went out after the bier of Abner,

D. "since it is said, 'And King David followed the bier' (2 Sam. 3:31)."

E. They said to him, "This action was only to appease the people."

F. And when they provide him with the funeral meal, all the people sit on the ground, while he sits on a couch.

3. **Special rules pertinent to the king because of his calling**

MISHNAH-TRACTATE SANHEDRIN 2:4

A. [The king] calls out [the army to wage] a war fought by choice on the instructions of a court of seventy-one.

B. He [may exercise the right to] open a road for himself, and [others] may not stop him.

C. The royal road has no required measure.

D. All the people plunder and lay before him [what they have seized], and he takes the first portion.

E. "He should not multiply wives to himself" (Deut. 17:17) – only eighteen.

F. R. Judah says, "He may have as many as he wants, so long as they do not entice him [to abandon the Lord (Deut. 7:4)]."

G. R. Simeon says, "Even if there is only one who entices him [to abandon the Lord] – lo, this one should not marry her."

H. If so, why is it said, "He should not multiply wives to himself"?

I. Even though they should be like Abigail [1 Sam. 25:3].

J. "He should not multiply horses to himself" (Deut. 17:16) – only enough for his chariot.

K. "Neither shall he greatly multiply to himself silver and gold" (Deut. 17:16) – only enough to pay his army.

L. "And he writes out a scroll of the Torah for himself" (Deut. 17:17)

M. When he goes to war, he takes it out with him; when he comes back, he brings it back with him; when he is in session in court, it is with him; when he is reclining, it is before him,

N. as it is said, "And it shall be with him, and he shall read in it all the days of his life" (Deut. 17:19).

MISHNAH-TRACTATE SANHEDRIN 2:5

A. [Others may] not ride on his horse, sit on his throne, handle his scepter.
B. And [others may] not watch him while he is getting a haircut, or while he is nude, or in the bath-house,
C. since it is said, "You shall surely set him as king over you" (Deut. 17:15) – that reverence for him will be upon you.

The philosophical cast of mind is amply revealed in this well-formed and highly formalized essay, which in concrete terms effects a taxonomy through the matching of data of an identical class, a study of the genus, national leader, and its two species, [1] king, [2] high priest: how are they alike, how are they not alike, and what accounts for the differences. The premise is that national leaders are alike and follow the same rule, except where they differ and follow the opposite rule from one another. But that premise also is subject to the proof effected by the survey of the data consisting of concrete rules, those systemically inert facts that here come to life for the purpose of establishing a proposition. By itself, the fact that, e.g., others may not ride on his horse, bears the burden of no systemic proposition. In the context of an argument constructed for nomothetic, taxonomic purposes, the same fact is active and weighty. The logic of coherence undertakes the search for points in common and therefore also points of contrast. We seek connection between fact and fact, sentence and sentence in the subtle and balanced rhetoric of the Mishnah, by comparing and contrasting two things that are like and not alike.

At the logical level, too, the Mishnah falls into the category of familiar philosophical thought. Once we seek regularities, we propose rules. What is like another thing falls under its rule, and what is not like the other falls under the opposite rule. Accordingly, as to the species of the genus, so far as they are alike, they share the same rule. So far as they are not alike, each follows a rule contrary to that governing the other. So the work of analysis is what produces connection, and therefore the drawing of conclusions derives from comparison and contrast: the *and,* the *equal.* The proposition then that forms the conclusion concerns the essential likeness of the two offices, except where they are different, but the subterranean premise is that we can explain both likeness and difference by appeal to a principle of fundamental order and unity. The high priest and king fall into a single genus, but speciation, based on traits particular to the king, then distinguishes the one from the other.

IV

The other quite remarkable quality of the intellectual character distinguishing the Mishnaic stage in the formation of Judaism is one without precedent in any prior writing of Judaism, whether in the Rabbinic stream or any other. I refer to the persistent introduction of conflicting opinion, in the form – as we saw just now in the passage in Sanhedrin – of the opposed and conflicting positions of two named sages, both of which as a matter of definition cannot be right. To place the matter of the systematic presentation of thought through the medium of conflicting propositions, which characterizes the Mishnah first of all in the Rabbinic writings, we turn to the great British classicist and historian of science, G. E. R. Lloyd. He describes this matter in language that serves equally well for the various Judaic systems:

> The Egyptians...had various beliefs about the way the sky is held up. One idea was that it is supported on posts, another that it is held up by a god, a third that it rests on walls, a fourth that it is a cow or a goddess...But a story-teller recounting anyone such myth need pay no attention to other beliefs about the sky, and he would hardly have been troubled by any inconsistency between them. Nor, one may assume, did he feel that his own account was in competition with any other in the sense that it might be more or less correct or have better or worse grounds for its support than some other belief.[3]

If we examine the two creation-myths of Genesis, or the two stories of the Flood, we see how readily conflicting stories might be joined together, and how little credence was placed on the possibility that one theory of matters, embodied in one version, might be correct, the other wrong. Not only so, but, as the sages of the Mishnah and the Talmuds themselves realized, the Pentateuchal laws do not form an internally harmonious statement but set forth rules in conflict with one another. The recognition of those contradictions and the work of negotiating the differences and even harmonizing them – all that awaited the great minds of the sages of the Mishnah and the Talmuds, who did the necessary work of jurisprudence and philosophy to present a completely coherent statement of the Torah. In search of dispute and debate, articulated and pursued, we simply look in vain through the entire heritage of Israelite Scriptures and through all extra-scriptural writings of various Judaic systems. In no prior or even contemporary writing deriving from a Judaism, in no systematic composition in response to passages of Scripture, deriving from a Christianity, do we find two or more opinions set side by side as positions equally deserving consideration. We find either a single position, or a position and a mock-debate weighted in favor of one side, as in the "woe unto you, scribes, Pharisees, hypocrites," passages of Mark and Matthew, on the other.

Greek philosophy and Mishnaic law and theology (continued in the Tosefta and the two Talmuds), by contrast, articulately faced the possibility that differing opinion competed and that the thinker must advocate the claim that his theory was right, the other's wrong. Conflicting principles both cannot be right, and merely announcing an opinion without considering alternatives and proposing to falsify them does not suffice for intellectual endeavor. And with the recognition of that possibility of not only opinion but argument, Greek philosophy engaged in debate:

> When we turn to the early Greek philosophers, there is a fundamental difference. Many of them tackle the same problems and investigate the same natural phenomena [as Egyptian and other science], but it is tacitly assumed that the various theories and explanations they propose are directly competing with one another. The urge is towards finding the best explanation, the most adequate theory, and they are then forced to consider the grounds for their ideas, the evidence and arguments in their favor, as well as the weak points in their opponents' theories.[4]

And what was true of science pertained to civilization in all aspects:

> In their very different spheres of activity, the philosopher Thales and the law-giver Solon may be said to have had at least two things in common. First, both disclaimed any supernatural authority for their own ideas, and, secondly, both accepted the principles of free debate and of public access to the information on which a person or an idea should be judged. The essence of the Milesians' contribution was to

introduce a new critical spirit into man's attitude to the world
of nature, but this should be seen as a counterpart to, and
offshoot of, the contemporary development of the practice of
free debate and open discussion in the context of politics and
law throughout the Greek world.[5]

In the indicative trait at hand, the systematic presentation of
conflicting opinions on a single program of inquiry, the Mishnah and
its continuator-documents take their place, therefore, within the
Greek philosophical tradition.

The Mishnah bears another trait in common with philosophical
writing. It is clearly meant to be memorized, the formulation and
language bearing powerful marks of a mnemonic program, e.g., organization of topical units within a distinctive pattern of language, so
that, when the topic shifts, the language pattern changes as well. So
too, sets of threes or fives – standard mnemonic devices, three establishing a series, therefore a pattern, and five corresponding to the
physical mnemonic of the fingers – predominate. The Mishnah, all
the more so the two Talmuds, represent notes on how thought is to be
reconstituted, the concentrate that yields the juice when water is
added, so to speak. These traits – orality, mnemonic construction,
and the character of brief notes meant for amplification and exposition within a disciplined framework – all together mark the Mishnah
as a document that is meant for the life-situation of a learning
community, just as the Classical philosophical writings were meant
for public discourse.

For Classical philosophy learning takes place (at least in imagination) in person, in public and through universally accessible debate.
The same evidence and arguments must appeal to all parties, and the
same principles of rational inquiry govern everyone. That is why the
ideal circumstances for philosophizing present themselves in collective argument, conducted (at least in theory and intent) orally,
through exchange; or in public exposition, in lecture-form, of well-
considered knowledge. Plato's dialogues, Aristotle's lectures, define
the norm, even though other contexts of philosophical speech are
attested. The public circumstance – dialogue through debate or
lecture – defines the rhetorical premise and even dictates the form,
whether dialogue, for Plato's Socrates, or lecture notes, for Aristotle.
Arguments conducted for all concerned parties, aimed at showing for
a wide audience the reasons for sound convictions, form the where-
withal of rigorous and also effective thought. These convictions form
the basis of Western intellectual life at its origins, with Plato and

Aristotle, and, as we shall see, they are shared by the framers of the Mishnah and, in a different manner, the Talmuds as well, as we shall see in Chapter Four.

Ancient Israelite Scriptures yield few comparable kinds of writing, that is to say, written down notes for a public exposition, on the one side, or a script for the reenactment of an exchange of views, on the other. True, one may well claim that parts of Job are meant for public performance, but in the main, the Wisdom literature, even parts of it devoted to propositions of general intelligibility and moral virtue such as Ecclesiastes and Proverbs, in no way approach the philosophical, and I claim, the Mishnaic (and Talmudic) conception of a public engagement in the form of a dialogue rich in argument and other exchange. The counseling father and the counseled son do not present themselves as exceptions to the rule. Whether written to be read in private or publicly sung and declaimed, these writings do not exhibit in common with those of Plato and Aristotle a single salient trait. That is to say, we look in vain in the writings of other Judaic systems, such as those collected in the Old Testament Apocrypha and Pseudepigrapha, in the library found at Qumran, in the papyri discovered at Elephantine, for instance, for anything comparable to notes for a public argument.

And the Mishnah's, the Tosefta's, and the Talmuds' innovation in form corresponds to its intellectual novelty. In no prior writing is a debate conducted, or the premise of a debate allowed to govern; opinions conflict throughout, but never compete in articulate fashion as they do in the dialogic writing of the Mishnah and analytical dialectics of the Mishnah and Talmuds. For the received Israelite writing in Hebrew and Aramaic prior to the Mishnah contains no counterpart to a document made up of disputes, with conflicting opinions given in accord with named authorities on a common agendum of difference. The dispute-form, indicative of the Mishnah and amplified in the Talmuds, finds no counterpart in a single earlier writing in Israel. In all of Hebrew Scriptures, for example, with their rich record of conflicting viewpoint we have nothing like a public dispute, a debate comprising balanced, reasonable arguments (prophets, for instance, do not debate with kings or priests, and only Moses debates with God, and then not on equal terms). Not only so, but while more than a single opinion may register in a given context, one opinion is never juxtaposed with some other and set out with arguments in behalf of the superiority of one position over another, or one explanation over another, for the purposes of a reasoned exchange of opinion and argument. That is to say, Elijah and the priests of Baal do not enjoy equal time to explain why fire consumed Elijah's but not the priests' offerings.

The singularity of the dispute-form proves still more striking when we examine the genre of Israelite literature to which the Mishnah most obviously is commonly alleged to correspond, law codes.[6] The manner in which laws are set forth in Exodus (JE), the Holiness Code (P), Deuteronomy, let alone the library at Qumran and in the Elephantine papyri, for example, in no way proves congruent with the manner in which the Mishnah sets forth laws. To take two striking differences already adumbrated, the former attribute nothing to named authorities, the latter names authorities in nearly every composition; further, the former never contain articulated debates on laws but only apodictic laws; the latter is made up of explicit disputes of rulings on a shared agendum of issues. A third difference, from Scripture's codes in particular, is to be noted: the absence of a myth of authority, corresponding to "The Lord spoke to Moses saying, speak to the children of Israel and say to them." To take an obvious point of comparison, set side by side, the Mishnah's presentation of Sabbath law and that in the Dead Sea library bear few points of formal comparability at all.

True, the Mishnah's law refers constantly to the substance of Scripture, even though citations of scriptural proof-texts prove rare and at best episodic. That makes all the more remarkable the persistence of disputes as the norm, unattributed, normative law as the mere background for the setting of vivid discourse. It is equally true that the Mishnah's law intersects with the law portrayed in prior collections, which is hardly surprising given the reference-point of all collections in Scripture. That again underscores the significant point: while in some details, the snippets of laws preserved at Qumran intersect in contents with bits of the laws of the Mishnah and related writings, in form we find only differences.[7] While the Mishnah frames much of its materials in the form of public exchanges, the other Judaisms' law codes give no hint as to their framers' expectations on how their writings were to be received and read. The Mishnah is a document to be memorized and performed – a kind of mimetic version of the law – and the formal traits that so indicate in the case of the Mishnah simply do not characterize those other law codes at all.[8] It is the striking fact, therefore, that the first piece of writing in the history of Judaic religious systems to set forth a program of debate is the Mishnah.[9] And the only subsequent documents that carried forward the disputes and debates of the Mishnah are the two Talmuds. Elsewhere, differing opinions prove abundant.

But occasions in which differing opinions are set forth in the form, and for the purpose, of debate prove few indeed.

The Mishnah, start to finish, forms a vast arena for debate. And, as Lloyd points out, beyond the recognition that "natural phenomena are not the products of random or arbitrary influences but regular and governed by determinable sequences of cause and effect,"[10] it is debate that forms the distinguishing mark of Greek science and philosophy, and it is with the Mishnah that debate entered the public discourse of the Judaism put forth by our sages of blessed memory. In the Mishnah's representation of matters, the sages always "knew and criticized one another's ideas," just as did the early Greek philosophers. And, in the context of prior Israelite writing, they find no antecedents or models or precedents for their insistence upon debate, (implicit) face-to-face exchange of contradictory views, with provision for sorting out difference through reasoned exchange.[11]

V

But if the method proves congruent with that of Greek philosophy, the message of the document adheres to the Pentateuchal program. It exaggerates only a little to say that, what we have, at the Mishnaic and later stages of Judaism, is a philosophical recapitulation of the law and lore of Scripture, specifically, the Pentateuch as Aristotle would have presented it. The modes of thought and analysis come from Athens, but the laws, directly from Sinai. The thousands of rules and cases (with sages' disputes thereon) that comprise the document upon close reading turn out to express in concrete language abstract principles of hierarchical classification. These define the document's method and mark it as a work of a philosophical character. Not only so, but a variety of specific, recurrent concerns, for example, the classification of types of causation and their consequences, the relationship of being to becoming, actual to potential, the principles of economics, the politics, correspond point by point to comparable ones in Graeco-Roman philosophy, particularly Aristotle's tradition. This stress on proper order and right rule and the formulation of a philosophy, politics, and economics, within the principles of natural history set forth by Aristotle, explain why the Mishnah makes a statement to be classified as philosophy, concerning the order of the natural world in its correspondence with the supernatural world.

The system of philosophy expressed through concrete and detailed law presented by the Mishnah, consists of a coherent logic and topic, a cogent world-view and comprehensive way of living. It is a world-view which speaks of transcendent things, a way of life in response to the supernatural meaning of what is done, a heightened and deepened perception of the sanctification of Israel in deed and in deliberation. Sanctification thus means two things, first, distinguishing Israel in all its dimensions from the world in all its ways; second, establishing the stability, order, regularity, predictability, and reliability of Israel in the world of nature and supernature in particular at moments and in contexts of danger. Danger means instability, disorder, irregularity, uncertainty, and betrayal. Each topic of the system as a whole takes up a critical and indispensable moment or context of social being. Through what is said in regard to each of the Mishnah's principal topics, what the system expressed through normative rules as a whole wishes to declare is fully expressed. Yet if the parts severally and jointly give the message of the whole, the whole cannot exist without all of the parts, so well joined and carefully crafted are they all. The details become clear in our survey of the document's topical program.

VI

So much for the balance: the Mishnah in dialogue with Scripture. But the Mishnah takes its leave of Scripture in its reluctance to engage with history — whether narrative, whether interpretation — in the manner of the Pentateuch and the Prophets. If in the context of ideas I had to point to a single, decisive point of differentiation between the Mishnah and Scripture, it would be to the intense interest of Scripture in history, meaning, setting forth lessons drawn from the particularities of context and continuity, explicating the teleology of events, and the complete disinterest of the Mishnah in the same matter. The Mishnah refers to things that happened, but it produces no history. And Rabbinic Judaism from the stage of the Mishnah forward followed suit, leaving for the Talmuds the huge task of reorienting this system of Judaism to its Scriptural foundations in historical narrative.

Since Rabbinic literature contains not a single sustained history book, comparable for example to Joshua, Judges, Samuel, and Kings, on the one side, or to Josephus's narratives, on the other, let me provide a picture of how the Mishnah treats questions that writings of other Judaisms, including Scripture, take up in narrative, teleological form. Rabbinic literature starting with the Mishnah addresses historical questions in its own way. (How Midrash-compilations treat history will be examined in context.) Since every Judaism takes up the past ("history") and uses the formulation of the past in the presentation of its systemic message, the inquiry into Rabbinic literature requires us to find out how writers write the counterpart to history.

The (superficially) ahistorical system set forth by the framers of the Mishnah identifies as a sample passage of the document examples of how the framers of the system deal with history and the laws of history. Because of the critical importance of the Mishnah in Rabbinic literature, we give a generous sample of its treatment of a single topic across the surface of the document, three of the six divisions, specifically: paragraphs of Rosh Hashanah Chapter Four, Taanit Chapter Four, and, of primary interest, Zebahim Chapter Fourteen. To understand what is at issue, we must recall that the framers of the Mishnah present us with a kind of historical thinking quite different from the one that they, along with all Israel, had inherited in Scripture. The legacy of prophecy, apocalypse, and mythic-history handed on by the writers of the books of the Hebrew Scriptures of ancient Israel, for instance, Jeremiah, Daniel, and Genesis, Exodus, and Deuteronomy, respectively, exhibits a single and quite familiar conception of history. First of all, history refers to events seen whole. Events bear meaning, form a pattern, and, therefore, deliver God's message and judgment.

The upshot is that every event, each one seen on its own, must be interpreted in its own terms, not as part of a pattern but as significant in itself. What happens is singular, therefore an event to be noted and points toward lessons to be drawn for where things are heading and why. If things do not happen at random, they also do not form indifferent patterns of merely secular, social facts. What happens is important because of the meaning contained therein. That meaning is to be discovered and revealed through the narrative of what has happened. So for all Judaisms until the Mishnah, the writing of history serves as a form or medium of prophecy. Just as prophecy takes up the interpretation of historical events, so historians retell these events in the frame of prophetic theses. And out of the two – historiography as a mode of mythic reflection, prophecy as a means of mythic construction – emerges a picture of future history, that is, what is going to happen. That picture, framed in terms of visions and supernatural symbols, in the end focuses, as much as do prophecy and history-writing, upon the here and now.

History consists of a sequence of one-time events, each of them singular, all of them meaningful. These events move from a beginning somewhere to an end at a foreordained goal. History moves toward eschatology, the end of history. The teleology of Israel's life finds its definition in eschatological fulfillment. Eschatology therefore constitutes not a choice *within* teleology, but the definition *of* teleology. That is to say, a theory of the goal and purpose of things (teleology) is shaped solely by appeal to the account of the end of times (eschatology). History done in this way then sits enthroned as the queen of theological science. Events do not conform to patterns. They form patterns. What happens matters because events bear meaning, constitute history.

Now, as is clear, such a conception of mythic and apocalyptic history comes to realization in the writing of history in the prophetic pattern or in the apocalyptic framework, both of them mythic modes of organizing events. We have every right to expect such a view of matters to lead people to write books of a certain sort, rather than of some other. In the case of Judaism, obviously, we should expect people to write history books that teach lessons or apocalyptic books that through pregnant imagery predict the future and record the direction and end of time. And in antiquity that kind of writing proves commonplace among all kinds of groups and characteristic of all sorts of Judaisms but one. And that is the Judaism of the Mishnah. Here we have a Judaism that does not appeal to history as a sequence of one-time events, each of which bears meaning on its own. What the Mishnah has to say about history is quite different, and, consequently, the Mishnah does not conform in any way to the scriptural pattern of representing, and sorting out, events: history, myth, apocalypse.

The first difference appears right at the surface. The Mishnah contains no sustained narrative whatsoever, a very few tales, and no large-scale conception of history. It organizes its system in non-historical and socially unspecific terms. That is to say, there is no effort at setting into a historical context, e.g., a particular time, place, a circumstance defined by important events, any of the laws of the Mishnah. The Mishnah's system is set forth out of all historical framework, as we observed earlier. That is a medium for the presentation of a system that has no precedent in prior systems of Judaism or in prior kinds of Judaic literature. The law codes of Exodus and Deuteronomy, for example, are set forth in a narrative framework, and the priestly code of Leviticus, for its part, appeals to God's revelation to Moses and Aaron, at specific times and places. In the Mishnah we have neither narrative nor setting for the representation of law.

Instead of narrative which, as in Exodus, spills over into case-law, the Mishnah gives description of how things are done in general and universally, that is, descriptive laws. Instead of reflection on the meaning and end of history, it constructs a world in which history plays little part. Instead of narratives full of didactic meaning, the

Mishnah's authorship as we shall see in a moment provides lists of events so as to expose the traits that they share and thus the rules to which they conform. The definitive components of a historical-eschatological system of Judaism – description of events as one time happenings, analysis of the meaning and end of events, and interpretation of the end and future of singular events – none of these commonplace constituents of all other systems of Judaism (including nascent Christianity) of ancient times finds a place in the Mishnah's system of Judaism. So the Mishnah finds no precedent in prior Israelite writings for its mode of dealing with things that happen. The Mishnah's way of identifying happenings as consequential and describing them, its way of analyzing those events it chooses as bearing meaning, its interpretation of the future to which significant events point – all those in context were unique. In form the Mishnah represents its system outside of all historical framework.

Yet to say that the Mishnah's system is ahistorical could not be more wrong. The Mishnah presents a different kind of history, the kind, as I shall explain, that social science, in the tradition of philosophy, yields: the laws of society, the rational explanation of the rules that govern events, the ordering and regularization of the chaos of happenstance. Its authorship revises the inherited conception of history and reshapes that conception to fit into its own system. When we consider the power of the biblical myth, the force of its eschatological and messianic interpretation of history, the effect of apocalypse, we must find astonishing the capacity of the Mishnah's framers to think in a different way about the same things. As teleology, the system of the Mishnah was constructed outside the eschatological mode of thought in the setting of the biblical world of ancient Israel.

This formation of a systemic teleology without resort to eschatology, in a world in which statements of goals and ends of things otherwise ordinarily took the form of the story of the end of the world as people knew it and the beginning of a messianic, perfect age, thus proves amazing. By "history," as the opening discussion makes clear, I mean not merely events, but how events are so organized and narrated as to teach (for them, theological, for us, religions-historical or social) lessons, reveal patterns, tell us what we must do and why, what will happen to us tomorrow. In that context, some events contain richer lessons than others; the destruction of the Temple of Jerusalem teaches more than a crop failure, being kidnapped into slavery more than stubbing one's toe. Furthermore, lessons taught by events – "history" in the didactic sense – follow a progression from trivial and private to consequential and public.

The framers of the Mishnah explicitly refer to very few events, treating those they do mention within a focus quite separate from what happened – the unfolding of the events themselves. They rarely create or use narratives. More probative still, historical events do not supply organizing categories or taxonomic classifications. We find no tractate devoted to the destruction of the Temple, no complete chapter detailing the events of Bar Kokhba, nor even a sustained celebration of the events of the sages' own historical life. When things that have happened are mentioned, it is neither in order to narrate, nor to interpret and draw lessons from, the event. It is either to illustrate a point of law or to pose a problem of the law – always *en passant,* never in a pointed way. So when sages refer to what has happened, this is casual and tangential to the main thrust of discourse. Famous events, of enduring meaning, such as the return to Zion from Babylonia in the time of Ezra and Nehemiah, gain entry into the Mishnah's discourse only because of the genealogical divisions of Israelite society into castes among the immigrants (M. Qiddushin 4:1).

Where the Mishnah provides little tales or narratives, moreover, they more often treat how things in the cult are done in general than what, in particular, happened on some one day. It is sufficient to refer casually to well-known incidents. Narrative, in the Mishnah's limited rhetorical repertoire, is reserved for the narrow framework of what priests and others do on recurrent occasions and around the Temple. In all, that staple of history, stories about dramatic events and important deeds, in the minds of the Mishnah's jurisprudents provide little nourishment. Events, if they appear at all, are treated as trivial. They may be well-known, but are consequential in some way other than is revealed in the detailed account of what actually happened. Let me now show some of the principal texts that contain and convey this other conception of how events become history and how history teaches lessons.

VII

Sages' treatment of events determines what in the Mishnah is important about what happens. Since the greatest event in the century-and-a-half, from circa 50 to circa 200, in which the Mishnah's materials came into being, was the destruction of the Temple in 70, we must expect the Mishnah's treatment of that incident to illustrate the document's larger theory of history: what is important and unimportant about what happens. The treatment of the destruction occurs in two ways. First, the destruction of the Temple constitutes a noteworthy fact in the history of the law. Why? Because various laws about rite and cult had to undergo revision on account of the destruction. The following provides a stunningly apt example of how the Mishnah's philosophers regard what actually happened as being simply changes in the law. We begin with Mishnah-tractate Rosh Hashanah Chapter Four.

ROSH HASHANAH CHAPTER FOUR

4:1–3

A. The festival day of the New Year which coincided with the Sabbath –
B. in the Temple they would sound the *shofar*.
C. But not in the provinces.
D. When the Temple was destroyed, Rabban Yohanan ben Zakkai made the rule that they should sound the *shofar* in every locale in which there was a court.
E. Said R. Eleazar, "Rabban Yohanan b. Zakkai made that rule only in the case of Yabneh alone."
F. They said to him, "All the same are Yabneh and every locale in which there is a court.

M. Rosh Hashanah 4:1

A. And in this regard also was Jerusalem ahead of Yabneh:
B. in every town which is within sight and sound [of Jerusalem], and nearby and able to come up to Jerusalem, they sound the *shofar*.
C. But as to Yabneh, they sound the *shofar* only in the court alone.

M. Rosh Hashanah 4:2

A. In olden times the *lulab* was taken up in the Temple for seven days, and in the provinces, for one day.
B. When the Temple was destroyed, Rabban Yohanan ben Zakkai made the rule that in the provinces the *lulab* should be taken up for seven days, as a memorial to the Temple;
C. and that the day [the sixteenth of Nisan] on which the *omer* is waved should be wholly prohibited [in regard to the eating of new produce] [M. Suk. 3:12].

M. Rosh Hashanah 4:3

First, let us examine the passage in its own terms, and then point to its consequence for the argument about history. The rules of sounding the *shofar* run to the special case of the New Year which coincides with the Sabbath, M. 4:1A–C. Clearly, we have some diverse materials here since M. 4:1A–D (+ E–F), are formally different from M. 4:3. The point of difference, however, is clear, since M. 4:3A has no counterpart at M. 4:1A–C, and this is for redactional reasons. That is, to connect his materials with what has gone before, the redactor could not introduce the issue of M. 4:1A–C with the formulary, *In olden times... When the Temple was destroyed....* Consequently, he has used the more common, mild apocopation to announce his topic, and then reverted to the expected formulary pattern, which, I think, characterized M. 4:1A–C as much as M. 4:3. M. 4:2A assumes a different antecedent construction from the one we have, a formulary which lists points in which Jerusalem is ahead of Yabneh, and, perhaps, points in which Yabneh is ahead of Jerusalem. But M. 4:2 clearly responds to M. 4:1E's view. The meaning of the several entries is clear and requires no comment.

But the point as to the use and meaning of history does. What we see is that the destruction of the Temple is recognized and treated as consequential – but only for the organization of rules. The event forms division between one time and some other, and, in consequence, we sort out rules pertaining to the Temple and synagogue in one way rather than in another. That, sum and substance, is the conclusion drawn from the destruction of the Temple, which is to say, the use that is made of that catastrophe: an indicator in the organization of rules. What we see is the opposite of an interest in focusing upon the one-time meaning of events. Now it is the all-time significance of events in the making of rules. Events are now treated not as irregular and intrinsically consequential but as regular and merely instrumental.

The passages before us leave no doubt about what sages selected as important about the destruction: it produced changes in synagogue rites. Although the sages surely mourned for the destruction and the loss of Israel's principal mode of worship, and certainly recorded the event of the ninth of Ab in the year 70, they did so in their characteristic way: they listed the event as an item in a catalogue of things that are like one another and so demand the same response. But then the destruction no longer appears as a unique event. It is absorbed into a pattern of like disasters, all exhibiting similar taxonomic traits, events to which the people, now well-schooled in tragedy, knows full well the appropriate response. So it is in demonstrating regularity that sages reveal their way of coping. Then the uniqueness of the event fades away, its mundane character is emphasized. The power of taxonomy in imposing order upon chaos once more does its healing work. The consequence was reassurance that historical events obeyed discoverable laws. Israel's ongoing life would override disruptive, one-time happenings. So catalogues of events, as much as lists of species of melons, served as brilliant apologetic by providing reassurance that nothing lies beyond the range and power of ordering system and stabilizing pattern. Here is yet another way in which the irregular was made regular and orderly, subject to rules:

MISHNAH-TRACTATE TAANIT 4:6–7

A. Five events took place for our fathers on the seventeenth of Tammuz, and five on the ninth of Ab.

B. On the seventeenth of Tammuz

(1) the tablets [of the Torah] were broken,
(2) the daily whole offering was cancelled,
(3) the city wall was breached,
(4) Apostemos burned the Torah, and (5) he set up an idol in the Temple.

C. On the ninth of Ab

(1) the decree was made against our forefathers that they should not enter the land,
(2) the first Temple,
(3) the second [Temple] were destroyed,
(4) Betar was taken,
(5) the city was ploughed up [after the war of Hadrian].

D. When Ab comes, rejoicing diminishes.

M. Taanit 4:6

A. In the week in which the ninth of Ab occurs it is prohibited to get a haircut and to wash one's clothes.

B. But on Thursday of that week these are permitted,

C. because of the honor due to the Sabbath.

D. On the eve of the ninth of Ab a person should not eat two prepared dishes, nor should one eat meat or drink wine.

E. Rabban Simeon b. Gamaliel says, "He should make some change from ordinary procedures."

F. R. Judah declares people obligated to turn over beds.

G. But sages did not concur with him.

M. Taanit 4:7

I include M. Taanit 4:7 to show the context in which the list of M. 4:6 stands. The stunning calamities catalogued at M. 4:6 form groups, reveal common traits, so are subject to classification. Then the laws of M. 4:7 provide regular rules for responding to, coping with, these untimely catastrophes, all (fortuitously) in a single classification. So the raw materials of history are absorbed into the ahistorical, supernatural system of the Mishnah. The process of absorption and regularization of the unique and one-time moment is illustrated in the passage at hand.

A still more striking example of the reordering of one-time events into all-time patterns derives from the effort to put together in a coherent way the rather haphazard history of the cult inherited from Scripture, with sacrifices made here and there and finally in Jerusalem. Now, the entire history of the cult, so critical in the larger system created by the Mishnah's lawyers, produced a patterned, therefore sensible and intelligible, picture. As is clear, everything that happened turned out to be susceptible of classification, once the taxonomic traits were specified. A monothetic exercise, sorting out periods and their characteristics, took the place of narrative, to explain things in its own way: first this, and then that, and, in consequence, the other. So in the neutral turf of holy ground, as much as in the trembling earth of the Temple mount, everything was absorbed into one thing, all classified in its proper place and by its appropriate rule. Indeed, so far as the lawyers proposed to write history at all, they wrote it into their picture of the long tale of the way in which Israel served God: the places in which the sacrificial labor was carried on, the people who did it, the places in which the priests ate the meat left over for their portion after God's portion was set aside and burned up. This "historical" account forthwith generated precisely that problem of locating the regular and orderly, which the philosophers loved to investigate: what happens when a given set of cases is governed by two distinct rules, so that we do not know how to classify the cases? We see the intersection of conflicting, but equally correct, taxonomic rules at M. Zebahim 14:9, below. The passage that follows therefore is history, so far as the Mishnah's creators proposed to write history: the reduction of events to rules forming compositions of regularity, therefore meaning. We follow Mishnah-tractate Zebahim Chapter Fourteen.

MISHNAH-TRACTATE ZEBAHIM 14:4–8

I A. Before the tabernacle was set up, (1) the high places were permitted, and (2) [the sacrificial] service [was done by] the firstborn [Num. 3:12–12, 8:16–18].

   B. When the tabernacle was set up, (1) the high places were prohibited, and (2) the [sacrificial] service [was done by] priests.

   C. Most Holy Things were eaten within the veils, Lesser Holy Things [were eaten] throughout the camp of Israel.

M. Zebahim 14:4

II A. They came to Gilgal.

   B. The high places were prohibited.

   C. Most Holy Things were eaten within the veils, Lesser Holy Things, anywhere.

M. Zebahim 14:5

III A. They came to Shiloh.

   B. The high places were prohibited.

   C. (1) There was no roof-beam there, but below was a house of stone, and hangings above it, and (2) it was 'the resting place' [Deut. 12:9].

   D. Most Holy Things were eaten within the veils, Lesser Holy Things and second-tithe [were eaten] in any place within sight [of Shiloh].

M. Zebahim 14:6

IV A. They came to Nob and Gibeon.

   B. The high places were permitted.

   C. Most Holy Things were eaten within the veils, Lesser Holy Things, in all the towns of Israel.

M. Zebahim 14:7

V A. They came to Jerusalem.

   B. The high places were prohibited.

   C. And they never again were permitted.

   D. And it was 'the inheritance' [Deut. 12:9].

   E. Most Holy Things were eaten within the veils, Lesser Holy Things and second-tithe within the wall.

M. Zebahim 4:8

Let us rapidly review the formal traits of this lovely composition, because those traits justify my insistence that we are dealing with a patterning of events. This set of five formally balanced items bears remarkably few glosses. The form is best revealed at M. 14:5, 7. M. 14:6C is the only significant gloss. M. 14:4 sets up a fine introduction, integral to the whole despite its interpolated and extraneous information at A2, B2. M. 14:8C is essential; D is a gloss, parallel to M. 14:6C2. The unitary construction is self-explanatory. At some points it was permitted to sacrifice on high places, at others, it was not, a neat way of harmonizing Scripture's numerous contradictions on the subject. M. 14:4B depends upon Lev. 17:5. M. 14:5 refers to Joshua 4:19ff.; M. 14:6, to Joshua 18:1. The 'resting place' of Deut. 12:9 is identified with Shiloh. At this point the obligation to separate second tithe is incurred, which accounts for the conclusion of M. 14:4D. M. 14:7 refers to I Samuel 21:2, 7, after the destruction of Shiloh, and to I Kings 3:4. M. 14:8 then identifies the 'inheritance' of Deut. 12:9 with Jerusalem. The 'veils' are familiar at M. 5:3, 5, and the walls of Jerusalem, M. 5:6–8. Here is a classic case of how the Mishnah systematizes Scripture's information.

M. Zebahim 14:9

A. All the Holy Things which one sanctified at the time of the prohibition of the high places and offered at the time of the prohibition of high places outside –

B. lo, these are subject to the transgression of a positive commandment and a negative commandment, and they are liable on their account to extirpation [for sacrificing outside the designated place, Lev. 17:8–9, M. 13:1A].

C. [If] one sanctified them at the time of the permission of high places and offered them up at the time of the prohibition of high places,

D. lo, these are subject to transgression of a positive commandment and to a negative commandment, but they are not liable on their account to extirpation [since if the offerings had been sacrificed when they were sanctified, there should have been no violation].

E. [If] one sanctified them at the time of the prohibition of high places and offered them up at the time of the permission of high places,

F. lo, these are subject to transgression of a positive commandment, but they are not subject to a negative commandment at all.

M. Zebahim 14:9

Now we see how the Mishnah's sages turn events into rules and show the orderly nature of history. The secondary expansion of M. 14:4–8 is in three parts, A-B, C and E-F, all in close verbal balance. The upshot is to cover all sorts of circumstances within a single well-composed pattern. This is easy to represent by simple symbols. We deal with two circumstances and two sets of actions: The circumstance of the prohibition of high places, (-), and that of their permission (+), and the act of sanctification of a sacrifice (A) and offering it up, (B), thus:

A: $-A -B$ = negative, positive, extirpation
C: $+A +B$ = negative, positive
E: $+ DA +B$ = positive only.

We cannot have $+A +B$, since there is no reason to prohibit or to punish the one who sanctifies and offers up a sacrifice on a high place when it is permitted to do so (!). Accordingly, all possible cases are dealt with. In the first case, both sanctification and offering up take place at the time that prohibition of high places applies. There is transgression of a positive commandment and a negative commandment. The negative is Deut. 12:13, the positive, Deut. 12:14. *Take heed that you do not offer your burnt-offerings at every place that you see; but at the place which the Lord will choose in one of your tribes, there you shall offer your burnt-offerings...* The mixtures, C and E, then go over the same ground. If sanctification takes place when it is permitted to sanctify animals for use in high places, but the offering up takes place when it is not allowed to do so (e.g., the former for M. 14:4, the latter, M. 14:6), extirpation does not apply (Lev. 17:5–7). When we then reverse the order (e.g., M. 14:6, M. 14:7), there is no negative (Deut. 12:13), but the positive commandment (Deut. 12:14) has been transgressed. But matters do not stop here. The rule-making out of the raw materials of disorderly history continues unabated.

M. Zebahim 14:10

A. These are the Holy Things offered in the tabernacle [of Gilgal, Nob, and Gibeon]:
B. Holy Things which were sanctified for the tabernacle.
C. Offerings of the congregation are offered in the tabernacle.
D. Offerings of the individual [are offered] on a high place.

E. Offerings of the individual which were sanctified for the tabernacle are to be offered in the tabernacle.

F. And if one offered them up on a high place, he is free.

G. What is the difference between the high place of an individual and the high place of the community?

H. (1) Laying on of hands, and (2) slaughtering at the north [of the altar], and (3) placing [of the blood] round about [the altar], and (4) waving, and (5) bring near.

I. R. Judah says, "there is no meal-offering on a high place [but there is in the tabernacle]"

J. and (1) the priestly service, and (2) the wearing of garments of ministry, and (3) the use of utensils of ministry, and (4) the sweet-smelling savor and (5) the dividing line for the [tossing of various kinds of] blood, and (6) the rule concerning the washing of hands and feet.

K. But the matters of time, and remnant, and uncleanness are applicable both here and there [by contrast to M. 14:3F-I].

M. Zebahim 14:10

When M. 14:4–8 refer to a high place that was permitted, and refer also to the presence of veils, it is assumed that there were both a tabernacle (hence the veils) and also high places. This must mean Gilgal, M. 14:5 and Nob and Gibeon, M. 14:7. Now the issue is, if there are both a tabernacle and a high place, which sorts of offerings belong to which kind of altar? It follows that the pericope treats the situations specified at M. 14:5, 7, a secondary expansion. A is answered by B. C-F go on to work out their own interests, and cannot be constructed to answer A, because they specify *are offered in the tabernacle* as a complete apodosis, which A does not require and B clearly does not want. B tells us that even though it is permitted to offer a sacrifice on a high place, a sacrifice which is set aside for the tabernacle (obviously) is to be offered there. Then C-F work the matter out. C and D are clear as stated. Holy Things that are sanctified for the tabernacle are offerings of the congregation (C). It is taken for granted that they are meant for the tabernacle, even when not so designated as specified by B. Individuals' sacrifices are assumed to be for high places unless specified otherwise (D). Obviously, if they are sanctified for the tabernacle, E, they are sacrificed there. But there is no reason to inflict liability if they are offered on a high place, F. The whole is carefully worked out, leaving no unanswered questions.

G then asks what difference there is between the high place which serves an individual, and "the high place" – the tabernacle – which serves the congregation, that is, the ones at Gilgal, Nob, and Gibeon. H specifies five items, J, six more, and Judah brings the list up to twelve. K completes the matter. The reference to *Time* requires explanation, since it is shorthand. The word refers to the priest's improper intention to eat the flesh or burn the sacrificial parts after the appropriate time, and the priest's doing so imparts to the meat or sacrificial parts the status of *refuse.* The word-choice – time – is unexpected. It conveys, "an attitude as to the time of disposing of the sacrificial parts of meat at a time other than the right time, e.g., too soon or, as here, too late." The inclusion of M. Zeb. 14:9, structurally matching M. Taanit 4:7, shows us the goal of the historical composition. It is to set forth rules that intersect and produce confusion, so that we may sort out confusion and make sense of all the data. The upshot may now be stated briefly: the authorship at hand had the option of narrative, but chose the way of philosophy: generalization through classification, comparison and contrast.

The Mishnah absorbs into its encompassing system all events, small and large. With what happens the sages accomplish what they do with everything else: a vast labor of taxonomy, an immense construction of the order and rules governing the classification of everything on earth and in Heaven. The disruptive character of history – one-time events of ineluctable significance – scarcely impresses the philosophers. They find no difficulty in showing that what appears unique and beyond classification has in fact happened before and so falls within the range of trustworthy rules and known procedures. Once history's components, one-time events, lose their distinctiveness, then history as a didactic intellectual construct, as a source of lessons and rules, also loses all pertinence. So lessons and rules come from sorting things out and classifying them, that is, from the procedures and modes of thought of the philosopher seeking regularity. To this labor of taxonomy, the historian's way of selecting data and arranging them into patterns of meaning to teach lessons, proves inconsequential. One-time events are not what matters. The world is composed of nature and supernature. The repetitious laws that count are those to be discovered in Heaven and, in Heaven's creation and counterpart, on earth. Keep those laws and things will work out. Break them, and the result is predictable: calamity of whatever sort will supervene in accordance with the rules. But just because it is predictable, a catastrophic happening testifies to what has always been and must always be, in accordance with reliable rules and within categories already discovered and well explained. That is why the lawyer-philosophers of the mid-second century produced the

Mishnah – to explain how things are. Within the framework of well-classified rules, there could be messiahs, but no single Messiah.

Up to now I have contrasted "history" with "philosophy," that is, disorderly and unique events as against rules governing all events and emerging inductively from them. I therefore have framed matters in such a way that the Mishnah's system appears to have been ahistorical and anti-historical. Yet in fact the framers of the Mishnah recognized the past-ness of the past and hence, by definition, laid out a conception of the past that constitutes a historical doctrine. Theirs was not an anti-historical conception of reality but a deeply historical one, even though it is a different conception of the meaning of history from the familiar one. It was, in a single word, social scientific, not historical in the traditional sense of history-writing. Let me explain this difference, since it is fundamental to understanding the Mishnah's system as essentially philosophical and, in our terms, scientific.

For modern history-writing, what is important is to describe what is unique and individual, not what is ongoing and unremarkable. History is the story of change, development, movement, not of what does not change, develop, or move. For the thinkers of the Mishnah, historical patterning emerges as today scientific knowledge does, through taxonomy, the classification of the unique and individual, the organization of change and movement within unchanging categories. That is why the dichotomy between history and eternity, change and permanence, signals an unnuanced exegesis of what was, in fact, a subtle and reflective doctrine of history. That doctrine proves entirely consistent with the large perspectives of scribes, from the ones who made omen-series in ancient Babylonia to the ones who made the Mishnah.

How, then, in the Mishnah does history come to full conceptual expression? History as an account of a meaningful pattern of events, making sense of the past and giving guidance about the future, begins with the necessary conviction that events matter because they form series, one after another. And when we put a series together, we have a rule, just as when we put cases together, we can demonstrate the rule that governs them all. The Mishnah's authorship therefore disposes of historical events just as it sorts out anything else of interest: correct composition of contracts, appropriate disposition of property, proper conduct on a holy day, all things imputed through specific events, formed so that we can derive out of the concrete the abstract and encompassing rule. What we see, therefore, is the congruence of language and thought, detail and main point, subject-matter and sheltering system.

That is why we may not find surprising the Mishnah's framers' reluctance to present us with an elaborate theory of events, a fact fully consonant with their systematic points of insistence and encompassing concern. Events do not matter, one by one. The philosopher-lawyers exhibited no theory of history either. Their conception of Israel's destiny in no way called upon historical categories of either narrative or didactic explanation to describe and account for the future. The small importance attributed to the figure of the Messiah as an historical-eschatological figure, therefore, fully accords with the larger traits of the system as a whole. If what is important in Israel's existence is sanctification, an ongoing process, and not salvation, understood as a one-time event at the end, then no one will find reason to narrate history.

The theology of the Mishnah encompasses history and its meaning, but, we now realize, history and the interpretation of history do not occupy a central position on the stage of Israel's life portrayed by the Mishnah. Later on, at the Talmudic level, history will regain its place on center-stage. For the Mishnah, the critical categories derive from the modalities of holiness. What can become holy or what is holy? These tell us what will attract the close scrutiny of our authorship and precipitate sustained thought, expressed through very concrete and picayune cases. If I had to identify the two most important foci of holiness in the Mishnah, they would be, in the natural world, the land, but only The Holy Land, the Land of Israel, and, in the social world, the people, but only The People of Israel. In the interplay among Land, People, and God, we see the inner workings of the theological vision of the sages of the Mishnah. So much for the Mishnah viewed on its own. Now let us examine the Mishnah's stage in the formation of Judaism in relationship to Scripture: how does the Mishnah present a topic that forms the centerpiece of the Pentateuch's composite system: the Sabbath?

4

THE MISHNAH IN PENTATEUCHAL CONTEXT

Continuity and change

Now that we have examined the Mishnah on its own, we are left with the question, how does the Mishnah mark a stage in the unfolding, from the Pentateuch forward, of a continuous religious tradition, Judaism? For to this point we have focussed on how the Mishnah innovates *tout court*. But how does the Mishnah both take up topics provided by Scripture and also impose the distinctive intellectual traits particular to the Mishnah, such as we have now examined at some length? To answer that question of continuity and change, we appeal to the work of comparison and contrast. That labor carries us from abstract theory to concrete law: the abstract theory is provided by the Pentateuch's presentation of a given topic. The concrete law emerges in a way in which the Mishnah actually sets forth the norms for that topic. So we turn to the substance of a particularly important topic, namely, the Sabbath, climax of creation for the Pentateuch, an indicative and central topic for the Mishnah, a matter of law for both, reaching even into the Ten Commandments. I provide an account of the Mishnah's law on that subject, in two tractates, Shabbat, on certain aspects of the Sabbath, and 'Erubin, Sabbath limits. Then I specify what I find to constitute the Mishnah's particular contribution to the unfolding of the topic at hand.

I

The Written Torah sets the stage. The Sabbath marks the celebration of creation's perfection (Gen. 2:1–3). Food for the day is to be prepared in advance (Ex. 16:22–26, 29–30). Fire is not to be kindled on that day, thus no cooking (Ex. 34:2–3). Servile labor is not to be carried on on that day by the householder and his dependents, encompassing his chattel (Ex. 20:5–11, Ex. 23:13, 31:12–17, 34:21). The "where" matters as much as the "when" and the "how:"

people are supposed to stay in their place: "Let each person remain in place, let no one leave his place on the seventh day" (Ex. 16:29–30), understanding by place the private domain of the household (subject to further clarification in due course). In the Mishnah and its continuator-documents, the Tosefta, the Yerushalmi, and the Bavli, no halakhic category defined by the Sabbath comes to more explicit formulation. And none reshapes the topic more distinctively than the one at hand.

II

In the setting of its topic, the Sabbath, the halakhah of Mishnah- and Tosefta-tractate Shabbat articulates only a few generative conceptions. But these, expressed in acute detail, encompass the whole. The result of the applied reason and practical logic, most, though not all, of the concrete rulings embody those few conceptions. Because of the promiscuous character of the illustrative compositions, the halakhah in its formulation in the Mishnah and the Tosefta appears prolix, when in fact it is intellectually quite economical. As a matter of fact the presentation of the halakhah serves the dual purpose of setting forth governing conceptions through exemplary cases, on the one side, and supplying information required for the correct observance of the Sabbath, on the other.

But the former task – instantiating, through exemplary cases, the generative conceptions of a broad and fundamental character – vastly predominates. Six governing principles cover nearly the entire Mishnah-tractate, and, it follows, nearly the whole of the halakhah (since the Tosefta mainly amplifies and refines the principles initially stated by the Mishnah, and the Talmuds contribute little halakhah to begin with). The generative problematics of the topic turns out to impart coherence to the presentation of the halakhah of Shabbat. The larger part of the halakhah, and much of the expository shank of the tractate of the law serve to set forth a single, encompassing conception, one that in its way recalls the governing conceptions embodied in the halakhah of Shebiit, 'Orlah, and (in its odd way) even Kilayim, as we saw. Israel at home, in its households ("tents"), recapitulates and realizes creation once again. In the present context, there are, by my way of seeing things, only six generative principles in all, and we find a place among those six for nearly the whole of the halakhah before us. In my catalogue at the end of each entry I specify the Mishnah-compositions that recapitulate the problematics under discussion; readers may stipulate that the corresponding passages of the Tosefta, Yerushalmi, and Bavli contribute their usual exercises of amplification and clarification and extension.

Now to summarize the Mishnah's presentation of the topic. Here we see the union of philosophy with the Pentateuch law, the way in which philosophy leads the framers of the Mishnah to reconsider the law and identify its governing logic. The conceptions are of two types, the one distinctive to the Sabbath, the other pertinent to a broad spectrum of halakhic categories but here illustrated by cases involving the Sabbath. We begin with the more general. The latter type supplies the larger number of generative conceptions, concerning, first, intentionality, second, causality (cause and effect), and, third, how many things are one and one many. These constitute philosophical, not theological problems. Let us consider the recurrent concerns that transcend the Sabbath altogether, starting with intentionality:

1. Intentionality – the classification of an action is governed by the intention by which it is carried out, so too the consequence:

    A. One is not supposed to extinguish a flame, but if he does so for valid reasons, it is not a culpable action; if it is for selfish reasons, it is. If one deliberately violated the Sabbath, after the Sabbath one may not benefit from the action; if it was inadvertent, he may. We consider also the intentionality of gentiles. One may not benefit indirectly from a source of heat. But what happens *en passant,* and not by deliberation, is not subject to prohibition. Thus if a gentile lit a candle for his own purposes, the Israelite may benefit, but if he did so for an Israelite, the Israelite may not benefit.

    B. If one did a variety of actions of a single classification in a single spell of inadvertence, he is liable on only one count.

    C. In the case of anything that is not regarded as suitable for storage, the like of which in general people do not store away, but which a given individual has deemed fit for storage and has stored away, and which another party has come along and removed from storage and taken from one domain to another on the Sabbath – the party who moved the object across the line that separated the two domains has become liable by reason of the intentionality of the party who stored away this thing that is not ordinarily stored.

D. The act must be carried out in accord with the intent for culpability to be incurred. The wrong intention invalidates an act, the right one validates the same act. Thus a person breaks a jar to eat dried figs from it, on condition that he not intend [in opening the jar] to make it into a utensil.

M. 2:5, T. 2:16, T. 2:14, T. 2:17–18, 21
M. 7:1–2, 10:4, 22:3–4

The principle that we take account of what one plans, not only what one does, and that the intentionality of an actor governs, yields at least four quite distinct results, none of them interchangeable with the others, but all of them subject to articulation in other contexts altogether, besides Shabbat.

To begin with, we deal with a familiar principle. Intentionality possesses taxonomic power. The status of an action – culpable or otherwise – is relative to the intent with which the action is carried out. That encompasses a gentile's action; he may not act in response to the will of an Israelite. But if he acts on his own account, then an Israelite *en passant* may benefit from what he has done. The law of Kilayim, Shebi'it, and and the shank of the Babas, goes over the same ground.

If the intention is improper, the action is culpable, if proper, it is not. But so far as inadvertence is the opposite of intentionality, second, the result of the failure to will or plan is as consequential as the act of will. If one acts many times in a single spell of inadvertence, the acts are counted as one. This too is an entirely familiar notion.

The third entry is the most profound, and it carries us nearest to the particularities of the halakhah of Shabbat. To understand it, we have to know that the halakhah in general takes account of what matters to people but treats as null what does not. Hence a sum of money or a volume of material deemed negligible is treated as though it did not exist. If one deliberately transports a volume of material of such insufficient consequence that no one would store that volume of that material, no violation of the law against transporting objects has taken place. Transporting objects from one domain to the other matters only when what is transported is valued. What, then, about a volume of material that people in general deem null, but that a given individual regards as worth something? For example, people in general do not save a useless sherd or remnant of fabric. But in a given case, an individual has so acted as to indicate he takes account of the sherd. By his action he has imparted value to the sherd, even though others would not concur. If then he has saved the negligible object, he has indicated that the sherd matters. If someone else takes the sherd out of storage and carries it from one domain to another, what is the result? Do we deem the one person's evaluation binding upon everyone else? Indeed we do, and the second party who does so is liable. The reason that ruling is not particular to the Sabbath becomes clear in the exegesis of the law, which carries us to a variety of other halakhic topics altogether, e.g., what is susceptible to uncleanness must be deemed useful, and what is held of no account is insusceptible, and what a given person deems useful is taken into account, and the rest follows.

The fourth matter involving intentionality is a commonplace of the halakhah and recapitulates the principle of the first. If someone acts in such a way as to violate the law but the act does not carry out his intent, he is not culpable; if he acts in accord with his intent and the intent is improper, he is culpable. So the match of intention and action serves to impose culpability.

In these ways, the particular law of Shabbat embodies general principles of intentionality that pertain to many other halakhic rubrics. While these four exercises in the practical application of the theory of intentionality encompass the halakhah of the Sabbath, none required the topic at hand in particular to make the point it wished to make; the applied reason and practical logic of intentionality yield only measured insight into the problematics of Shabbat.

The matter of causality produces a number of cases that make the same point, which is, we take account of indirect consequences, not only direct causality. But the consequences that we impute to indirect causality remain to be specified.

2. Indirect as well as direct consequences are taken into account.

   A. Since one may not perform an act of healing on the Sabbath, one may not consume substances that serve solely as medicine. But one may consume those that are eaten as food but also heal. One may lift a child, even though the child is holding something that one is not permitted to handle or move about; one may handle food that one may not eat (e.g., unclean) along with food that one may eat. One may not ask gentiles to do what he may not do, but one may wait at the Sabbath limit at twilight to do what one may ask another person to do. Thus: they do not go to the Sabbath limit to wait nightfall to bring in a beast. But if the beast was standing outside the Sabbath limit, one calls it and it comes on its own.

M. 3:3, 4, 5, M. 4:2, M. 14:3–4, 16:7–8,
21:1–3, 23:3–4, 24:1–4

Once we distinguish indirect from direct causality, we want to know the degree to which, if at all, we hold a person responsible for what he has not directly caused; what level of culpability, if any, pertains? The point is that what comes about on its own, and not by the direct action of the Israelite adult, is deemed null. If one is permitted to eat certain foods, then those foods may be eaten on the Sabbath even though they possess, in addition to nourishment, healing powers. Indirect consequences of the action are null. One may carry a child, even though the child is holding something one may not carry. We impose a limit on the effects of causation, taking account of direct, but not indirect, results of one's action. One may make the case that the present principle places limits upon the one that assigns intentionality taxonomic power; here, even though one may will the result, if one has not directly brought about the result, he is still exempt from liability. In no way is this law particular to the Sabbath.

The third generative conception that in no way limits itself to Sabbath law involves assessing the manner in which we classify actions and the definition thereof. It invokes the rules of classification, e.g., when does an action encompass many episodes, and when does a single deed stand on its own? Sages conceive that a single spell of inadvertence, covering numerous episodes or transactions, constitutes one unitary action, the episodes being joined by the inadvertence of the actor, the actions then being treated as indivisible by reason of a single overarching intentionality, as we have already noted. They further conceive that numerous actions of a single type entail a single count of guilt, the repeated actions of the same classification constituting one protracted deed. On the other hand, by reason of consciousness, the performance of many actions entails guilt on each count, for each action on its own carries out the actor's intentionality. The larger problem of the many and the one forms the generative problematic of entire tractates, e.g., tractate Keritot, and enormous, interesting compositions of halakhah are devoted to the way in which many things fall into a single classification, or a single category yields many subdivisions, e.g., tractate Peah (for land). In the present halakhic rubric, the generative conception generates an elegant composition, but not a rich body of exegesis.

3. In assessing culpability for violating the halakhah of the Sabbath, we reckon that an action not only may be subdivided but it may also be joined with another action, so that multiple actions yield a single count of culpability.

   A. Thus whoever forgets the basic principle of the Sabbath and performs many acts of labor on many different Sabbath days is liable only for a single sin-offering. He who knows the principle of the Sabbath and performs many acts of labor on many different Sabbaths is liable for the violation of each and every Sabbath.

   B. He who knows that it is the Sabbath and performs many acts of labor on many different Sabbaths is liable for the violation of each and every generative category of labor. He who performs many acts of labor of a single type is liable only for a single sin-offering.

   M. 7:1–2, 22:5

Clearly, the principle that an act on its own is classified, as to culpability, by the considerations of intentionality, on the one side, and the classification of actions, on the other, cannot limit itself to the matter of the Sabbath. And we shall meet it many times in other areas of law altogether, e.g., oaths, acts of the contamination of the Temple (one or many spells of inadvertence, one or many types of action), and so on without limit.

A program of questions of general applicability to a variety of topics of the halakhah clearly shaped the problematics of Shabbat. Intentionality, causality, and classification of the many as one and the one as many – these standard themes of philosophical inquiry turn out to shape the presentation of the halakhah at hand, and, as my references indicate, the exegetical problems deemed to inhere in the topic at hand transform much of the halakhah into an exercise in analytical thinking carried out in concrete terms – applied reason and practical logic of a philosophical character. If we were composing a handbook of halakhic exegesis for a commentator intent on covering the entire surface of the halakhah, the issue of the many and the one would take its place, alongside the issues of causality, direct and indirect, and the taxonomic power of intentionality. But the specificities of the halakhah of Shabbat in no way provided more than the occasion for a routine reprise of these familiar foci of exegesis.

If we had to stop at this point and generalize upon our results, we should conclude that the halakhah on the Sabbath serves as a mere vehicle for the transmission of philosophical principles of general applicability. Cases of applied reason and practical logic sustain concrete illustration of abstractions, occasions for solution, in detail, of the working of axiomatic givens, governing postulates in the solution of problems of theory set forth in matters of fact. No problematics distinctive to the topic at hand precipitates deep thought that surfaces, in due course, in the formulation of specific problems and cases. Were we to close the matter where we now stand, then, the halakhah of Shabbat would appear to have no bearing upon the theme of the Sabbath, and that theme would appear to be interchangeable with any other for the purposes of the exegesis of abstract principles. Then, if we distinguish the philosophical, deriving from principles of general applicability based on analysis of everyday things, from the theological, deriving from distinctive conceptions based on divinely revealed conceptions, we should consequently assign the halakhah a philosophical, but not a theological, task.

Such a result even merely on the face of things would prove dubious. For we should be left with a body of law disconnected from the religious life that accords to that law origins in revelation and authority in God's will. The halakhah would emerge as the concretization of philosophical reflections bear no consequence for the knowledge of God and what God has in mind for holy Israel. A mere medium of concretization of abstract thought, the halakhah would contain within itself no deep thought upon theological principles, thought deriving from the revealed Torah. But as we shall now see, alongside systematic thinking about philosophical problems subject to generalization throughout the law, the Oral Torah's halakhah of Shabbat states in practical terms a set of conceptions deriving from a close reading of the Written Torah's account of the Sabbath.

These conceptions, framed in the same manner of concretization – practical logic and applied reason – embody deep thought about issues particular to the Sabbath. They yield conclusions that form the foundations of a massive theological structure, one built out of what is conveyed by revelation and implicit in the Torah's account of matters. These conclusions, of a broad and general character, can have emerged only from the topic at hand. And the statement that sages wished to set forth can have come to systematic expression only in the particular setting defined by that topic – and the halakhah required for the concretization of the message deemed to inhere in that topic. I cannot overstate matters. The Sabbath, and only the Sabbath, could produce a suitable statement of the conclusions sages set before us. And once in hand, the same conclusions turn out to delineate a vast world of cogent construction: the rules of creation as God intended it to be, translated into conduct in the here and now. When people study the details of the halakhah, they encounter the concretization of governing conceptions revealed in the Torah in connection with the topic at hand and in no other conception. When people carry out the halakhah of Shabbat, meaning, refrain from the actions deemed improper on that holy day, they realize by what they do not do a conception of such grandeur and profundity as to make of holy Israel God's Sabbath-surrogate in the here and now: people who act like God on the Sabbath. To state the upshot in a simple way: in keeping the halakhah of Shabbat, Israel acts out the logic of creation, and this they do by what they do not do.

Let me specify what I conceive to be the encompassing principles, the generative conceptions that the laws embody and that animate the law in its most sustained and ambitious statements. They concern three matters, [1] space, [2] time, and [3] activity, as the advent of the Sabbath affects all three.

The advent of the Sabbath transforms creation, specifically reorganizing space and time and reordering the range of permissible activity. First comes the transformation of space that takes effect at sundown at the end of the sixth day and that ends at sundown of the Sabbath day. At that time, for holy Israel, the entire world is divided into public domain and private domain, and what is located in the one may not be transported into the other. What is located in public domain may be transported only four cubits, that is, within the space occupied by a person's body. What is in private domain may be transported within the entire demarcated space of that domain. All public domain is deemed a single spatial entity, so too all private domain, so one may transport objects from one private domain to another. The net effect of the transformation of space is to move nearly all permitted activity to private domain and to close off public domain for all but the most severely limited activities; people may not transport objects from one domain to the other, but they may transport objects within private domain, so the closure of public domain from most activity, and nearly all material or physical activity, comes in consequence of the division of space effected by sunset at the end of the sixth day of the week.

1. Space – on the Sabbath the household and village divide into private and public domain, and it is forbidden to transport objects from one domain to the other:

    A. Private domain is defined as at the very least an area ten handbreadths deep or high by four wide, public domain, an unimpeded space open to the public. There one may carry an object for no more than four cubits, which sages maintain is the dimension of man.

    B. The sea, plain, *karmelit* [neutral domain], colonnade, and a threshold are neither private domain nor public domain. They do not carry or put [things] in such places. But if one carried or put [something into such a place], he is exempt [from punishment].

    C. If in public domain one is liable for carrying an object four cubits, in private domain, there is no limit other than the outer boundaries of the demarcated area of the private domain, e.g., within the walls of the household.

    D. What is worn for clothing or ornament does not violate the prohibition against carrying things from private to public domain. If one transports an object from private domain to private domain without bringing the object into public domain, e.g., by tossing it from private to private domain, he is not culpable.

    M. 1:1, M. 6:1–9, 11:1–6

The point of the division into private and public domain emerges in the exposition of the distinction; it concerns transporting objects. One may cross the line, but not carry anything in so doing – hence the concern for what may or may not be worn as clothing. The same point emerges in the rule that one may move an object from one private domain to another, so long as public domain does not intervene. Carrying within public domain forms an equally important consideration; one may do so only within the space occupied by his very body, his person. But the four cubits a person occupies in public domain may be said to transform that particular segment of public domain into private domain, so the effect is the same. The delineation of areas that are not definitively public domain but also not private domain – the sea and the plain, which are not readily differentiated, the space within a colonnade, a threshold – simply refines and underscores the generative distinction of the two distinct domains.

So when it comes to space, the advent of the Sabbath divides into distinct domains for all practical purposes what in secular time is deemed divided only as to ownership, but united as to utilization. Sacred time then intensifies the arrangements of space as public and private, imparting enormous consequence to the status of what is private. There, and only there, on the Sabbath, is life to be lived. The Sabbath assigns to private domain the focus of life in holy time: the household is where things take place then. When, presently, we realize that the household (private domain) is deemed analogous to the Temple or tabernacle (God's household), forming a mirror image to the tabernacle, we shall understand the full meaning of the generative principle before us concerning space on the Sabbath.

Second comes the matter of time and how the advent of sacred time registers. Since the consequence of the demarcation on the Sabbath of all space into private and public domain effects, in particular, transporting objects from one space to the other, how time is differentiated will present no surprise. The effects concern private domain, the household. Specifically, what turns out to frame the halakhic issue is what objects may be handled or used, even in private domain, on the Sabbath. The advent of the Sabbath thus affects the organization of space and the utilization of tools and other objects, the furniture of the household within the designated territory of the household. The basic principle is simple. Objects may be handled only if they are designated in advance of the Sabbath for the purpose for which they will be utilized on the Sabbath. But if tools may be used for a purpose that is licit on the Sabbath, and if those tools are ordinarily used for that same purpose, they are deemed ready at hand and do not require reclassification; the accepted classification applies. What requires designation for Sabbath use in particular is any tool that may serve more than a single purpose, or that does not ordinarily serve the purpose for which it is wanted on the Sabbath. Designation for use on the Sabbath thus regularizes the irregular, but is not required for what is ordinarily used for the purpose for which it is wanted and is licitly utilized on the Sabbath.

2. Time: what is to be used on the Sabbath must be so designated in advance.

    A. For example, on the Sabbath people do not put a utensil under a lamp to catch the oil. But if one put it there while it is still day, it is permitted. But they do not use any of that oil on the Sabbath, since it is not something which was prepared [before the Sabbath for use on the Sabbath.

B. What one uses on the Sabbath must be designated in advance for that purpose, either in a routine way (what is ordinarily used on the Sabbath, e.g., for food preparation, does not have to be designated especially for that purpose) or in an exceptional manner. But within that proviso, all utensils may be handled on the Sabbath, for a permitted purpose. If something is not ordinarily used as food but one designated it for that purpose, e.g., for cattle, it may be handled on the Sabbath.

M. 3:6, 17:1–8, 18:2, 20:5, 22:2

The advent of sacred time calls into question the accessibility and use of the objects and tools of the world, but with a very particular purpose in mind. That purpose emerges when we note that if an object is ordinarily used for a purpose that is licit on the Sabbath, e.g., for eating, it need not be designated for that purpose for use on the Sabbath. Since on the Sabbath it is used for its ordinary, and licit, purpose, that suffices. So the advent of the Sabbath requires that things licit for use on the Sabbath be used in the manner that is standard. If one wishes to use those things for a given purpose that is licit on the Sabbath, but that those objects do not ordinarily serve, then in advance of the Sabbath one must designate those objects for that purpose, that is, regularize them. That rule covers whole, useful tools, but not broken ones or tools that will not serve their primary purpose.

The Sabbath then finds all useful tools and objects in their proper place; that may mean, they may not be handled at all, since their ordinary function cannot be performed on the Sabbath; or it may mean, they may be handled on the Sabbath exactly as they are handled every other day, the function being licit on the Sabbath; or it may mean, they must be designated in advance of the Sabbath for licit utilization on the Sabbath. That third proviso covers utensils that serve more than a single function, or that do not ordinarily serve the function of licit utilization on the Sabbath that the householder wishes them to serve on this occasion. The advent of the Sabbath then requires that all tools and other things be regularized and ordered. The rule extends even to utilization of space, within the household, that is not ordinarily used for a (licit) purpose for which, on the Sabbath, it is needed. If guests come, storage-space used for food may be cleared away to accommodate them, the space being conceived as suitable for sitting even when not ordinarily used for that purpose. But one may not clear out a store room for that purpose. One may also make a path in a store room so that one may move about there. One may handle objects that, in some way or another, can serve a licit purpose, in the theory that that purpose inheres. But what is not made ready for use may not be used on the Sabbath. So the advent of the Sabbath not only divides space into public and private, but also differentiates useful tools and objects into those that may or may not be handled within the household.

We come to the third generative problematics that is particular to the Sabbath. The effect upon activity that the advent of the Sabbath makes concerns constructive labor. I may state the generative problematics in a simple declarative sentence: In a normal way one may not carry out entirely on his own a completed act of constructive labor, which is to say, work that produces enduring results. That is what one is supposed to do in profane time. What is implicit in that simple statement proves profound and bears far-reaching implications. No prohibition impedes performing an act of labor in an other-than-normal way, e.g., in a way that is unusual and thus takes account of the differentiation of time. Labor in a natural, not in an unnatural, manner is prohibited. But that is not all. A person is not forbidden to carry out an act of destruction, or an act of labor that produces no lasting consequences. Nor is part of an act of labor, not brought to conclusion, prohibited. Nor is it forbidden to perform part of an act of labor in partnership with another person who carries out the other requisite part. Nor does one incur culpability for performing an act of labor in several distinct parts, e.g., over a protracted, differentiated period of time. The advent of the Sabbath prohibits activities carried out in ordinary time in a way deemed natural: acts that are complete, consequential, and in accord with their accepted character.

3. Activity: on the Sabbath one is liable for the intentional commission of a completed act of constructive labor, e.g., transporting an object from one domain to the other, if one has performed, in the normal manner, the entire action beginning to end.

   A. If one has performed only part of an action, the matter being completed by another party, he is exempt. If one has performed an entire action but done so in an-other-than-ordinary manner, he is exempt. If one transports an object only to the threshold and puts it down there, he is exempt, even though, later on, he picks it up and completes the transportation outward to public domain.

B. If one performed a forbidden action but did not intend to do so, he is exempt. If one performed a forbidden action but in doing so did not accomplish his goal, he is exempt. If one transported an object or brought an object in – if he did so inadvertently, he is liable for a sin offering. If he did so deliberately, he is subject to the punishment of extirpation.

C. All the same are the one who takes out and the one who brings in, the one who stretches something out and the one who throws [something] in – in all such cases he is liable. By observing Sabbath prohibitions prior to sunset, one takes precautions to avoid inadvertent error.

D. One is liable for constructive, but not destructive acts of labor, and for acts of labor that produce a lasting consequence but not ephemeral ones.

E. One is liable for performing on the Sabbath classifications of labor the like of which was done in the tabernacle. They sowed, so you are not to sow. They harvested, so you are not to harvest. They lifted up the boards from the ground to the wagon, so you are not to lift them in from public to private domain. They lowered boards from the wagon to the ground, so you must not carry anything from private to public domain. They transported boards from wagon to wagon, so you must not carry from one private domain to another.

F. But moving the object must be in the normal manner, not in an exceptional way, if culpability is to be incurred.

G. An entire act of labor must involve a minimum volume, and it must yield an enduring result. An act of destruction is not culpable. Thus, as we recall, he who tears [his clothing] because of his anger or on account of his bereavement, and all those who effect destruction, are exempt.

H. Healing is classified as an act of constructive labor, so it is forbidden; but saving life is invariably permitted, as is any other action of a sacred character that cannot be postponed, e.g., circumcision, saving sacred scrolls from fire, saving from fire food for immediate use, and tending to the deceased, along with certain other urgent matters requiring a sage's ruling.

M. 1:1, 2, 3, 10–11, 2:7, 8, 7:2, M. 7:3–4,
M. :1–6, 9:5–7, 10:1, 10:2–4, 10:5–6, 12:1–5,
M. 13:2–7, 14:1–2, 15:1–3, 16:1–8, 18:3, 19:1–6,
T. 15:11ff., M. 22:1, 22:6, 23:5, 24:5

This systematic, extensive, and richly detailed account of the activity, labor, that is forbidden on the Sabbath but required on weekdays introduces these considerations, properly classified:

A. Preconditions

1. intentionality: the act must carry out the intention of the actor, and the intention must be to carry out an illicit act of labor
2. a single actor: culpability is incurred for an act started, carried through, and completed by a single actor, not by an act that is started by one party and completed by another
3. analogy: an act that on the Sabbath may be carried out in the building and maintenance of the tabernacle (Temple) may not be performed in the household, and on that analogy the classification of forbidden acts of labor is worked out

B. Considerations

1. routine character: the act must be done in the manner in which it is ordinarily done
2. constructive result: the act must build and not destroy, put together and not dismantle; an act of destruction if not culpable

C. Consequences

1. completeness: the act must be completely done, in all its elements and components
2. permanent result: the act must produce a lasting result, not an ephemeral one
3. consequence: to impart culpability, a forbidden act of labor must involve a matter of consequence, e.g., trans-

port of a volume of materials that people deem worth storing and transporting, but not a negligible volume.

What is the upshot of this remarkable repertoire of fundamental considerations having to do with activity, in the household, on the holy day? The halakhah of Shabbat in the aggregate concerns itself with formulating a statement of how the advent of the Sabbath defines the kind of activity that may be done by specifying what may not be done. That is the meaning of repose, the cessation of activity, not the commencement of activity of a different order. To carry out the Sabbath, one does nothing, not something. And what is that "nothing" that one realizes through inactivity? One may not carry out an act analogous to one that sustains creation. An act or activity for which one bears responsibility, and one that sustains creation, is [1] an act analogous to one required in the building and maintenance of the tabernacle, [2] that is intentionally carried out [3] in its entirety, [4] by a single actor, [5] in the ordinary manner, [6] with a constructive and [7] consequential result – one worthy of consideration by accepted norms. These are the seven conditions that pertain, and that, in one way or another, together with counterpart considerations in connection with the transformation of space and time, generate most of the halakhah of Shabbat.

This survey of the halakhah of Shabbat suffices to demonstrate that nearly the entirety of the halakhic corpus is set forth to make a single point. It is to show ordinary times, what it means to sanctify the Sabbath. But while we now can identify the generative problematics of the halakhah, the religious principles of the halakhah remain to be seen. A few obvious conceptions animate the law. Like God at the completion of creation, the halakhah of the Sabbath defines the Sabbath to mean to do no more, but instead to do nothing. At issue in Sabbath rest is not ceasing from labor but ceasing from labor of a very particular character, labor in the model of God's work in making the world. Then why the issues of space, time, and activity? Given the division of space into public domain, where nothing much can happen, and the private domain of the household, where nearly everything dealt with in the law at hand takes place, we realize that the Sabbath forms an occasion of the household in particular. There man takes up repose, leaving off the tools required to make the world, ceasing to perform the acts that sustain the world. But what is that message concerning the Israelite household within the construction of creation that can have been set forth only in the framework of the particular topic of the halakhah before us? Before we identify that vast context in which the humble matters at hand take on consequence, we have first to survey the complementary halakhah of 'Erubin.

III

The halakhah set forth by tractate 'Erubin focuses on the verses that link the act of eating with the locus of residence:

> See! The Lord has given you the Sabbath, therefore on the sixth day he gives you bread for two days; remain every man of you in his place; let no man go out of his place on the seventh day. So the people rested on the seventh day.
>
> Exodus 16:29–30

The prohibition of "going out of one's place" on the Sabbath is linked to eating meals in one's place on the holy day. The juxtaposition of a double-supply of bread for Friday and Saturday and remaining in place leaves no doubt that [1] one stays home, on the one side, and that [2] home is where one eats, on the other. By extension, one must remain within the limits of one's residence on the Sabbath.

On the Sabbath one is to remain in place, meaning, within the limits of private domain. But what is "private domain"? As we shall see, the transformation into a large condominium of initially private domain permits utilization of a substantial area beyond the limits of one's own property. Therefore what is private, what is shared on the Sabbath forms the generative problematic of the halakhah – that, and the meaning of "eating in his place." Sages find in Scripture evidence for the proposition that a shared meal forms a fictive representation of the condominium status of a properly delineated set of private properties. So too, the formation of a common outer boundary accomplishes the same goal, e.g., for an entire village. It follows that acts of the commingling of domains – the Hebrew is 'erub – accomplishes the goal of forming a large shared domain for Sabbath utilization.

To capture the governing premise of the halakhah of 'Erubin, one might paraphrase the familiar Latin apophthegm, *ubi bene, ibi patria* ("where things are good, there is my homeland") in this wise: *ubi pane, ibi domus*, ("where the bread is, there is my household"). That is because, for various purposes of carrying or travel on the Sabbath, one may establish residence – in place of the household where he normally resides – by identifying a place for eating other than the

136

regular one. And that conception that where one eats, there is place of residence, bears profound practical consequences for Sabbath observance in particular. For one thing it gives a new definition for "household," one that removes the household from the profoundly material framework in which it functions as the smallest whole building block of the social order. The Written Torah defines the Sabbath in part by sending Israel to its tents on that occasion. Repose involves entry into a stationary condition. The given of the halakhah of 'Erubin is that people are to stay in their place on the Sabbath day. That means each person has a place, defined as four cubits (enough for a burial plot), and, further, that he may move from that place for the distance of two thousand cubits in any direction.

Scripture yields the proposition at hand, though if that is the case, then Scripture is remarkably reticent to define any details of the law. Here is how the Talmud finds that law in the Written Torah:

A. If he does not recognize [any landmark], or he is not an expert in the law, and [if he] said, "My place of Sabbath residence is in the place where I am now located," he has acquired two thousand cubits in all directions from the place where he is located:

B. As to these two thousand cubits, where do they occur in Scripture?

C. It is as has been taught on Tannaite authority:

D. "Abide you every man in his place" (Ex. 16:29) —this refers to four cubits.

E. "Let no man go out of his place (Ex. 16:29) —this refers to two thousand cubits.

F. And how do we know this?

G. Said R. Hisda, "We derive the meaning of 'place' from the meaning of 'place' at Ex. 21:13, 'I will appoint you a place where he may flee,' and we derive the sense of 'flight' from the meaning of 'flight' at Num. 35:26, 'Beyond the border of his city of refuge, where he flees,' and we derive the meaning of 'border' from the sense of 'border' at Num. 35:27, 'Outside the border,' and we derive the meaning of 'border' from 'without' and the meaning of 'without from the sense of 'without,' since it says, 'And you shall measure without the city for the east side two thousand cubits' (Num. 25:5)."

Bavli 'Erubin 4:7–9 III.1/50B

The exercise of literary analogy is somewhat recondite, but the basic mode of thought is not unfamiliar in our own day. Clearly, we deal with a topic set forth by Scripture but independently articulated by the halakhah of the Mishnah-Tosefta-Yerushalmi-Bavli.

At the heart of matters profound reflection on the meaning of what is private and what is shared takes place. The halakhah in detail therefore addresses the problem, how can Israelites on the Sabbath move about from one private domain to another, so arranging matters that shared and common ownership of private domain secures for all parties the right to carry things in the space held in common? One answer is, since where one eats, there one resides, prepare a symbolic, or fictive, meal, the right to which is shared by all. All householders thereby commingle their property rights, so that a common single estate will then be formed of various private domains. Another answer is, establish a boundary around the entire set of private domains, one that like a wall forms of them all a single property. The medium by which the one or the other procedure is carried out is called an *'erub*, a medium of commingling, thus referring to either the symbolic, shared meal or the equally fictive demarcation line, as the case requires: a meal of commingling, or a boundary-marker for commingling ownership of private property.

In play throughout the exposition of the halakhah of 'Erubin are these propositions that in due course will come to full exposition in the halakhah of Shabbat: [1] one may not transport objects from private to public domain, but [2] there are types of domain that are neither the one nor the other, specifically, the courtyard linking a number of private properties, and the alleyway onto which a number of courtyards debouch.

To these givens the halakhah of 'Erubin takes for granted a number of propositions, upon which all else is founded. These are as follows:

[1] Remaining in one's place does not mean one may not leave his house; one may move about his own property; he may move to the limit of 2,000 cubits from one's own residence.
[2] Through a fictive meal or an *'erub* – a meal of commingling – one may commingle ownership of a courtyard shared with others. Similarly, through a fictive meal, or a *shittuf,* a meal of partnership, an alleyway into which a number of courtyards debouch may be formed into a common courtyard; this is signalled by marking the alleyway as a single domain by establishing a

gateway, and then the shared meal establishes that all of the private domains are commingled as to ownership.

[3] One must remain in his own village, that is, the settled area and its natural environs.

[4] One may establish residence at some place other than his own household, by making provision for eating a meal at that other place. The meal must be located in its place by sundown on the Sabbath, but a verbal declaration accomplishes the same purpose. That fictive residence permits him to measure his allotted area for travel from that other place.

The halakhic exposition of the topic is signalled by the outline that follows:

i.   The Delineation of a Limited Domain

    A.   Forming an Alley-Way into a Single Domain
    B.   Forming an Area Occupied by a Caravan into a Single Domain for the Sabbath
    C.   A Well in Public Domain

ii.   The 'Erub and the Sabbath-Limit of a Town

    A.   The 'Erub: A Symbolic Meal for Establishing Joint Ownership of a Courtyard or for Establishing Symbolic Residence for Purposes of Travel on the Sabbath
    B.   The Erub and Violating the Sabbath-Limit
    C.   Defining the Sabbath-Limit of a Town

iii. The 'Erub and Commingling Ownership of a Courtyard or an Alleyway

    A.   The 'Erub and the Courtyard
    B.   Areas that May Be Deemed Either Distinct from One Another or as a Commingled Domain so that the Residents Have the Choice of Preparing a Joint 'Erub or Two Separate Ones
    C.   The Shittuf and the Alleyway
    D.   Neglecting the 'Erub for a Courtyard
    E.   An 'Erub for More than One Courtyard
    F.   The 'Erub and the Area of Roofs

iv.   Public Domain in General

At issue here is the definition of the Sabbath as the day to remain in place: "remain every man of you in his place; let no man go out of his place on the seventh day." "*His* place" explicitly means private domain. There, the Torah implicitly affirms, people may conduct life in an ordinary way. But "private domain" and householder are not deemed synonymous, and that marks an important judgment. Now "private domain" means "one's place," and that does not have to be the household. Not only so, but an individual is now free to designate his "place" as other than that of his home and extended family, the place where he functions as part of a unit of production.

"Private domain," whether or not the household within its walls, is where an Israelite is supposed to spend the Sabbath, and, the halakhah clearly indicates, that is the only normal situation for the Sabbath. Spending the Sabbath in public domain, domain not designated for one's place or residence for the holy span of time, means sitting in place and doing nothing. Private domain is where one may do what he likes. That is, it is there that, within the framework of the Sabbath they may handle what they wish, carry what they wish from spot to spot, conduct all licit actions, one more, within the limits of the Sabbath: actions that are not constructive with enduring results and that are consonant with the sanctity of the time. Beyond "his place," a householder may not conduct himself as if he owned the territory, meaning, handle whatever he wants, move about what he wishes, do whatever he chooses. Apart from walking about, for all practical purposes on the Sabbath all one may do in public domain by his mere presence is establish private domain, meaning, a space of four cubits; from that point he cannot budge.

If prior to the Sabbath, however, one has established a place of Sabbath residence, then he may move through private or public domain to a limit of two thousand cubits, but still, in public domain, he may transport nothing. If one's place of Sabbath residence is the household where he normally resides, he need do nothing; but he has the option of selecting some other spot as "his place" for the purpose of the Sabbath, and then he may move about within the range of two thousand cubits from another starting point than the household. But either way, the bulk of the halakhah of 'Erubin concerns conduct in private domain. But that is deceiving. For central to the halakhah is encompassing the extension of private domain to the outermost possible limits, the walls of the town, real or fictive, the entirety of the private domain, now melded, held by joint residents of a courtyard or the set of courtyards that debouch into an alleyway, or the alleyways that all together comprise a village. That commingling of ownership of pieces of private domain into one vast, still-private domain ("his place" vastly extended, but also diluted by the commingled ownership of others) is accomplished by relinquishing one's exclusive proprietorship of his own sector of private domain.

The upshot is, through the medium of an 'erub, an act of commingling of domains, a householder gives up his unlimited power over his own share of private domain in order to acquire limited power over a much larger share of land that is in that same status. And, through that same medium, one may not only commingle his rights of ownership, he may also remove himself from the property that is usually his private domain and establish another domain. It comes down to the same thing. The advent of the Sabbath redefines what is meant by private domain, losing the individual from the group as much as losing the proprietary rights of the householder from his own domain but extending his rights over the domain of others. The Sabbath then brings about a reorganization of the division of property and society alike. As we shall see in the final unit of this chapter, at stake is a much deeper conception of the human condition on the Sabbath: where and who man is on the day of repose. Let us examine the generative interests of the halakhah in its own terms.

The halakhah, then, refers to media of commingling, ways in which private ownership for the purposes of creating a common private domain on the Sabbath is shared among householders and their counterparts. This each does by giving up sole ownership-rights to his own property to the specified others, but at the same time gaining rights to their property. The 'erub is the medium for transforming private property into a common domain among householders, as much as it has the power to form a realm of private property within or encompassing also the public domain. The former is accomplished by a meal, the latter by a fence. The 'erub, whether meal or fence, establishes common ownership for all participants, redefining the meaning of "private property" from what is owned by an individual to what is owned by the resident sector of the community of Israel in a particular here and now. What is at stake in both the formation of a large private domain or the establishment out of public domain of what is private is the same: the possibility of conducting life on the Sabbath in the normal manner. Now all property is private for the purposes of conducting the required affairs of the household – eating meals, carrying objects from place to place within the designated territory – but privacy of ownership gains a new meaning, no longer individual, but now communal.

A medium of commingling or 'erub may take the form of a physical line of demarcation, e.g., a symbolic fence, or it may take the form of a meal shared among householders. In the latter instance, the act of eating together (or, more accurately, the possibility of doing so) defines property as shared. That is because, as I said at the outset, eating defines residence. People who share a common meal – even in theory – then are treated as a cogent social unit, an extended household, possessed of the lands of all adherents thereto. The topical program of the halakhah covers two issues:

[1]   the 'erub and the Sabbath limits of a town; and
[2]   the 'erub and the commingling of ownership of a domain of ambiguous status.

In this context what people want to know about each of the two topics is: how is an 'erub provided? what sort of food is used? what do we do if the fictive meal is invalidated? We further ask about the negative side of matters, the consequence of violating the laws of the Sabbath limit. We deal with the 'erub that serves the village as a whole as against the 'erub that sets limits for the individual's travel in one direction and permits his travel in another. Finally, we inquire about the 'erub that serves the courtyard: those who must, and those who need not, set out an 'erub to establish joint domain over the shared quarters, with attention first to the courtyard, then to the alleyway. Once we know who must set forth the 'erub for courtyards and alleyways, we describe the sort of meal that is required, then deal with one who neglects to participate in the meal of commingling for a courtyard and the consequences of his inaction. What precipitates detailed inquiry – the problematics of the halakhah as it is articulated – emerges at the interstices, the primary issues of the topic having been settled. The three units of the halakhah that form the shank of the tractate – the final unit provides a reprise of the opening unit of the halakhah of Shabbat, carrying across the demarcation line between public and private domain – focus upon the margins of matters.

The first of the three units of the halakhah treats special problems of a demarcated domain other than the ordinary courtyard. The household is the model, with its walls and gateway. But households are assumed not to stand on their own but rather to form part of larger aggregates of enclosed space, on the one side, and persons are assumed to take up residence in locations other than conventional households, on the other. The former encompass the alley-way, the latter, the caravansary. In addition we deal with the area around a well and a fenced in field not serving as a human habitation. In converting into areas that unambiguously are classified as private domain, we deal with the formation of arrangements of materials into representations of the markings of gateways or courtyards, namely, gaps delineated as entry-space and walls, respectively. The act of forming these fictive representations realizes the intent to treat the affected space as private, so to classify its formerly-anomalous status by an act that confirms the intentionality. But the law provides for symbolic representations, not requiring the actual construction of conventional barriers.

The first of these anomalous areas, the alleyway, is converted into private domain ("households") by the provision of a symbolic gateway, the whole being walled in any event. So what the alleyway contributes is formal closure to the existing domain, marking off the entire area of private domain, subdivided into individual ownership, now defined by the shared entry-way as a single continuous property. What happens, then, is that the several householders concur for the purpose of the Sabbath on sharing ownership of the entire property. Accepting the symbol of closure, the householders convert their individually-owned private domains into a shared but still domain.

The second of the areas is delineated by the formation of a fence of a sort. A well, which is private domain, has to be differentiated from public domain, so that when animals drink or people draw water, they do not transport the water from the private domain of the well to the public domain of the ground around the well; the fence encompasses sufficient space for the whole to form a single, private domain. The fence around the well, which is private domain, permits drinking without by the act of drinking carrying the water – in one's person or the body of the beast – from the one domain – the well's private domain – to the other, the area, beyond the well, where the beast is standing. By extending the enclosed space around the well, the householder forms of the whole a single, private domain. Here the issue is establishing private domain out of public domain. The ambiguity, for the purpose of the Sabbath, is that public domain now supplies a place of personal residence. Constructing the symbolic demarcation resolves that ambiguity, establishing that the function of the plot – residence of persons – is confirmed by the fictive form, a fence establishing private use.

In these makeshift arrangements, the halakhah's details embody the main point. It is that "residence" requires the confluence of formal and functional indicators. It is not enough for the courtyards to share a common alleyway, even though, functionally, they form a single domain. A symbolic gateway must formally confirm the arrangement, and so too with the ropes around the camp-ground of the caravan and corners that in an imaginary way form an enclosure of the space around the well.

The questions concerning the 'erub-meal – as distinct from the 'erub-fence – carry us deeper into the condition of the householder on the Sabbath; the meal is shared, so establishing as "his place" all those who have a right to share in that meal. Once more, then, the commingling of ownership bears the meaning that rights of private property and possession on the Sabbath give way in the formation of a vast community, closed to the world but fully communitarian in rights of ownership. We shall presently ask for suitable metaphors for the clarification of the matter, and then the appropriate myth for the explanation thereof. In connection with the meal of commingling, two distinct considerations come under analysis.

First, just as courtyards are joined by a symbolic gateway at the entrance of the alleyway that they share, so the households of a given courtyard also may be formed into a single private domain. This is accomplished through the provision of a symbolic, fictive meal that (in theory) all may eat in common. The 'erub-meal then signifies that all who share it commingle their property into a single property; that is then the "his place" of all of the householders and their dependants, thus one large private domain.

Second, just as fellow-travellers form out of public domain a common, shared private domain, thus establishing for the purpose of the Sabbath a point of residence other than the established one (the household of each traveller, respectively), so individuals may provide a domain for themselves other than the established one.

So in both cases what the 'erub accomplishes is to confirm the householder's act of will: here I share my property and give up ownership; there I demarcate property as mine for the pertinent purpose and so establish ownership. It is a symbolic transaction, precipitated by the advent of the seventh day at its intersection with the intangible lines of order that mark out the spaces of the world.

In the second unit of the halakhah, we define the character of the fictive fusion meal, whatever purpose it is meant to serve (courtyards, alleyways). The principle is that it must be theoretically-edible food, even though it is subject to an ad hoc prohibition, and it may not be food that is absolutely forbidden. It must be situated where it is theoretically accessible, that is, within private domain. Now since the meal establishes either common ownership or common residence, we turn to how individuals benefit from this provision of the halakhah. An individual has the right to move from his place of residence for a distance of 2,000 cubits on the Sabbath day. Beyond that space, as we recall, he may move only four cubits, that is, within the space occupied by his own body. By situating an 'erub-meal as the indicator of Sabbath residence, an individual has the power to change his residence from the normal one to some other place. That secures the right to move over the space of 2,000 cubits other than the territory delineated by his regular residence, his household. Positioning the 'erub at the outer edge of his village, then, he may make it possible to travel to a neighboring village. In addition to using the 'erub-meal for that purpose, under certain conditions he may accomplish the same end through a verbal declaration, but he must refer to a particular, identifiable place.

A town may form a single private domain if its territory is demarcated in an appropriate way, by a wall or its surrogate. The boundaries may be established and augmented through established physical markers, e.g., walls, turrets, ruins, and the like. The gaps in the demarcation-lines may be up to fifty cubits, indicated by a rope. So much for a town divided among numerous householders. A town originally held by a single householder is preserved as private domain, encompassing many owners, by means of a fictive meal.

Clearly a number of distinct problems are joined together by the common principles involved in 'Erubin: commingling ownership of courtyards out of the domain of individual householders; that of alleyways out of courtyards; that of an entire village out of distinct walled territories; the space permitted to an individual to traverse from his established residence; and on and on. But among them, the most important is commingling ownership of a courtyard or an alleyway. The alleyway joining a number of courtyards, which we met at the outset, recurs in the provision of a fictive fusion meal of partnership, called a shittuf, that functions for the alley as the fictive fusion meal of shared ownership, called, we know, an 'erub-meal, serves for the courtyard. There is no functional difference between the two meals. The same principles apply, though in some details the one meal meets requirements not demanded of the other.

As we should expect, in the same context we deal with interstitial cases, where a rite of commingling may or may not serve, that is, areas that may be classified as distinct or as commingled. Here is the apex of the halakhah's power to identify and resolve interstitial problems, e.g., roofs that are not differentiated sheltering houses that are. So we turn into a vast private households that form courtyards, courtyards that debouch into a common alley, and the alleyways of an entire town, all sheltered within common walls or the equivalent thereof. The conclusion of the presentation of the law – public domain in general, as distinct from the much differentiated treatment of private domain and individual residence – recapitulates the opening unit of Shabbat: carrying in public domain in general, now special problems in the same connection.

So, throughout, we deal with a symbolic transaction, namely, the commingling whether of abstract ownership or of abstract lines of delineation of property. In both matters we wish to establish the ways of overcoming, on the Sabbath, the boundaries, whether of private ownership or of demarcation of territory. What we want is to establish the means of sharing what is private, so that many commingle rights of ownership, and unifying what is divided, so that many properties are formed into one. What is at stake? It is the definition, on the Sabbath, of holy Israel. The key-point here is that individuals who do not participate in the rite of commingling ownership do not benefit from the provision of the law. Here Israel defines itself by common ownership of property, excluding nonconforming Israelites and gentiles. Israel now is the community, the rest, individuals of no standing. In contemporary categories, we may define Israel as a communitarian society, called into existence at the moment of sanctification of time at sunset at the advent of the seventh day. So much for the contents of the law of the Mishnah concerning the Sabbath.

IV

We turn now to analyze the relationship of Scripture and the generative premises of the law as set forth in the Mishnah. We begin with the obvious question, which Scripture does not precipitate in its statement of the matter, why do sages devote their reading of the halakhah of 'Erubin above all to differentiating public from private domain? When we consider the choices represented by this reading of the topic, we realize that the halakhah has independently developed a subject that, to begin with, Scripture introduces without elaboration. Yet all of 'Erubin and a fair component of Shabbat focus upon that matter. The answer derives from the governing theology of the Sabbath. The Written Torah at Gen. 1:1–2:3 represents the Sabbath as the climax of creation.

The theology of the Sabbath put forth in the Oral Torah's halakhah derives from a systematization of definitions implicit in the myth of Eden that envelopes the Sabbath. Sages' thinking about the Sabbath invokes in the formation of the normative law defining the matter the model of the first Sabbath, the one of Eden. The two paramount points of concern – [1] the systematic definition of private domain, where ordinary activity is permitted, and [2] the rather particular definition of what constitutes a prohibited act of labor on the Sabbath – precipitate deep thought and animate the handful of principles brought to concrete realization in the two tractates. As we see when we deal with the halakhah of Shabbat, while "Thou shalt not labor" of the Ten Commandments refers in a generic sense to all manner of work; but in the halakhah of Shabbat, "labor" bears very particular meanings and is defined in a quite specific, and somewhat odd, manner. We can make sense of the halakhah of Shabbat-'Erubin only by appeal to the story of Creation, the governing metaphor derived therefrom, the sages' philosophical reflections that transform into principles of a general and universal character the case at hand. Here we focus on 'Erubin, and in due course we turn to Shabbat.

Why the stress on space and activity? What is it about the Sabbath of creation that captures sages' attention? We work back from the large structures of the halakhah to the generative thought – how sages thought, and about what did they think? – that gives definition to those structures. And, among available formulations, clearly they gave priority to the Creation-story of Gen. 1:1–2:3, which accounts for the origin of the Sabbath. The halakhah turns out to realize in detailed, concrete terms generalizations that sages locate in and derive from the story of creation. And what they find is a metaphor for themselves and their Israel, on the one side, and the foundation for generalization, out of the metaphor, in abstract terms susceptible to acute concretization, on the other. That is to say, the Sabbath of Eden forms the model: like this, so all else. And sages, with their remarkable power to think in general terms but to convey thought in examples and details, found it possible to derive from the model the principles that would accomplish their goal: linking Israel to Eden through the Sabbath, the climax of their way of life, the soul of their theological system.

Only when we know what is supposed to take place on the Sabbath – in particular in the model of the Sabbath that originally celebrated creation – to the exclusion of the model of the Sabbath that would focus the halakhah upon the liberation of slaves from Egypt (Deuteronomy's version) or the cessation of labor of the household, encompassing animals and slaves (Exodus's version) – only then shall we find the key to the entire matter of the Sabbath of the halakhah of the Oral Torah. Then we may identify the setting in which the rules before us take on meaning and prove to embody profound religious thinking. But we cannot treat 'Erubin out of the larger halakhic context. And, as a matter of fact, I find the halakhah that presents the model of how sages think about the Sabbath and accounts for the topical program of their thought – the fully articulated source of the governing metaphor – is Shebi'it, as we saw in Chapter 2.

That tractate describes the observance of the Sabbath that is provided every seventh year for the Land of Israel itself. The Land celebrates the Sabbath, and then, Israel in its model. The Land is holy, as Israel is holy, and the Priestly Code leaves no doubt that for both, the Sabbath defines the rhythm of life with God: the seventh day for Israel, the seventh year for the Land. For both, moreover, to keep the Sabbath is to be like God. And, specifically, that is when God had completed the work of creation, pronounced it good, sanctified it – imposed closure and permanence, the creation having reached its conclusion. God observed the Sabbath, which itself finds its definition as the celebration and commemoration of God's own action. This is what God did, this is what we now do. What God did concerned creation, what we do concerns creation. And all else follows. The Sabbath then precipitates the imitation of God on a very particular occasion and for a very distinctive purpose. And given what we have identified as sages' governing theology – the systematic account of God's perfect justice in creation, yielding an account and explanation of all else – we find ourselves at the very center of the system. The meeting of time and space on the seventh day of creation – God having formed space and marked time – finds its counterpart in the ordering of Israelite space at the advent of time, the ordering of that space through the action and inaction of the Israelites themselves.

Now what about our topic and its halakhic development? 'Erubin, with its sustained exercise of thought on the commingling of ownership of private property for the purpose of Sabbath observance and on the commingling of meals to signify shared ownership, accomplishes for Israel's Sabbath what Shebi'it achieves for the Land's. On the Sabbath inaugurated by the Sabbatical Year the Land, so far as it

THE MISHNAH IN PENTATEUCHAL CONTEXT

is otherwise private property, no longer is possessed exclusively by the householder. So too, the produce of the Land consequently belongs to everybody. It follows that the halakhah of 'Erubin realizes for the ordinary Sabbath of Israel the very same principles that are embodied in the halakhah of Shebi'it. That halakhah defines the Sabbath of the Land in exactly the same terms: the Land is now no longer private, and the Land's produce belongs to everybody. The Sabbath that the Land enjoys marks the advent of shared ownership of the Land and its fruit. Sharing is so total that hoarding is explicitly forbidden, and what has been hoarded has now to be removed from the household and moved to public domain, where anyone may come and take it.

Here we find the Sabbath of Creation overspreading the Sabbath of the Land, as the Priestly Code at Genesis 1 and at Leviticus Lev. 25:1–8 define matters. The latter states,

> When you enter the land that I am giving you, the land shall observe a Sabbath of the Lord. Six years you may sow your field and six years you may prune your vineyard and bather in the yield. But in the seventh year the land shall have a Sabbath of complete rest, a Sabbath of the Lord; you shall not sow your field or prune your vineyard. You shall not reap the aftergrowth of your harvest or gather the grapes of your untrimmed vines; it shall be a year of complete rest for the land. But you may eat whatever the land during its Sabbath will produce – you, your male and female slaves, the hired-hand and bound laborers who live with you, and your cattle and the beasts in your land may eat all its yield.

The Sabbatical year bears the message, therefore, that on the Sabbath, established arrangements as to ownership and possession are set aside, and a different conception of private property takes over. What on ordinary days is deemed to belong to the householder and to be subject to his exclusive will on the Sabbath falls into a more complex web of possession. The householder continues to utilize his property but not as a proprietor does. He gives up exclusive access thereto, and gains in exchange rights of access to other peoples' property. Private property is commingled; everybody shares in everybody's. The result is, private property takes on a new meaning, different from the secular one. So far as the householder proposes to utilize his private property, he must share it with others, who do the same for him. To own then is to abridge ownership in favor of commingling rights thereto, to possess is to share. And that explains why the produce of the Land belongs to everyone as well, a corollary to the fundamental postulate of the Sabbath of the Land.

What, about Eden on the Sabbath, defines the governing metaphor out of which the principles of the halakhah work themselves out in the articulation of acute details that yields our halakhah. Working back from the details to the organizing topics, and from the topics to the principles that govern, we find ourselves able to frame the right question. It is, What qualities of Eden impress sages? With the halakhah as the vast corpus of facts, we focus upon two matters: [1] time and space, [2] time and activity. How is space demarcated at the specified time, how is activity classified at that same time? The former works itself out in a discussion of where people may move on the Sabbath and how they may conduct themselves (carry things as they move). The latter finds its definition in the model of labor that is prohibited. With Eden as the model and the metaphor, we take a simple sighting on the matter. First, Adam and Eve are free to move in Eden where they wish, possessing all they contemplate. God has given it to them to enjoy. If Eden then belongs to God, he freely shares ownership with Adam and Eve. And – all the more so – the produce of Eden is ownerless. With the well-known exception, all the fruit is theirs for the taking. So we find ourselves deep within the halakhah of Shebi'it, as already spelled out.

It is in this context that we return to the halakhah of Shabbat-'Erubin, with special reference to the division of the world into private and public domain, the former the realm of permitted activity on the Sabbath, the latter not. If we may deal with an 'erub-fence or an 'erub meal, how are we to interpret what is at stake in these matters? It is in both instances to render private domain public through the sharing of ownership. The 'erub-fence for its part renders public domain private, but only in the same sense that private domain owned by diverse owners is shared, ownership being commingled. The 'erub-fence signals the formation for purposes of the sanctification of time of private domain – but with the owner-ship commingled. So what is "private" about "private domain" is different on the Sabbath from in secular time. By definition, for property to be private in the setting of the Sabbath, it must be shared among householders. On the Sabbath, domain that is totally private, its ownership not commingled for the occasion, becomes a prison, the householder being unable to conduct himself in the normal manner in the courtyard beyond his door, let alone in other courtyards in the same alleyway, or in other alleyways that debouch onto the same street. And the halakhah makes provision for those – whether Israelite or gentile – who do not offer their proprietorship of their households for commingling for the Sabbath.

What happens, therefore, through the 'erub-fence or 'erub meal is the re-definition of proprietorship: what is private is no longer personal, and no one totally owns what is his, but then everyone (who wishes to participate, himself and his household together) owns a share everywhere. So much for the "in his place" part of "each man in his place." His place constitutes an area where ordinary life goes on, but it is no longer "his" in the way in which the land is subject to his will and activity in ordinary time. If constructing a fence serves to signify joint ownership of the village, now turned into private domain, or constructing the gateway, of the alleyway and its courtyards, what about the meal? The 'erub-meal signifies the shared character of what is eaten. It is food that belongs to all who wish to share it. But it is the provision of a personal meal, also, that allows an individual to designate for himself a place of Sabbath residence other than the household to which he belongs.

So the Sabbath loosens bonds, those of the householder to his property, those of the individual to the household. It forms communities, the householders of a courtyard into a community of shared ownership of the entire courtyard, the individual into a community other than that formed by the household to which he belongs – now the community of disciples of a given sage, the community of a family other than that in residence in the household, to use two of the examples common in the halakhah. Just as the Sabbath redefines ownership of the Land and its produce, turning all Israelites into a single social entity, "all Israel," which, all together, possesses the Land in common ownership, so the Sabbath redefines the social relationships of the household, allowing persons to separate themselves from the residence of the household and designate some other, some personal, point of residence instead.

The main point of the law of private domain in 'Erubin (as well as Shabbat) seen in the model of Shebi'it then is to redefine the meaning of "private domain," where each man is to remain in "his" place. The law aims to define the meaning of "his," and to remove the ownership of the land and its produce from the domain of a householder, rendering ownership public and collective. Taking as our model Shebi'it, we note that in the year that is a Sabbath, the land is held to be owned by nobody and everybody, and the produce of the Land belongs to everyone and no one, so that one may take and eat but thank only God. It is no one's, so everone may take; it is everyone's, so everyone may eat, and God alone is to be acknowledged. Since, on the Sabbath, people are supposed to remain within their own domain, the counterpart to Shebi'it will provide for the sharing of ownership, thus for extending the meaning of "private domain" to encompass all the partners in a shared locus. "Private domain," his place, now bears a quite different meaning from the one that pertains in profane time. The Sabbath recapitulates the condition of Eden, when Adam and Eve could go where they wished and eat what they wanted, masters of all they contemplated, along with God. Israel on the Sabbath in the Land, like Adam on the Sabbath of Eden that celebrates Creation, shares private domain and its produce.

From the matter of ownership and possession, we turn to the issue of work on the Sabbath. Here again, Scripture's declaration on the matter is subjected to radical reconception by the sages of the Mishnah. Scripture declares that Israel on the Sabbath in the Land like God on the Sabbath of Eden rests from the labor of creation. That means, no acts of work – and the halakhah commences where Scripture concludes, an archetypal case of independent development of a received subject. That brings us to the question, What about that other principle of the Sabbath, the one set forth by the halakhah of Shabbat? The richly detailed halakhah of Shabbat defines the matter in a prolix, yet simple way. It is that on the Sabbath it is prohibited deliberately to carry out in a normal way a completed act of constructive labor, one that produces enduring results, one that carries out one's entire intention: the whole of what one planned, one has accomplished, in exactly the proper manner. That definition takes into account the shank of the halakhah of Shabbat as set forth in the Mishnah-tractate, and the amplification and extension of matters in the Tosefta and the two Talmuds in no way revises the basic principles. Here there is a curious, if obvious, fact: it is not an act of labor that itself is prohibited (as the Ten Commandments in Exodus and Deuteronomy would have it), but an act of labor of a very particular definition.

No prohibition impedes performing an act of labor in an other-than-normal way. In theory, one may go out into the fields and plough, if he does so in some odd manner. He may build an entire house, so long as it collapses promptly. The issue of activity on the Sabbath therefore is removed from the obvious context of work, conventionally defined. Now the activity that is forbidden is of a very particular sort, modeled in its indicative traits after a quite specific paradigm. A person is not forbidden to carry out an act of destruction, or an act of labor that produces no lasting consequences. He may start an act of labor if he does not complete it. He may accomplish an act of labor in some extraordinary manner. None of these acts of labor are forbidden, even though, done properly and with consequence, they represent massive violations of the halakhah. Nor is part of an act of labor that is not brought to conclusion prohibited. Nor is it forbidden to perform part of an act of labor in partnership with another person who carries out the other requisite part. Nor does one incur culpability for performing an act of labor in several distinct parts, e.g., over a protracted, differentiated period of time. A person may not willingly carry out the entirety of an act of constructive labor, start to finish. The issue is not why not, since we know the answer: God has said not to do so. The question is, whence the particular definition at hand?

Clearly, a definition of the act of labor that is prohibited on the Sabbath has taken over and recast the commonsense meaning of the commandment not to labor on the Sabbath. For considerations enter that recast matters from an absolute to a relative definition. One may tie a knot – but not one that stands. One may carry a package, but not in the usual manner. One may build a wall, only if it falls down. And, as I have stressed, one may do pretty much anything without penalty – if he did not intend matters as they actually happened. The metaphor of God in Eden, as sages have reflected on the story of Creation, yields the governing principles that define forbidden labor. What God did in the six days of creation provides the model.

Let us review the main principles item by item. They involve the three preconditions. The act must fully carry out the intention of the actor, as creation carried out God's intention. The act of labor must be carried out by a single actor, as God acted alone in creating the world. An act of labor is the like of one that is required in the building and maintenance of God's residence in this world, the tabernacle. The act of labor prohibited on the Sabbath involves two considerations. The act must be done in the ordinary way, just as Scripture's account leaves no doubt, God accomplished creation in the manner in which he accomplished his goals from creation onward, by an act of speech. And, weightier still, the forbidden act of labor is one that produces enduring consequences. God did not create only to destroy, but he created the enduring world. And it goes without saying, creation yielded the obvious consequences that the act was completely done in all ways, as God himself declared.

The act was one of consequence, involving what was not negligible but what man and God alike deemed to make a difference. Sages would claim, therefore, that the activity that must cease on the Sabbath finds its definition in the model of those actions that God carried out in making the world.

That such a mode of thought is more than a mere surmise, based on the congruence of the principles by which labor forbidden on the Sabbath spin themselves out of the Creation-story, emerges when we recall a striking statement. It is the one that finds the definition of forbidden labor in those activities required for the construction and maintenance of the tabernacle, which is to say, God's residence on earth. The best statement, predictably, is the Bavli's:

> People are liable only for classifications of labor the like of which was done in the tabernacle. They sowed, so you are not to sow. They harvested, so you are not to harvest. They lifted up the boards from the ground to the wagon, so you are not to lift them in from public to private domain. They lowered boards from the wagon to the ground, so you must not carry anything from private to public domain. They transported boards from wagon to wagon, so you must not carry from one private domain to another.
>
> Bavli Shabbat 4:2 I.4/49B

Sages found in the analogy of how, in theory, the tabernacle was maintained, the classifications of labor that pertain. In the tabernacle these activities are permitted, even on the Sabbath. In God's house, the priests and Levites must do for God what they cannot do for themselves – and the identification of acts of labor forbidden on the Sabbath follows.

The details of the halakhah then emerge out of a process in which two distinct sources contribute. One is the model of the tabernacle. What man may do for God's house he may not do for his own – God is always God, the Israelite aspires only to be "like God," to imitate God, and that is a different thing. The other is the model of the creation of the world and of Eden. Hence to act like God on the Sabbath, the Israelite rests; he does not do what God did in creation. The former source supplies generative metaphors, the like of which may not be done; thus acts like sowing, like harvesting, like lifting boards from public to private domain, and the like, are forbidden. The latter source supplies the generative principles, the abstract definitions involving the qualities of perfection and causation: intentionality, completion, the normality of the conduct of the action, and the like. The mode of analogical thinking governs, but, as we see, a double metaphor pertains, the metaphor of God's activity in creation, the metaphor of the priests' and Levites' activity in the tabernacle. Creation yields those large principles that we have identified: the traits of an act of labor for God in creation define the prohibited conditions of an act of labor on the Sabbath. By appeal to those two metaphors, we can account for every detail of the halakhah.

Now what has Scripture contributed to all this? Everything – and nothing. Scripture defines the encompassing structure, in which all details find their place, proportion, and implicit meanings. The philosophical interest in generalization and harmonization provides the jurisprudence of the topic: the details of the law as they form a coherent whole. The Mishnaic stage carries forward the program of thought characteristic of the age between the Pentateuch and the Mishnah, which itself built upon a reading of the Pentateuch that, I have argued, coheres with the clear construction of the document read whole.

What is the upshot? On the Sabbath Israel goes home to Eden. How best to make the statement that the Land is Israel's Eden, that Israel imitates God by keeping the Sabbath, meaning, not doing the things that God did in creating the world but ceased to do on the Sabbath, and that to restore its Eden, Israel must sustain its life – nourish itself – where it belongs? To set forth those most basic convictions about God in relationship to man and about Israel in relationship to God, I can imagine no more eloquent, no more compelling and appropriate, medium of expression than the densely detailed halakhah of Shebi'it, Shabbat, and 'Erubin. Indeed, outside of the setting of the household, its ownership, utilization, and maintenance, I cannot think of any other way of fully making that statement stick. In theory implausible for its very simplicity (as much as for its dense instantiation!), in halakhic fact, compelling, the Oral Torah's statement accounts for the human condition. Israel's Eden takes place in the household open to others, on the Sabbath, in acts that maintain life, share wealth, and desist from creation.

The key words, therefore, are in the shift from the here and now of time in which one works like God, to the *then* and the *there* when one desists from working, just as God did at the moment the world was finished, perfected, and sanctified. Israel gives up the situation of man in ordinary time and space, destructive, selfish, dissatisfied and doing. Then, on the Sabbath, and there, in the household, with each one in place, Israel enters the situation of God in that initial, that perfected and sanctified then and there of creation: the activity that consists in sustaining life, sharing dominion, and perfecting repose through acts of restraint and sufficiency. Here we see the outcome of independent thinking about a received subject: a profound recapitulation of Scripture's own deepest layers of reflection, now in the detailed and concrete language of actuality. Here is what the halakhah, articulated by the sages of tractates Shabbat and 'Erubin, in accord with sound philosophical principles of analysis, does best.

5

THE TALMUDS
The conclusive statement

The Talmuds of the Land of Israel (circa 400 CE) and Babylonia (circa 600 CE) mark the fourth and conclusive stage in the formation of Judaism. As different in character and purpose from all prior documents as the Mishnah is from Scripture, the Talmuds drew together the entire received heritage of law and theology and restated the whole in a new intellectual idiom and in a definitive formulation. The mode of thought characteristic of the Talmuds, particularly the second of the two, is the dialectical argument of propositional analysis. The definitive formulation joined the Mishnah's emphasis upon sanctification and a timeless world of the present tense with the Pentateuch's, and Scripture's, stress upon salvation in a historical world of purposeful events leading to the climax and conclusion of history. So while the Mishnah framed a vision of a restoration of Eden in the eternal Sabbath, whether now, whether then, the Talmuds offered a glimpse of an end-time, a goal toward which Israel, vanguard of humanity, would find its way.

The Judaism that emerged in the conclusive statement of the Talmud of Babylonia called Israel to a life of sanctification in the here and now that would come to realization in the moment of salvation at the end of days. This synthesis into a single system – a world view, a way of life, a theory of who and what is Israel – came to full realization when the Talmuds recast the Mishnah – its method and its message – and so dictated the future of Judaism. Here we focus on the method, and in Chapter Six turn to the message that characterized the Talmudic stage in the formation of Judaism.

I

The advent of the Mishnah precipitated a remarkable period of legal and theological activity and creativity, the third century CE marking the seed-time of Rabbinic Judaism, as much as the seventh, with the advent of the Talmud of Babylonia, would witness its harvest. It would be difficult to point to a time of greater imagination and innovation, with entirely unprecedented types of writing undertaken to serve as media for thoughts never before contemplated. Having given a full and systematic statement to the modes of thought and foci of reflection of the first and second centuries, themselves resting on deep inquiry into the implications of the Pentateuch characteristic of unknown sages from the fifth century to the first, the Mishnah, in negative and positive ways, dictated the long future.

The character of the Mishnah as an autonomous work of philosophical rationalism defined the task of its principal continuators, the Talmud of the Land of Israel and the Talmud of Babylonia, over the next four hundred years. When, in circa 200, the Mishnah reached closure and was received and adopted as law by the state-sanctioned Jewish governments both in the Roman empire (in the land of Israel), and in Iran (in Babylonia), the function and character of the document precipitated a considerable crisis. Politically and theologically presented as the foundation for the everyday administration of the affairs of Jewry, the Mishnah ignored the politics of the sponsoring regimes, the patriarchate in the Land of Israel, the exilarchate in Babylonia, that governed the Jewish communities of the respective provinces. Essentially ahistorical, speaking of the Temple and the high priest and the king as the political institutions of Israel, the code hardly identified as authoritative any known political institution, let alone the constituted ones.

True, that political-institutional flaw (from the viewpoint of the sponsoring authorities) can scarcely have proved critical. But silence of the authorship of the Mishnah on the theological call for their document presented not a chronic but an acute problem. Since Jews generally accepted the authority of Moses at Sinai, failure to claim for the document a clear and explicit relationship to the Torah of Moses defined that acute issue. Why should people accept as authoritative the rulings of this piece of writing, so different from Scripture? Omitting reference to a theological, as much as to a political myth, the authorship of the Mishnah also failed systematically to signal the relationship between their document and Scripture. Since, for all Judaisms, the Hebrew Scriptures in general, and the Pentateuch, in particular, represented God's will for Israel, silence on that matter provoked considerable response.

Laws issued to define what people were supposed to do could not stand by themselves; they had to receive the imprimatur of Heaven, that is, to be given the status of revelation. Accordingly, to make its way in Israelite life, the Mishnah as a constitution and code demanded for itself a theory of beginnings at (or in relation to) Sinai, with Moses, from God. The character of the Mishnah itself hardly won confidence that, on the face of it, the document formed part of, or derived from Sinai. It was originally published through oral formulation and oral transmission, that is, in the medium of memorization. But it had been in the medium of writing that, in the view of all of Israel until about 200 CE, God had been understood to reveal the divine word and will. The Torah was a written book. People who claimed to receive further messages from God usually wrote them down. They had three choices in securing acceptance of their account. All three involved linking the new to the old.

In claiming to hand on revelation, they could, first, sign their books with the names of biblical heroes. Second, they could imitate the style of biblical Hebrew. Third, they could present an exegesis of existing written verses, validating their ideas by supplying proof texts for them. From the closure of the Torah literature in the time of Ezra, circa 450 BCE to the time of the Mishnah, nearly seven centuries later, we do not have a single book alleged to be holy and at the same time standing wholly out of relationship to the Holy Scriptures of ancient Israel. The Pseudepigraphic writings bearing names such as Jeremiah, Moses, the Patriarchs, Enoch, and even Adam, fall into the first category, the Essene writings at Qumran into the second and third, Psalms and law codes in the Davidic and Mosaic manner, respectively. We may point also to the Gospels, which take as a principal problem demonstrating how Jesus had fulfilled the prophetic promises of the Old Testament and in other ways carried forward and even embodied Israel's Scripture.

Insofar as a piece of Jewish writing did not find a place in relationship to Scripture, its author laid no claim to present a holy book. The contrast between Jubilees and the Testaments of the Patriarchs, with their constant and close harping on biblical matters, and the several books of Maccabees, shows the differences. The former claim to present God's revealed truth, the latter, history. So a book was holy because in style, in authorship, or in (alleged) origin it continued Scripture, finding a place therefore (at least in the author's mind) within the canon, or because it provided an exposition on Scripture's meaning. But the Mishnah made no such claim. It entirely ignored the style of biblical Hebrew, speaking in a quite different kind of Hebrew altogether. It is silent on its authorship through sixty-two of the sixty-three tractates (the claims of Abot are post facto). In any event, nowhere does the Mishnah contain the claim that God had inspired the authors of the document. These are not given biblical names and certainly are not alleged to have been biblical saints. Most of the book's named authorities flourished within the same century as its anonymous arrangers and redactors, not in remote antiquity. Above all, the Mishnah contains scarcely a handful of exegeses of Scripture. These, where they occur, play a trivial and tangential role. So here is the problem of the Mishnah: different from Scripture in language and style, indifferent to the claim of authorship by a biblical hero or divine inspiration, stunningly aloof from allusion to verses of Scripture for nearly the whole of its discourse – yet authoritative for Israel.

So the Mishnah was not a statement of theory alone, telling only how matters will be in the eschaton. Nor was it a wholly sectarian document, reporting the view of a group without standing or influence in the larger life of Israel. True, in some measure it bears both of these traits of eschatology and sectarian provenance. But the Mishnah was (and is) law for Israel. It entered the government and courts of the Jewish people, both in the motherland and also overseas, as the authoritative constitution of the courts of Judaism. The advent of the Mishnah therefore marked a turning in the life of the nation-religion. The document demanded explanation and apology. And the one choice one did not face, as a Jew in third-century Tiberias, Sepphoris, Caesarea, or Beth Shearim, in Galilee, was ignore the Mishnah and the issues inherent in its character as a piece of writing given political standing by the ethnarch. True, one might refer solely to ancient Scripture and tradition and live life out within the inherited patterns of the familiar Israelite religion-culture.

But as soon as one dealt with the Jewish government in charge of everyday life – went to court over the damages done to a crop by a neighbor's ox, for instance – one came up against a law in addition to the law of Scripture, a document the principles of which governed and settled all matters. So the Mishnah rapidly came to confront the life of Israel. The people who knew the Mishnah, the rabbis or sages, came to dominate that life. And their claim, in accord with the Mishnah, to exercise authority and the right to impose heavenly sanction came to perplex. There were two solutions to the problem set forth by the character of the Mishnah, each one reaching fruition in the Talmudic stage of Judaism:

160

[1] THE MISHNAH AS AN AUTONOMOUS, FREESTANDING COMPONENT OF THE TORAH OF SINAI: One response was represented by the claim that the authorities of the Mishnah stood in a chain of tradition that extended back to Sinai; stated explicitly in the Mishnah's first apologetic, tractate Abot, that circulated from approximately a generation beyond the promulgation of the Mishnah itself, that view required amplification and concrete demonstration. This approach treated the word *torah* as a common noun, as the word that spoke of a status or classification of sayings. A saying was *torah*, that is, enjoyed the status of torah or fell into the classification of *torah*, if it stood in the line of tradition from Sinai.

[2] THE MISHNAH IS SUBORDINATE TO THE WRITTEN PART OF THE TORAH BUT CAN BE SHOWN TO STAND ON THE WRITTEN TORAH'S AUTHORITY: A second took the same view of *torah* as a common noun. This response was to treat the Mishnah as subordinate to, and dependent upon, Scripture. Then *torah* was what fell into the classification of the revelation of *Torah* by God to Moses at Sinai. The way of providing what was needed within that theory was to link statements of the Mishnah to statements ("proof texts") of Scripture. The Tosefta, circa 300, a compilation of citations of, and comments upon the Mishnah, together with some autonomous materials that probably reached closure in the period in which the work of redaction of the Mishnah was going on, as well as the Talmuds systematically did just that. So, in the third century, did commentaries on the legal passages of the Pentateuch in Numbers and Deuteronomy, Sifré to Numbers and Sifré to Deuteronomy, respectively; both linked to Scripture cited passages of the Mishnah and the Tosefta.

The former solution treated Torah with a small t, that is to say, as a generic classification, and identified the Mishnah with the Torah revealed to Moses at Sinai by claiming a place for the Mishnah's authorities in the process of tradition and transmission that brought torah – no longer, the Torah, the specific writing comprising the Five Books of Moses – to contemporary Israel, the Jewish people. It was a theological solution, expressed through ideas, attitudes, implicit claims, but not through sustained rewriting of either Scripture or the Mishnah.

The latter solution, by contrast, concerned the specific and concrete statements of the Mishnah and required a literary, not merely a theological, statement, one precise and specific to passages of the Mishnah, one after the other. What was demanded by the claim that the Mishnah depended upon, but therefore enjoyed the standing of, Scripture, was a line-by-line commentary upon the Mishnah in light of Scripture. But this – the approach of the Tosefta and both Talmuds – I stress, also treated *torah* as a common noun.

[3] THE REDEFINITION OF THE TORAH: The third way emerged in Sifra, a sustained and profound, philosophical reading of the book of Leviticus. Sifra's solution would set aside the two solutions, the theological and the literary, and explore the much more profound issues of the fundamental and generative structure of right thought, yielding, as a matter of fact, both Scripture and the Mishnah. This approach insisted that *torah* always was a proper noun. There was, and is, only The Torah. But this – The Torah – demanded expansion and vast amplification. When we know the principles of logical structure and especially those of hierarchical classification that animate The Torah, we can undertake part of the task of expansion and amplification, that is, join in the processes of thought that, in the mind of God, yielded The Torah. For when we know how God thought in giving The Torah to Moses at Sinai and so accounting for the classifications and their ordering in the very creation of the world, we can ourselves enter into The Torah and participate in its processes.

Presenting the two Torahs in a single statement constituted an experiment in logic, that logic, in particular, that made cogent thought possible, and that transformed facts into propositions, and propositions into judgments of the more, or the less, consequential. While the Mishnah's other apologists wrote the written Torah into the Mishnah, Sifra's authorship wrote the oral Torah into Scripture. That is to say, the other of the two approaches to the problem of the Mishnah, the one of Sifra, to begin with claimed to demonstrate that the Mishnah found its correct place within the written Torah itself. Instead of citing verses of Scripture in the context of the Mishnah, the authorship of Sifra cited passages of the Mishnah in the context of Scripture, Leviticus in particular.

What the three accounts of the Mishnah's relationship to the Pentateuchal Torah achieved, each in its own way, cohered to yield a single consequence. All three insisted on a privileged position for the Mishnah within, or at least in intimate relationship to, the Torah of Sinai. That explains two facts that together demonstrate the absolute uniqueness of the Mishnah in Rabbinic literature. First, the Mishnah as a document acknowledged no prior writing, except – and then only episodically – for Scripture itself. Second, the Mishnah alone among Rabbinic documents itself received sustained and systematic commentaries in the model of those accorded to Scripture. Every document that followed the Mishnah, that is to say, the entirety of Rabbinic literature except for the Mishnah, took shape as a commentary to a prior document, either Scripture or the Mishnah itself. So the entirety of Rabbinic literature testifies to the unique standing of the Mishnah, acknowledging its special status, without parallel or peer, as the oral part of the Torah. The Talmuds, particularly the Talmud of Babylonia, 600 CE, made the Mishnah work, and they imposed upon the Mishnah that definition that it would enjoy for the next fourteen hundred years.

II

That is not because the Talmuds set forth an autonomous message in the context of Mishnah-exegesis, as the Mishnah does in the setting of Pentateuchal exegesis. Little of what the Talmuds' authorships present in their own name, not as commentary, thus in a propositional form, derives cogency and force from a received statement, and most of it does not. True, many of the propositions of the two Talmuds, in the nature of things, address the meaning of paragraphs of the Mishnah, and most of the documents are laid out as a commentary to either the Mishnah or Scripture. But the authorship of each of the compositions and the framer of the respective composites has selected out of Scripture and the Mishnah the passages or topics it wishes to amplify. And both documents introduce topics not formerly addressed, or treated in the Mishnah very differently, form and substance, from in the Talmuds.

So the Talmuds not only commented upon, but essentially reworked, the received Judaism represented by the Mishnah. The writers of the Mishnah created a coherent document, with a topical program formed in accord with the logical order dictated by the characteristics of a given topic, and with a set of highly distinctive formulary and formal traits as well. But these are obscured when the document is taken to bits and reconstituted in the way in which the Talmuds are. For the Mishnah was read by the Talmuds as a composite of discrete and essentially autonomous rules, a set of atoms, not an integrated molecule, so to speak. In so doing, the most striking formal traits of the Mishnah are obliterated. More important, the

Mishnah as a whole and complete statement of a viewpoint no longer exists. Its propositions are reduced to details. But what is offered instead? The answer is, a statement that, on occasion, recasts details in generalizations encompassing a wide variety of other details across the gaps between one tractate and another. This immensely creative and imaginative approach to the Mishnah vastly expands the range of discourse. But the consequence is to deny to the Mishnah both its own mode of speech and its distinctive and coherent message. So the two Talmuds formulate their own hermeneutics, to convey their theological system:

[1] defining the Torah and
[2] demonstrating its perfection and comprehensive character: unity, harmony, lineal origin from Sinai.

Both Talmuds take an independent stance when facing the Mishnah, making choices, reaching decisions of their own. Both Talmuds' framers deal with Mishnah-tractates of their own choice, and neither provides a Talmud to the entirety of the Mishnah. What the Mishnah therefore contributed to the Talmuds was not received in a spirit of humble acceptance by the sages who produced either of the two Talmuds. Important choices were made about what to treat, hence what to ignore. The exegetical mode of reception did not have to obscure the main lines of the Mishnah's system. But it surely did so. The discrete reading of sentences, or, at most, paragraphs, denying all context, avoiding all larger generalizations except for those tran-scending the specific lines of tractates – this approach need not have involved the utter reversal of the paramount and definitive elements of the Mishnah's whole and integrated world view (its "Judaism"). But doing these things did facilitate the revision of the whole into a quite different pattern. That represents a re-presentation of the Torah, one of considerable originality indeed.

A second trait, already familiar to us, joins with the foregoing. The Mishnah rarely finds it necessary to adduce proof-texts from the written Torah in support of its statements. The Talmuds, by contrast, find it appropriate whenever possible to cite Scriptural proof-texts for the propositions of the Mishnah. While the various tractates of the Mishnah relate in different ways to Scripture, the view of the framers of the Talmud on the same matter is not differentiated. So far as they are concerned, proof-texts for Mishnaic rules are required. These will be supplied in substantial numbers. And that is the main point. The Mishnah now is systematically represented as not standing free and separate from Scripture, but dependent upon it. The authority of the Mishnah's laws then is reinforced. But the autonomy of the Mishnah as a whole is severely compromised. Just as the Mishnah is represented in the Talmud as a set of rules, rather than as a philosophical essay, so it is presented, rule by rule, as a secondary and derivative development of Scripture. It would be difficult to imagine a more decisive effort to re-formulate the Torah than is accomplished by this work.

The undifferentiated effort to associate diverse Mishnah laws with Scripture is to be viewed together with the systematic breakup of the Mishnah into its diverse laws. The two quite separate activities produce a single effect in both Talmuds. They permit the Talmuds to represent the state of affairs pretty much as the framers of the Talmuds wish to do. Theology as a creative venture here determines to (re)define the Torah. And how is this done? Everything is shown to be continuous: Scripture, Mishnah, the Tosefta where cited, the authoritative sayings labeled Tannaite where used, ending in — the Talmud itself (whichever Talmud we examine, the effect being the same)! Then all things, as now shaped by the rabbis of the Talmud(s), have the standing of Scripture and represent the authority of Moses (now called "our Rabbi"). Accordingly, once the Mishnah enters either of the two Talmuds it nowhere emerges intact. It is wholly preserved, but in bits and pieces, shaped and twisted in whatever ways the Talmuds wish. The Torah now forms a single, continuous statement. And that is the work of the first Talmud, not only of the second.

The question has now to be asked, when do the Talmuds speak for themselves not for the Mishnah? Second, what sorts of units of discourse contain such passages that bear what is "Talmudic" in the two Talmuds? These two questions produce the same answers for both Talmuds, allowing us to characterize the topical or propositional program of the two Talmuds.

[1] THEORETICAL QUESTIONS OF LAW NOT ASSOCIATED WITH A PARTICULAR PASSAGE OF THE MISHNAH. In the first of the two Talmuds there is some tendency, and in the second, a very marked tendency, to move beyond the legal boundaries set by the Mishnah's rules themselves. More general inquiries are taken up. These of course remain within the framework of the topic of one tractate or another, although there are some larger modes of thought characteristic of more than a single tractate.

[2] EXEGESIS OF SCRIPTURE SEPARATE FROM THE MISHNAH. It is under this rubric that we find the most important instances in which the Talmuds present materials essentially independent of the Mishnah.

[3] HISTORICAL STATEMENTS. The Talmud contains a fair number of statements that something happened, or narratives about how something happened. While many of these are replete with biblical quotations, in general they do not provide exegesis of Scripture, which serves merely as illustration or reference point.

[4] STORIES ABOUT, AND RULES FOR, SAGES AND DISCI-PLES, SEPARATE FROM DISCUSSION OF A PASSAGE OF THE MISHNAH. The Mishnah contains a tiny number of tales about rabbis. These highly formalized and abbreviated testimonies serve principally as precedents for, or illustrations of, rules. The Talmuds by contrast contain a sizable number of well-amplified stories about sages and their relationships to other people.

When the Talmuds present us with ideas or expressions of a world related to, but fundamentally separate from, that of the Mishnah, that is, when the Talmuds wish to say something other than what the Mishnah says and means, they will take up one of two modes of discourse. Either we find exegesis of biblical passages, with the value system of the rabbis read into the Scriptural tales; or we are told stories about holy men and paradigmatic events, once again through tales told in such a way that a didactic purpose is served. It follows that the Talmuds form composites of three kinds of materials:

[1] exegeses of the Mishnah (and other materials classified as authoritative, that is, Tannaite),
[2] exegeses of Scripture, and
[3] accounts of the men who provide both.

It is at that third type of writing that the new stage in Judaism takes shape: the reintroduction into the Judaic system of concern for men and their works, events and their meaning, and not only principles and their secondary articulation. If the Mishnah, then, turned stories into propositions for analysis and extension, the Talmuds (and related Midrash-compilations) transformed propositions into stories for imaginative recapitulation. Both Talmuds then constitute elaborate reworkings of the two antecedent documents: the Mishnah, lacking much reference to Scripture, and the Scripture itself. The Talmuds bring the two together into a synthesis of their compilers' own making, both in reading Scripture into Mishnah, and in reading Scripture alongside of, and separate from, Mishnah.

If, therefore, we want to point to what is Talmudic in either of the two Talmuds it is the exegesis of Scripture, on the one side, and the narration of historical or biographical tales about holy men, on the other. Since much of the biblical exegesis turns upon holy men of biblical times, we may say that the Talmuds speak for themselves alone, as distinct from addressing the problems of the Mishnah, when they tell about holy men now and then. But what is genuinely new in the Talmuds, in comparison and contrast to the Mishnah, is the inclusion of extensive discourse on the meaning imputed to Scripture.

It follows that the two Talmuds stand essentially secondary to two prior documents: Mishnah (encompassing for this purpose the whole corpus labeled Tannaite, whenever and wherever produced, much being later than the Mishnah and some being Babylonian), on the one side, and Scripture, on the other. The Mishnah is read in the Talmuds pretty much within the framework of meaning established by the Mishnah itself. Scripture is read as an account of a world remarkably like that of the rabbis of the Talmuds. When the rabbis speak for themselves, as distinct from the Mishnah, it is through exegesis of Scripture. (But any other mode of reading Scripture, to them, would have been unthinkable. They took for granted that they and Scripture's heroes and sages lived in a single timeless plane.)

Let us now turn to three more questions, the answers to which equally characterize both Talmuds' programs of exegesis, the counterpart to the topical program of the Mishnah:

[1] What do rabbis in the two Talmuds do in common when they read the Mishnah?

[2] What are their modes of thought, their characteristic ways of analysis?

[3] What do we learn about their world view from the ways in which they receive and interpret the world view they have inherited in the Mishnah?

Here we enter the Talmudic stage. These are the very questions, we now realize, that the Talmuds answer on their own account, not only the Mishnah's. The Talmudic exegetes of the Mishnah brought to the document no distinctive program of their own. The exegetes did not know in advance of their approach to a law of the Mishnah facts about the passage not contained within the boundaries of the language of the Mishnah passage itself (except only for facts contained within other units of the same document). Rejecting propositions that were essentially *a priori*, they proposed to explain and expand precisely the wording and the conceptions supplied by the document under study.

In not a single instance did the Mishnah-exegetes in either Talmud appear to twist and turn the language and message of a passage, attempting to make the words mean something other than what they appear to say anyhow. The framers of both Talmuds' reading of the Mishnah take as the measure of truth the clear and present sense of the Mishnah's own language and formulations, rarely asking the Mishnah's rule to confirm a judgment extrinsic to the Mishnah's message. While the Talmuds follow a coherent hermeneutics that is very much their own, there is no exegetical program revealed in the Talmuds' reading of the Mishnah other than that defined, to begin with, by the language and conceptions of one Mishnah passage or another. Seen whole, the Talmuds appear to be nothing more than secondary developments of the Mishnah. If there is nothing *in particular* that is Talmudic, nonetheless, there is much *in general* that in both Talmuds is Talmudic. This is in entirely familiar respects.

First, the Mishnah was set forth by Judah the Patriarch, who sponsored the document, whole and complete, a profoundly unified, harmonious document. The Talmud insists upon obliterating the marks of coherence. It treats in bits and pieces what was originally meant to speak whole. That simple fact constitutes what is original, stunningly new and, by definition, Talmudic. Second, the Mishnah, also by definition, delivered its message in the way chosen by Judah the Patriarch. That is to say, by producing the document as he did, the Patriarch left no space for the very enterprises of episodic exegesis undertaken so brilliantly by his immediate continuators and heirs.

True, a rather limited process of explanation and gloss of words and phrases, accompanied by a systematic inquiry into the wording of one passage or another, got underway, probably at the very moment, and within the very process, of the Mishnah's closure. But insofar as the larger messages and meanings of the document are conveyed in the ways Judah the Patriarch chose through formalization of language, through contrasts, through successive instances of the same – normally unspecified, general proposition, e.g. the need for exegesis was surely not generated by his own program for the Mishnah. Quite to the contrary, Judah chose for his Mishnah a mode of expression and defined for the document a large-scale structure and organization, which, by definition, were meant to stand firm and autonomous. Rabbi's Mishnah speaks clearly and for itself.

The true power of the two Talmuds emerges when we realize that the Mishnah did not merely come to closure. At the very moment at which it was completed, the Mishnah also formed a closed system, that is, a whole complete statement that did not require facts outside of its language and formulation, so made no provision for commentary and amplification of brief allusions, as the Talmuds' style assuredly does. The Mishnah refers to nothing beyond itself except, episodically, Scripture. It promises no information other than what is provided within its limits. It raises no questions for ongoing discussion beyond its decisive, final, descriptive statements of enduring realities and fixed relationships.

The Talmuds' single irrevocable judgment is precisely opposite: this text needs a commentary. The Talmuds' first initiative is to reopen the Mishnah's closed system, almost at the moment of its completion and perfection. That at the foundations is what is Talmudic about the Talmuds: their daring assertion that the concluded and completed demanded clarification and continuation. Once that assertion was made to stick, nothing else mattered very much. The two Talmuds' message was conveyed in the very medium of the Talmud: a new language, focused upon a new grid of discourse to re-view a received writing.

In the two Talmuds in common we address a program of criticism of the Mishnah framed by independent and original minds. How is this made manifest? Let us quickly bypass the obvious points of independent judgment, the matter of insistence that the very word choices of the Mishnah require clarification, therefore prove faulty. The meanings and amplification of phrases represent the judgment that Judah's formulation, while stimulating and provocative, left much to be desired. These indications of independence of judgment among people disposed not merely to memorize but to improve upon the text provided by Judah the Patriarch hardly represent judgments of substance. Rather, let us turn to the two most striking:

[1] the provision of Scriptural proof-texts for the propositions of various passages of the Mishnah;
[2] the rewriting, in the Mishnah's own idiom, if not in its redactional and disciplinary patterns, of much of the law.

As to the former, of course, the message is familiar and clear. The propositions of the Mishnah cannot stand by themselves but must be located within the larger realm of Scriptural authority. As to the latter, the Tosefta's compositions and other Tannaite passages, serving as an exegetical complement to the Mishnah's corresponding passages, imitate the Mishnah. For they are phrased in the way in which the Mishnah's sentences are written (as distinct from the utterly different way in which the Talmuds' own sentences are framed, e.g., in Hebrew rather than in the Talmuds' Aramaic). And yet they show equivalent independence of mind. They indicate that, where sages of the time of the Talmuds took up Mishnaic passages, they were not at all limited to the work of gloss and secondary expansion. They recognized and exercised a quite remarkable freedom of initiative. They undertook to restate in their own words, but imitating the Mishnah's style, the propositions of the Mishnah passage at hand.

That is, they both cite what the Mishnah said and also continue, in imitation of the Mishnah's language, the discourse of the Mishnah passage itself. These Toseftan or other Tannaite complements to the Mishnah – a vast number of them demonstrably written after the closure of the Mishnah – are Talmudic in two senses. First, they come to expression in the period after the Mishnah had reached closure, as is clear from the fact that the exact language of the Mishnah is cited prior to the labor of extension expansion and revision. So they are the work of the Talmuds' age and authority. Second, they derive from precisely the same authorities responsible for the formation of the Talmud as a whole. But then, shifting from Hebrew to Aramaic, the Talmud of Babylonia makes its own systematic, dialectical inquiry into the implications of the received law, as we shall see later in this chapter.

Accordingly, both the insistence upon adducing proof-texts for passages the Patriarch judged not to need them and the persistent revision and expansion of the Mishnah, even in clumsy imitation of the Mishnah's syntax, rhetoric, and word choices, tell us once more this simple truth: the Talmuds are distinctively Talmudic precisely when the Mishnah itself defines the Talmuds' labor, dictates its ideas, displays its rhetoric, determines its results.

The very shift in usable language, from "the Mishnah" (as a whole) to "the Mishnah passage" or "the Mishnaic law at hand" indicates the true state of affairs. On the surface, in all manner of details, the two Talmuds are little more than secondary and derivative documents, explaining the Mishnah itself in trivial ways, or expanding it in a casuistic and logic-chopping manner. But viewing that same surface from a different, more distant perspective and angle, we see things quite differently. In detail the Talmuds changed nothing. Overall, the Talmuds left nothing the same. And, it follows, in general, the two Talmuds stand close together, not only in form, but in program and much else.

In the two Talmuds we find little to deem Talmudic in particular. But in them both, equally, there is much that is talmudic in general. The particular bits and pieces are Mishnaic. But – as I have stressed in pointing to the theological character of both Talmuds – the Talmuds leave nothing of the Mishnah whole and intact. Their work upon the whole presents an essentially new construction. Through the Mishnah, Judah contributed to the Talmuds most of the bricks, but little of the mortar, and none of the joists and beams. The design of the whole bore no relationship to the Patriarch's plan for the Mishnah. The sages of the Talmud did the rest. They alone imagined, then built, the building. They are the architects, theirs is the vision. The building is a monument to the authority of the sage above all.

What is most definitively indicative of the Talmudic sages' freedom of imagination is the exercise – by each set of authors – of free choice even among the Mishnah's tractates awaiting exegesis. We do not know why some tractates were chosen for Talmudic expansion and others left fallow. We may speculate that the Yerushalmi's omission of all reference to the entire division of Holy Things, on the everyday conduct of the Temple, and to most of the division of Purities, on the sources of uncleanness, objects subject to uncleanness, and modes of removing contamination, constitutes a radical revision of the law of Judaism. What for Judah the Patriarch was close to fifty percent of the whole story in volume, forming two of his six divisions in structure, for that Talmud's designers (I assume early as much as late), was of no importance. That is an amazing fact, attesting on its own to the Talmuds' formulation of their own program and statement, independent of that of the Mishnah even while expressed wholly in the form of a commentary to the Mishnah. Here too, we find the Torah once more subject to (re)-definition; nothing of course would be omitted; but choices clearly were made about what is to be brought to the fore.

Both Talmuds in common address the tractates of Appointed Times, Women, and Damages, the second, third, and fourth divisions of the Mishnah. That is then where the comparisons and contrasts have to take place. Interest in the division of Appointed Times involved extensive discussion of the conduct of the cult on extraordinary days.

Perhaps at issue here was not what had to be omitted (the cult on appointed times) but what people wanted to discuss, the home and village on those same holy occasions. So the former came in the wake of the latter. Inclusion of the divisions of Women, on the family and the transfer of women from father to husband and back, and Damages, on civil law and institutions, is not hard to explain. The sages fully expected to govern the life of Israel, the Jewish people, in its material and concrete aspects. These divisions, as well as some of the tractates of the division on Appointed Times, demanded and received attention. Ample treatment of the laws in the first division, governing the priests' rations and other sacred segments of the agricultural produce of the Holy Land, is to be expected among authorities living not only in, but also off, the Holy Land.

If we stand back and reflect on the Mishnah's program, we recognize how different is that of the respective Talmuds. The Mishnah covers a broad variety of topics. The Talmuds contribute none of their own, but trawl across the entire surface of the Mishnah. The Mishnah is organized topically. The Talmuds may be broken down into discrete compositions and neatly-joined composites, none of them framed as freestanding, topical formations, all of them in one way or another depending upon the Mishnah for order and coherence. The Mishnah lays out rules and facts about a world beyond itself. The Talmuds negotiate rules and recast facts into propositions that concern the Mishnah – a different focus of discourse and perspective altogether. Continuous with the Mishnah, the two Talmuds in point of fact redirect the Mishnah not only by destroying its integrity and picking and choosing with its topical (and propositional) program, but also by forming of the detritus of the received writing a statement of their own. But it was not a statement that, in the end, concerned the Mishnah at all, rather, a statement about the Torah, and a statement of the Torah.

In accepting authority, in centering discourse upon the ideas of other men, in patiently listing even the names behind authoritative laws from olden times to their own day, the sages and framers of the Talmud accomplished exactly the opposite of what we might have supposed they wanted to do. They made a commentary. On the surface, that suggests they wanted merely to continue and strengthen the received tradition. But they obliterated the text. They loyally explained the Mishnah. But they turned the Mishnah into something else than what it had been. They patiently hammered out chains of tradition, binding themselves to the authority of the remote and holy past. But it was, in the end, a tradition of their own design and choosing. That is, it was not tradition but a new creation. And so these Talmuds of ours, so loyal and subservient to the Mishnah of Judah the Patriarch, turn out to be less reworkings of received materials than works – each one of them – of remarkably independent judgment. The Talmuds speak humbly and subserviently about received truth, always in the name only of Moses and of sages of times past. But in the end it is truth not discovered and demonstrated, but determined and invented and declared.

The Talmudic stage comes to expression in literary terms as much as in doctrinal ones. The redactional program of the men responsible for laying out the materials of Talmuds may now be described. There is a pronounced tendency in both Talmuds to move from close reading of the Mishnah and then Tosefta outward to more general inquiry into the principles of a Mishnah passage and their interplay with those of some other, superficially unrelated passage, and, finally, to more general reflections on law not self-evidently related to the Mishnah passage at hand or to anthologies intersecting only at a general topic. Unlike the Mishnah, the Talmuds reveal no effort to systematize sayings in larger constructions, or to impose a pattern upon all individual sayings. If the Mishnah is framed to facilitate memorization, then we must say that the Talmuds' materials are not framed with mnemonics in mind. If the Mishnah focuses upon subsurface relationships in syntax, the Talmud in the main looks like notes of a discussion. These notes may serve to recreate the larger patterns of argument and reasoning, a summary of what was thought and perhaps also said. The Talmud preserves and expresses concrete ideas, reducing them to brief but usually accessible and obvious statements. The Mishnah speaks of concrete things in order to hint at abstract relationships, which rarely are brought to the surface and fully exposed.

The Mishnah hides. The Talmuds spell out. The Mishnah hints. The Talmuds repeat ad nauseam. The Mishnah is subtle, the Talmuds, obvious; the one is subtle, restrained and tentative, the others aimed at full and exhaustive expression of what is already clear. The sages of the Mishnah rarely represent themselves as deciding cases. Only on unusual occasions do they declare the decided law, at best reticently spelling out what underlies their positions. The rabbis of the Talmuds harp on who holds which opinion and how a case is actually decided, presenting a rich corpus of rulings and precedents. They seek to make explicit what is implicit in the law. The Mishnah is immaterial and spiritual, the Talmud earthy and social. The Mishnah deals in the gossamer threads of philosophical principle, the Talmud in the coarse rope that binds this one and that one into a social construction.

The Mishnah speaks of a world in stasis, an unchanging, eternal present tense where all the tensions of chaos are resolved. The Talmuds address the real Israel in the here and now of ever-changing times, the gross matter of disorder and history. Clearly, the central traits of the Mishnah, revealed in the document at its time of closure in circa 200, were revised and transformed into those definitive of the Talmud at its time of closure in circa 400 for the earlier Talmud, 600 for the later. We know only that when we compare the Mishnah to the Talmuds we find in each case two intertwined documents, quite different from one another both in style and in values. Yet they are so tightly joined that the Talmud appears in the main to provide mere commentary and amplification for the Mishnah. So in important, superficial traits the two Talmuds are indistinguishable.

III

What distinctively characterizes the Talmudic stage in the formation of Judaism is the dialectical argument, the mode of Mishnah- and halakhah-analysis that defines the age of conclusion. Dialectical argument – the movement of thought through contentious challenge and passionate response, initiative and counter-ploy – characterizes the Talmud of Babylonia in particular, but finds a limited place, also, in other Rabbinic documents. That mode of receiving tradition – critical, penetrating, uncompromising ("let logic pierce the mountain") – imparted to Rabbinic Judaism its character as a compelling, dynamic, open-ended system, able to receive into itself whatever time and circumstance would bring, and to naturalize within its system all things that, in their inner logic, could be shown to conform.

A definition is therefore called for of that trait of important writings and the culture that they embody and transmit to all time to come. The dialectical, or moving, argument is important because, in the sustained conflict provoked by the testing of proposition in contention, argument turns fact into truth. Making a point forms of data important propositions. The exchanges of propositions and arguments, objects and ripostes, hold together, however protracted. "Dialectical" means, moving or developing an idea through questions and answers, sometimes implicit, but commonly explicit. What "moves" is the flow of argument and thought, from problem to problem. The movement is generated specifically by the raising of contrary questions and theses. What characterizes the dialectical argument in Rabbinic literature is its meandering, its moving hither and yon. It is not a direct or straight-line movement, e.g., thesis, antithesis, synthesis. Rather, the Rabbinic dialectical argument – the protracted, sometimes meandering, always moving flow of contentious thought – raises a question and answers it, then raises a question about the answer, and, having raised another question, then gives an answer to that question, and continues in the same fashion. So it moves hither and yon; it is always one, but it is never the same, and it flows across the surface of the document at hand.

Those second and third and fourth turnings differentiate a dialectical from a static argument, much as the bubbles tell the difference between still and sparkling wine. The always-sparkling dialectical argument is one principal means by which the Talmud or some other Rabbinic writing accomplishes its goal of showing the connections between this and that, ultimately demonstrating the unity of many "thises and thats." These efforts at describing the argument serve precisely as well as program notes to a piece of music: they tell us what we are going to hear; they cannot play the music.

The dialectical argument opens the possibility of reaching out from one thing to something else, not because people have lost sight of their starting point or their goal in the end, but because they want to encompass, in the analytical argument as it gets underway, as broad and comprehensive a range of cases and rules as they possibly can. The movement from point to point in reference to a single point that accurately describes the dialectical argument reaches upward toward a goal of proximate abstraction, leaving behind the specificities of not only cases but laws, carrying us upward to the law that governs many cases, the premises that undergird many rules, and still higher to the principles that infuse diverse premises; then the principles that generate other, unrelated premises, which, in turn, come to expression in other, still-less intersecting cases. The meandering course of argument comes to an end when we have shown how things cohere.

What then is at stake in the dialectical argument? I see three complementary results. All of them, in my view, prove commensurate to the effort required to follow protracted, sometimes tedious disquisitions.

First, we test every allegation by a counter-proposition, so serving the cause of truth through challenge and constant checking for flaws in an argument.

Second, we survey the entire range of possibilities, which leaves no doubts about the cogency of our conclusion.

Third, quite to the point, by the give and take of argument, we ourselves are enabled to go through the thought processes set forth in the subtle markings that yield our reconstruction of the argument. We not only review what people say, but how they think: the processes of reasoning that have yielded a given conclusion. Sages and disciples become party to the modes of thought; in the dialectical argument, they are required to replicate the thought-processes themselves.

IV

Here we come to the critical question, how can we account for the Talmud's resort to dialectical argument, which had no precedent whatsoever in prior Israelite writing of any kind? What gave the sages the courage to admit into the inner sanctum of intellect so corrosive and unsettling a force as unrelenting criticism: thesis, antithesis, yielding the same process again and again? Dialectics certainly did not respond to the demand of Mishnah-exegesis. Not only so, but both Talmuds more often than not accomplish their goals without resort to contentious argument, let alone to the asking and answering of questions for substantive, not merely rhetorical purposes. But the Talmud's single indicative trait, even though not a paramount or ubiquitous one, is its dialectics, and we have every reason to want to know why. Because they inherited a corpus of conflict, a heritage of contending statements of norms and laws, the heirs of the Mishnah, proposing to continue the work of the Mishnah, found in dialectics the appropriate medium of expression and thought for accomplishing their task of confronting contention and resolving disharmony. If the Torah was to be perfected, as the Psalmist held, then it was through dialectics that the Rabbinic sages would both demonstrate the perfection of the Mishnah, the transcription of the oral Torah of Sinai, and also remove the imperfections of the law that the Torah handed on to Israel.

To understand what identified dialectical inquiry as the medium of choice for accomplishing the goals of the framers of the Talmud's composites and authors of its compositions, we have to review the Talmud's own tasks, outlined earlier. Organized around the Mishnah in the form of a commentary to that document, the Talmud that together with the Mishnah comprises the Talmud of Babylonia, also known as the Bavli, accords privileged standing to the Mishnah.

The form of the Talmud, its principles of organization and its systematic program, all accord priority to the Mishnah. But that is misleading. For, bearing secondary developments and also sizable topical appendices, as well as free-standing composites of Scripture-commentary, the Talmud of the Bavli vastly exceeds the requirements of a Mishnah commentary. Not only so, but when we understand the actual task of the compilers of the Talmud and authors of its compositions – not only the formal requirements they adopted for themselves – we shall see why dialectics solved a considerable intellectual problem that they addressed.

The Talmud created in Babylonia joins together a variety of composites of cogent compositions. By no means do all of these composites take the task of Mishnah-commentary and propose only to explain or amplify the law of the Mishnah, or its language, or its Scriptural bases. These composites divide into various types, each with its own rhetorical protocol and exegetical or expository and argumentative task. All but one type bear in common the purpose of compiling bodies of information, e.g., exegesis of verses of Scripture, lower-critical comments upon the sense and meaning of passages of the Mishnah, and the like. All express viewpoints, some contain disputes. The one type of composition (sometimes built into a composite) that conducts a sustained argument concerning an important thesis, sets forth a highly argumentative kind of writing. That writing takes the form of question-answer, aiming at dialogue, the dialectical argument.

Not by any measure the paramount type of composite in the Talmud, the dialectical argument imparts flavor to the whole Talmud by imposing tension and supplying movement, focus and purpose. By its movement, from question to answer, point to point, problem to problem, case to case, the dialectical argument also gives the Talmud the quality of dynamism. The rigor required to participate in a challenging exchange defines the intellectual quality of the whole document, even though most of the sustained discussions prove merely illuminating, not contentious. For its part the dialectical argument asks for not merely information but analysis, not merely acute reading of existing language but formulation of new points of interest altogether.

Dialectics defined the ideal method for the Mishnah-analysis undertaken by the Talmud. The character of the Mishnah defined the challenge that was met by the selection and utilization of the dialectical argument, which, in all writings of all Judaisms from the beginnings before 586 BCE to the third century CE, has no precedent.

Nor does the dialectical argument appear elsewhere than in the two Talmuds. And, truth be told, dialectics predominates only in the final compilation of the Rabbinic canon, the Talmud of Babylonia. A large-scale structure of lists, the Mishnah's generalizations (e.g., the king ranks higher in the political hierarchy than the high priest) rarely come to articulation; the mass of detail invited close study and analysis. The general had to emerge out of the concrete and specific, and generalizations valid at one point had to be tested against those emergent elsewhere; implications of generalizations for encompassing principles here required comparison and contrast with those that formed the foundations of a legal unit on an unrelated topic elsewhere. All of this work of construction would turn the Mishnah's details into large-scale compositions of encompassing significance.

But the Mishnah by itself did not exhaust the resources of normative rulings that formed the heritage of its time and sages. And the Talmud, for its part, though organized around the Mishnah, in fact took as its problem the law of the Mishnah, along with other law not found in the Mishnah. The privileging of the Mishnah did not extend to the laws that it set forth. If the framers of the Mishnah hoped to bring order out of chaos by giving the authoritative selection of the law – not merely a collection of their preferences and choices among laws – they were to find only disappointment. Repudiating the privileging of the Mishnah, reducing the document to a mere framework for the organization of something greater, the writers of the Talmud's compositions and compilers of its composites redefined matters and assigned to themselves a far more important task than merely glossing a fixed code.

That choice formed their response to a simple fact: the Mishnah collected only a small portion of the law that had come into being in the first and second centuries. I have already made reference to the Tosefta, which collected autonomous law, not only recapitulations of the Mishnah's law, and to other formulations assigned to authors in the time of the Mishnah but not collected in the Mishnah or the Tosefta, only in the Talmuds themselves. Indeed, a sizable corpus of opinion, rulings, cases and disputes, circulated from the period in which the Mishnah emerged but found (or was given) no place within the Mishnah. Some of these materials came to rest in the compilation of supplements to the Mishnah called the Tosefta. Corresponding to the Mishnah in its topical organization and program, the Tosefta exceeded the Mishnah in sheer volume by at least four times – perhaps more. Other laws were formulated along with attributions to the same authorities, called Tannaite sages, who occur in the

Mishnah. These laws scarcely differentiated themselves from those in the Mishnah, except in contents. Still more laws circulated, whether or not attributed to the names of authorities who occur also in the Mishnah, bearing the mark TNY – yielding "it was formulated as a Tannaite rule" – and these too enjoyed the same standing and authority as Tannaite sayings collected in the Mishnah or the Tosefta.

If therefore, a coherent and uniform principled system of norms was to reach full articulation, the laws, and not the Mishnah, would form the arena for systematic study. That is to say, if a cogent system was to emerge out of the heritage of normative rulings out of Tannaite sponsorship, the entire mass of normative rulings would require analysis; points of contradiction would have to be sorted out; harmony between and among diverse laws would have to be established. To accomplish the task of analysis of sayings, formulation and testing of generalizations, above all, the discovery of the principles embedded in the normative rules governing discrete cases, the Talmud resorted to the dialectal argument. That would make possible the transformation of the Mishnah's lists, limited by their nature to data of a single kind, into the starting-points for series capable of infinite extension across data of diverse kinds, as I shall explain in due course.

The implications of the character of the heritage of norms that the Rabbinic sages addressed with the Mishnah in hand prove self-evident. Specifically, had the Rabbinic sages received only the Mishnah, the character of that document would have imposed a labor of mere amplification of a well-crafted document and application of a uniform law. That is not only because of the exquisite quality of the craftsmanship exhibited in the Mishnah's composition, but also because of the pristine clarity of its laws themselves. Where there is a difference of opinion, it is labeled by assigning to the minority view a name, with the majority, and normative, position given anonymously. So was schism signaled clearly if tacitly. Hence applying the law would have imposed no formidable burdens. And had the Babylonian sages of the third through seventh centuries received only a mass of laws, deriving from hither and yon, the primary work of selection and organization, not analysis and theoretical synthesis, would have occupied their best energies. But that is not how matters worked out. The Mishnah imposed structure and order. The boundaries of discourse therefore were laid out. But the Mishnah's selectivity defined the exegetical problematics for further inquiry. Accordingly, the Rabbinic sages addressed a dual challenge,

[1] both subjecting a well-crafted document to exegesis, amplification, and theoretical inquiry,
[2] but also sorting out conflicting data from other sources on the same matters that the said document took up.

It follows that the intellectual tasks confronting the heirs of the Mishnah were made complicated by the conflict between the status of the Mishnah and the sizable legacy of authoritative data transmitted along with the Mishnah. The Mishnah enjoyed privileged status. All other compositions and composites received the form of commentary to the Mishnah. But the exegesis of the Mishnah did not then define the sole intellectual labor at hand. For the privileging of the Mishnah proved incomplete, with a huge corpus of other rulings on the same agenda compiled in the Tosefta, with other bodies of rulings on elements of the same agenda compiled alongside the Tosefta, and with still other free-floating sayings endowed with Tannaite status to cope with as well. Mishnah-exegesis – words, phrases, sources in Scripture – then would ordinarily enjoy pride of position, at the head of any sustained composite. But, following that work, next in line would come the challenge of conflicting opinion on the Mishnah's topics and rulings. Not only so, but the privileging of the Mishnah would remain a mere formality, without a direct confrontation with the conflicting opinions preserved along with the Mishnah. The Mishnah had to be shown perfect in form, harmonious in contents, dominant in norm-setting, if that initial act of privileging were to signal long-term status as the authoritative statement.

The Mishnah's character as a mass of petty rulings defined a third task, one that was natural to the rigorous intellects who comprised the cadre of the Rabbinic sages. That was to require the quest for not only harmony but also generalization, the encompassing principle, the prevailing rule emerging from concrete data. For intellectuals of sages' sort sought not only information about details, but guidance on the main lines of thought. Not only so, but, engaged as they were in the administration of the life of the Jewish communities of Babylonia, theirs proved to be a practical reason and applied logic. They had not only to rule on cases covered by the Mishnah – and laws of its standing in addition – but also on cases not envisaged at all within the framework of the Mishnah. These cases of new kinds altogether, involving not only application of the law but penetration into the principles behind the law that could be made to cover new cases, demanded the formation of an analytical logic capable of generating the principles to produce new laws.

And that is where dialectics entered in, for both practical and theoretical reasons. Theoretical considerations come first. Crafted to begin with to produce clarity of definition, the mode of dialectical argument of Classical philosophy defined a reliable method to secure compelling definitions of important principles. To deal with conflicting opinion on definition, two or more rulings on the same problem had to be set side by side and given each its hearing. Perhaps the conflict could be resolved through making a distinction; in that case let one party challenge the other, with a harmonizing opinion then registering. Perhaps the conflict revealed principles that were at odds. These required articulation, analysis, juxtaposition and then, if possible, harmonization, if possible, reformulation at a higher level of abstraction. Perhaps rulings on one topic rested on a principle that affected, also, rulings on another topic altogether. Then the principle expressed by rulings on that unrelated topic had to be made articulate and brought into relationship with the underlying principle operative elsewhere. And again, a given set of rulings served to illustrate a single point in common, and that point in common was to be formulated as a hypothesis of general intelligibility and applicability. Rulings on one topic rested on a principle that also affected rulings on another topic altogether. Then the principle expressed by rulings on that unrelated topic had to be made articulate and brought into relationship with the underlying principle operative elsewhere.

And again, a given set of rulings served to illustrate a single point in common, and that point in common was to be formulated as a hypothesis of general intelligibility and applicability. How better to test a hypothesis than in a dialogue between proponents and opponents, the latter raising contrary cases, the former overcoming contradiction, the former amplifying and extending their hypothesis, the latter proposing to limit it. The upshot is, the very character of the corpus of law received by the Rabbinic sages in Babylonia insured that a vast repertoire of conflict and contention would define the work of those responsible for the orderly application of the law – the Mishnah's law but not that alone – to the everyday affairs of the community of holy Israel. Given the range of data to be addressed, the mode of question-answer, challenge out of conflicting data and response through resolution of conflict, served as the principal medium of thought. The very character of the corpus of norms generated the kind of conflict best resolved through the challenge and response embodied in question-answer rhetoric of dialectics. The specific purpose of the Rabbinic sages' reading of the norms – the formulation of an internally coherent, proportionate, and harmonious statement – coincided with the promise of dialectic, which is to expose conflict and find ways through reason of resolving it. But if theory made dialectics the method of choice, politics reenforced the theoretical usefulness of that method of thought and expression.

Moreover, practical considerations, both intellectual and political in character, underscored the usefulness of dialectics. Framed in a rhetoric aimed at effecting agreement out of conflict, preserving civility and rationality in confrontation of opinion, received tradition, or ideas, dialectics moreover took a form exceedingly suitable to the situation of the sages. All of them proud, accomplished, certain of their knowledge, and opinionated, sages required a medium of thought that would accord recognition and respect to all participants. Simply announcing opinions – solutions to problems, rulings on cases, theories for analytical consideration – accomplished little, when the participants to public discourse addressed one another as equals and laid a heavy claim upon a full hearing for their respective views.

And even if the Rabbinic sages had proved to be men of limited intellect, politics pointed toward dialogue and argued in favor of a rhetoric of dialectics. None possessed access to coercive force, other than that of intellectual power and moral authority. For, lacking an efficient administration capable of imposing order, they could hope to accomplish their goals through persuasion, not coercion. Denied the services of a police force or army, effective principally through public opinion and persuasion (relying heavily, for instance, upon ostracism as a social penalty), the Rabbinic sages could best impose their will by means of powerful argument. The power of rationality, moreover, proved singularly congruent to sages' circumstance, since none of them enjoyed political sponsorship sufficient to compel the rest to conform, and all of the more influential ones jealously guarded their standing and prerogatives.

The mode of argument made possible through dialectics – two or more positions fully exposed, with arguments pro and con, a complete repertoire of positions and possibilities, laid out in the form of an exchange between and among equals, with point-by-point *Auseindersetzungen*, allowing for the full articulation of generalizations, exceptions based on cases, counter-arguments, and competing generalizations – that mode of argument alone could prove congruent to the politics of powerful intellects lacking worldly position to sustain their hypotheses. Accordingly, the Rabbinic sages chose wisely when they determined that argument in dialogic form, within dialectical logic, defined the best possible instrument with which to accomplish their task of explanation, analysis, and amplification of the law that they had received not only from the Mishnah but from other sources of the same status or origin.

V

What does all this mean for the Talmudic stage of Judaism? The main consequence for the Talmud of formation through dialectical arguments is simply stated. It is the power of that mode of the representation of thought to show us – as no other mode of writing (without abstract symbols) can show – not only the result but the workings of the logical mind. By following dialectical arguments, all those who take up the document enter into those same thought processes, and their minds then are formed in the model of rigorous and sustained, systematic argument. The reason is simply stated. When we follow a proposal and its refutation, the consequence thereof, and the result of that, we ourselves form partners to the logical tensions and their resolutions; we are given an opening into the discourse that lies before us. As soon as matters turn not upon tradition, to which we may or may not have access, but reason, specifically, challenge and response, proposal and counter-proposal, "maybe matters are just the opposite?" we find an open door before us.

For these are not matters of fact but of reasoned judgment, and the answer, "well, that's my opinion," in its "traditional form," namely, that is what Rabbi X has said so that must be so, finds no hearing. Moving from facts to reasoning, propositions to the process of counter-argument, the challenge resting on the mind's own movement, its power of manipulating facts one way rather than some other and of identifying the governing logic of a fact – that process invites the reader's or the listener's participation. The author of a dialectical composite presents a problem with its internal tensions in logic and offers a solution to the problem and a resolution of the logical conflicts.

What is at stake in the capacity of the framer of a composite, or even the author of a composition, to move this way and that, always in a continuous path, but often in a crooked one? The dialectical argument opens the possibility of reaching out from one thing to something else, and the path's wandering is part of the reason. It is not because people have lost sight of their starting point or their goal in the end, but because they want to encompass, in the analytical argument as it gets underway, as broad and comprehensive a range of cases and rules as they can. The movement from point to point in reference to a single point that accurately describes the dialectical argument reaches a goal of abstraction. At the point at which we leave behind the specificities of not only cases but laws, sages carry the argument upward to the law that governs many cases, the premises that undergird many rules, and still higher to the principles that infuse diverse premises; then the principles that generate other, unrelated premises, which, in turn, come to expression in other, still-less intersecting cases. The meandering course of argument comes to an end when we have shown how things cohere that we did not even imagine were contiguous at all.

The dialectical argument forms the means to an end. The distinctive character of the Talmud's particular kind of dialectical argument is dictated by the purpose for which dialectics is invoked. Specifically, the goal of all argument is to show in discrete detail the ultimate unity, harmony, proportion, and perfection of the law – not of the Mishnah as a document but of all the law of the same standing as that presented by the Mishnah. The hermeneutics of dialectics aims at making manifest how to read the laws in such a way as to discern that many things really say one thing. The variations on the theme then take the form of detailed expositions of this and that. Then our task is to move backward from result to the reasoning process that has yielded said result: through regression from stage to stage to identify within the case not only the principles of law that produce that result, but the processes of reasoning that link the principles to the case at hand. And, when we accomplish our infinite regression, we move from the workings of literature to its religious character and theological goal, the focus of the Talmudic culture: it is to know God in heaven, represented, on earth, by the Torah, its unity, its integrity. That theological observation carries us from the character of the Talmuds' particular statement to the contents of that statement: the reversion to history as Scripture portrays history.

6

THE TALMUDS IN PENTATEUCHAL CONTEXT

Israel in history

The scriptural record of Israel, Pentateuchal and prophetic alike, took as its premise a single fact. When God wished to lay down a judgment, he did so through the medium of events, whether a burning bush, whether a lost battle. History, composed of singular events, therefore spoke God's message. Prophets found vindication through their power to enunciate and even (in the case of Moses) to make, and change, history. Revealing God's will, history moreover consisted of a line of one-time events, all of them heading in a single direction, a line that began at creation and will end with redemption or salvation. Had the Talmuds carried forward the Mishnah's approach to history – its transformation of narrative into laws of the social order, its formation of events into classifications in groups and denial of the uniqueness of events – its stage of Judaism would have afforded no role to a principal voice of Israel's Scriptures. But the period in which the Talmuds and related compilations of Scripture-exegeses took shape and reached closure, the fifth century and beyond, encompassed events that the Rabbinic sages could not have ignored had they wanted to.

I

The advent of Christianity in the first and second centuries did not constitute an event of which the Mishnah's sages found they had to take notice; the Mishnah sets forth a stage in Judaism without attention to the new faith invoking the ancient Scriptures of Israel and challenging Israel's standing as God's people. The advent of the Christian empire to political power with Constantine's conversion in the early fourth century, in 312, changed everything. No stoic indifference, no policy of patient endurance could shelter Israel from the storm of doubt that swept over them. Christians could plausibly point to their entry into political hegemony as proof of God's favor.

But an event later in that same century, in 360⁻¹, turned the crisis represented by the Christian challenge from chronic to acute. An emperor came to the throne who rejected Christianity and restored paganism; and to spite the Christians, the emperor Julian further- more told the Jews they could rebuild the Temple in Jerusalem. But the project came to naught. And for a long time to come, Christians would point not only to the destruction of Jerusalem in 70 CE but to the fiasco in 361 CE as evidence that the Torah had come to fulfill- ment in Christ.

A quarter-century after Julian, John "of the golden tongue" (= Chrysostom), who was born in 347 and died in 407, in a set of sermons preached in 386–7 addressed the issue of Judaism in a series of sermons accusing Christians of backsliding. The point relevant here is simple: Jesus had predicted the destruction of the Temple. Not long before, the apostate emperor and the Jews had tried to rebuild it. They did not succeed. That proves that the temple no longer serves to legitimate Jewish religion. All of these commonplaces point to a single issue: was, and is, Jesus the Christ? And Christians adduced the facts of history to answer that question in the affirmative. Chrysostom's eight sermons, *Adversus Judaeos*, given in Antioch, explicitly introduced the Jerusalem fiasco into the interpretation of Scripture through historical events. He held that, for their part the Jews did not understand their own Scripture because they did not grasp "the true meaning of the prophecies, because they did not understand the significance of the 'times' the prophets were discussing. They stubbornly refused to apply texts to Christ." Because the Jews rejected the Messiah, gentiles took their place. Because of the same error, they were punished with the destruction of Jerusalem and the Temple, which just now had *not* been rebuilt though the emperor had planned to restore it. The Jewish law was no longer valid: "Just as the Old Testament was a shadow of the reality fulfilled in the New Testament, so the Jewish law was valid only as a guide to Christ." "Since Christ had come, continuing to observe the law was like going back into the desert from the Promised Land." The present power of the Church moreover proved that Christ was the Messiah and that the Church was favored by God. So the issue of Jesus's Messiahship enjoyed priority over all others. The relationship of the destruction of Jerusalem and the divinity of Jesus took pride of place. The longest homily and the most theological-historical, the fifth, is summarized by Wilken as follows:

...the chief topic of the sermon: The greatest proof that Christ is truly God is that he 'predicted the temple would be destroyed, that Jerusalem would be captured, and that the city would no longer be the city of the Jews as it had been in the past.' If only ten, twenty, or fifty years had passed since the destruction of the temple, one might understand doubts about Jesus' prophecy, but over three centuries have passed and there is not 'a shadow of the change for which you are waiting.' ...If the Jews had never attempted to rebuild the temple during this time, one might say that they could do so only if they made the effort. But the course of events shows the reverse, for the Jews have attempted to rebuild the temple, not once, but three times, and were unsuccessful in every effort...The failure of Julian's effort to rebuild the temple in Jerusalem, then, is proof that Christ was not an ordinary man among men, but the divine son of God. His word was more powerful than the feeble efforts of men, for by his word alone he defeated the emperor Julian and the whole Jewish people. The prophecy of Christ is proven true by the historical facts'. The fulfillment of the ancient prophecies and the continued existence of the Church is evidence of the power and divinity of Christ.[1]

And from this all the rest followed. So the Rabbinic sages found urgent the historical question: if the Torah is true, why is Israel in trouble all the time? For if Constantine had become a Christian, if Julian's promise of rebuilding the Temple had produced nothing, if Christian emperors had secured control of the Empire for Christ and even abridged long-standing rights and immunities of Israel, as they did, then what hope could remain for Israel? Of greater consequence, was not history vindicating the Christian claim that God had saved humanity through the suffering people of God, the Church? Christians believed that the conversion of Constantine and the Roman government proved beyond a doubt that Christ was King-Messiah. For Israel the interpretation of the political happenings of the day required deep thought about the long-term history of humanity. Conceptions of history carried with them the most profound judgments on the character of the competing nations: the old people, Israel, and the Christians, a third race, a no-people – as some called themselves – now become the regnant nation, the Church. We do not know that the conversion of Constantine and events in its aftermath provoked sages to devote thought to the issues of history and its meaning. We know only that they compiled documents rich in thought on the subject. What they said, moreover, bore remarkable pertinence to the issues generated by the history of the century at hand. They set forth two messages, one concerning history, the other concerning the end of history and the advent of the Messiah. In this way, the Talmudic stage came full circle, restoring history and prophecy to the very heart of the Judaism of the dual Torah, which, in its Mishnaic formulation, treated the past as paradigmatic for an eternal present and by "Messiah" meant a classification of the priesthood.

II

To incorporate into Judaism a doctrine of history, the Rabbinic sages paid systematic attention to the narratives of the Pentateuch, finding in them instruction for the new age. As they composed commentaries to the Mishnah, so they worked out commentaries to Pentateuchal books, each of them pointed and purposive, all of them making coherent statements, respectively. It was in their commentary to Genesis, called Genesis Rabbah ("an amplification of Genesis"), circa 450 CE, that the Rabbinic sages made their most explicit statement about the meaning and end of history. Why choose Genesis in particular? From the story of the beginnings of the world and of Israel they sought meaning for their own times. The book of Genesis became the principal mode of historical reflection and response for the sages of the age. But, trained by the Mishnah and the halakhah to think like philosophers, social scientists in particular, in the book of Genesis the framers of Genesis Rabbah intended to find those principles of society and of history that would permit them to make sense of the on-going history of Israel. They took for granted that Scripture speaks to the life and condition of Israel, the Jewish people. God repeatedly says exactly that to Abraham and to Jacob. The entire narrative of Genesis is so formed as to point toward the sacred history of Israel, the Jewish people: its slavery and redemption; its coming Temple in Jerusalem; its exile and salvation at the end of time. In the reading of the authors at hand, therefore, the powerful message of Genesis proclaims that the world's creation commenced a single, straight line of events, leading in the end to the salvation of Israel and through Israel all humanity. That message – that history heads toward Israel's salvation – sages derived from the book of Genesis and contributed to their own day. Therefore in their reading of Scripture a given story will bear a deeper truth about what it means to be Israel, on the one side, and what in the end of days will happen to Israel, on the other. But their reading makes no explicit reference to what, if anything, had changed in the age of Constantine. But we do find repeated references to the four kingdoms, Babylonia, Media, Greece, Rome – and beyond the fourth will come Israel, fifth and last. So sages' message, in their theology of history, was that the present anguish prefigured the coming vindication, of God's people.

Accordingly, sages read Genesis as the history of the world with emphasis on Israel. So the lives portrayed, the domestic quarrels and petty conflicts with the neighbors, all serve to yield insight into what was to be. Why so? Because the deeds of the patriarchs taught lessons on how the children were to act, and, it further followed, the lives of the patriarchs signaled the history of Israel. Israel constituted one extended family, and the metaphor of the family, serving the nation as it did, imparted to the stories of Genesis the character of a family record. History become genealogy conveyed the message of salvation. These propositions really laid down the same judgment, one for the individual and the family, the other for the community and the nation, since there was no differentiating. Every detail of the narrative therefore served to prefigure what was to be, and Israel found itself, time and again, in the revealed facts of the history of the creation of the world, the decline of humanity down to the time of Noah, and, finally, its ascent to Abraham, Isaac, and Israel.

What are the laws of history, and, more important, how do they apply to the crisis at hand? The principal message of the story of the beginnings, as sages read Genesis, is that the world depends upon the merit of Abraham, Isaac, and Jacob; Israel, for its part, enjoys access to that merit, being today the family of the patriarchs and matriarchs. That sum and substance constitutes the sages' doctrine of history: the family forms the basic and irreducible historical unit. Israel is not so much a nation as a family, and the heritage of the patriarchs and matriarchs sustains that family from the beginning even to the end. So the sages' doctrine of history transforms history into genealogy, just as Eusebius's doctrine of history turns history into chronology. The consequence, for sages, will take the form of the symbolization through family relationships of the conflict between (Christian) Rome and eternal Israel. The rivalry of brothers, Esau and Jacob then contains the history of the fourth century – from sages' viewpoint a perfectly logical mode of historical reflection. That, in detail, expresses the main point of the system of historical thought yielded by Genesis Rabbah.

Historical study commonly leads to the periodization of history, the division of time into a number of distinct epoches. That patterning of history, its division in eras each with its own definitive traits, indeed, constitutes one important exercise of historical thought of a social scientific order. Specifically, for the Rabbinic sages Rome then stands as the penultimate epoch; Israel for the end. For the present topic, we consider how the patriarchs, for their part, contribute to the periodization of history – itself a source of comfort to doubting Israel even now. For if there is a well-defined sequence, then we can understand where we are and wait patiently until we reach the next, and better age. Time and again events in the lives of the patriarchs prefigure the four monarchies, among which, of course, the fourth, last (but for Israel), and most intolerable was Rome. Here is an exercise in the recurrent proof of that single proposition.

A. "[And it came to pass, as the sun was going down,] lo, a deep sleep fell on Abram, and lo, a dread and great darkness fell upon him" (Gen. 15:12):

B. "...lo, a dread" refers to Babylonia, as it is written, "Then was Nebuchadnezzar filled with fury" (Gen. 3:19).

C. "...and darkness" refers to Media, which darkened the eyes of Israel by making it necessary for the Israelites to fast and conduct public mourning.

D. "...great..." refers to Greece.

G. "...fell upon him" refers to Edom, as it is written, "The earth quakes at the noise of their fall" (Jer. 49:21).

H. Some reverse matters:

I. "...fell upon him" refers to Babylonia, since it is written, "Fallen, fallen is Babylonia" (Is. 21:9).

J. "...great..." refers to Media, in line with this verse: "King Ahasuerus did make great" (Est. 3:1).

K. "...and darkness" refers to Greece, which darkened the eyes of Israel by its harsh decrees.

L. "...lo, a dread" refers to Edom, as it is written, "After this I saw..., a fourth beast, dreadful and terrible" (Dan. 7:7).

Genesis Rabbah XLIV:XVII.4

The fourth kingdom is part of that plan, which we can discover by carefully studying Abraham's life and God's word to him. The inevitable and foreordained salvation follows this same pattern of historical epoches:

A. "Then the Lord said to Abram, 'Know of a surety [that your descendants will be sojourners in a land that is not theirs, and they will be slaves there, and they will be oppressed for four hundred years; but I will bring judgment on the nation which they serve, and afterward they shall come out with great possessions']" (Gen. 15:13–14):

B. "Know" that I shall scatter them.

C. "Of a certainty" that I shall bring them back together again.

D. "Know" that I shall put them out as a pledge [in expiation of their sins].

E. "Of a certainty" that I shall redeem them.

F. "Know" that I shall make them slaves.

G. "Of a certainty" that I shall free them.

Genesis Rabbah XLIV:XVIII.1

Reading the verse as a paradigm for all time, we recognize its piquant relevance to the age of the document in which it occurs. There is oppression, but redemption is coming. The lives of the patriarchs bring reassurance. The proposition is that God has unconditionally promised to redeem Israel, but if Israel repents, then the redemption will come with greater glory. If Abraham, Isaac, and Jacob stand for Israel later on, then Ishmael, Edom, and Esau represent Rome. Hence whatever sages find out about those figures tells them something about Rome and its character, history, and destiny.

So Genesis is read as both a literal statement and also as an effort to prefigure the history of Israel's suffering and redemption. Ishmael, standing now for Christian Rome, claims God's blessing, but Isaac gets it, as Jacob will take it from Esau. Details, as much as the main point, yielded laws of history. In the following passage, the sages take up the detail of Rebecca's provision of a bit of water, showing what that act had to do with the history of Israel later on. The passage at hand is somewhat protracted, but it contains in a whole and cogent way the mode of thought and the results: salvation is going to derive from the merit of the matriarchs and patriarchs.

A. "Let a little water be brought" (Gen. 18:4):

B. Said to him the Holy One, blessed be he, "You have said, 'Let a little water be brought' (Gen. 18:4). By your life, I shall pay your descendants back for this: 'Then sang Israel this song," spring up O well, sing you to it'" (Num. 21:7)."

C. That recompense took place in the wilderness. Where do we find that it took place in the Land of Israel as well?

D.   "A land of brooks of water" (Deut. 8:7).

E.   And where do we find that it will take place in the age to come?

F.   "And it shall come to pass in that day that living waters shall go out of Jerusalem" (Zech. 14:8).

G.   ["And wash your feet" (Gen. 18:4)]: [Said to him the Holy One, blessed be he,] "You have said , 'And wash your feet.' By your life, I shall pay your descendants back for this: 'Then I washed you in water' (Ez. 16:9)."

H.   That recompense took place in the wilderness. Where do we find that it took place in the Land of Israel as well?

I.   "Wash you, make you clean" (Is. 1:16).

J.   And where do we find that it will take place in the age to come?

K.   "When the Lord will have washed away the filth of the daughters of Zion" (Is. 4:4).

L.   [Said to him the Holy One, blessed be he,] "You have said, 'And rest yourselves under the tree' (Gen. 18:4). By your life, I shall pay your descendants back for this: 'He spread a cloud for a screen' (Ps. 105:39)."

M.   That recompense took place in the wilderness. Where do we find that it took place in the Land of Israel as well?

N.   "You shall dwell in booths for seven days" (Lev. 23:42).

O.   And where do we find that it will take place in the age to come?

P.   "And there shall be a pavilion for a shadow in the day-time from the heat" (Is. 4:6).

Q.   [Said to him the Holy One, blessed be he,] "You have said, 'While I fetch a morsel of bread that you may refresh yourself' (Gen. 18:5). By your life, I shall pay your descendants back for this: 'Behold I will cause to rain bread from heaven for you' (Ex. 16:45)"

R.   That recompense took place in the wilderness. Where do we find that it took place in the Land of Israel as well?

S.   "A land of wheat and barley" (Deut. 8:8).

T.   And where do we find that it will take place in the age to come?

U.   "He will be as a rich grain field in the land" (Ps. 82:16).

V.   [Said to him the Holy One, blessed be he,] "You ran after the herd ['And Abraham ran to the herd' (Gen. 18:7)]. By your life, I shall pay your descendants back for this: 'And there went forth a wind from the Lord and brought across quails from the sea' (Num. 11:27)."

W.   That recompense took place in the wilderness. Where do we find that it took place in the Land of Israel as well?

X.   "Now the children of Reuben and the children of Gad had a very great multitude of cattle" (Num. 32:1).

Y.   And where do we find that it will take place in the age to come?

Z.   "And it will come to pass in that day that a man shall rear a young cow and two sheep" (Is. 7:21).

AA. [Said to him the Holy One, blessed be he,] "You stood by them: 'And he stood by them under the tree while they ate' (Gen. 18:8). By your life, I shall pay your descendants back for this: 'And the Lord went before them' (Ex. 13:21)."

BB. That recompense took place in the wilderness. Where do we find that it took place in the Land of Israel as well?

CC. "God stands in the congregation of God" (Ps. 82:1).

DD. And where do we find that it will take place in the age to come?

EE. "The breaker is gone up before them...and the Lord at the head of them" (Mic. 2:13).

Genesis Rabbah XLVIII:X.2

The passage presents a sizable and beautifully disciplined construction, making one point again and again. Everything that the matriarchs and patriarchs did brought a reward to his descendants. The enormous emphasis on the way in which Abraham's deeds prefigured the history of Israel, both in the wilderness, and in the Land, and, finally, in the age to come, provokes us to wonder who held that there were children of Abraham beside Israel. The answer then is clear. We note that there are five statements of the same proposition, each drawing upon a clause in the base verse. The extended statement moreover serves as a sustained introduction to the treatment of the individual clauses that now follow, item by item. When we recall how Christian exegetes imparted to the Old Testament the lessons of the New, we realize that sages constructed an equally epochal and encompassing reading of Scripture. They now understood the meaning of what happened then, and, therefore, they also grasped from what had happened then the sense and direction of events of their own day. So history yielded patterns, and patterns proved points, and the points at hand indicated the direction of Israel. The substance of historical doctrine remains social in its focus. Sages present their theory of the meaning of history within a larger theory of the identification of Israel. Specifically, they see Israel as an extended family, children of one original ancestral couple, Abraham and Sarah. Whatever happens, then, constitutes family history, which is why the inheritance of merit from the ancestors protects their children even now, in the fourth century.

What, one asks, did sages find to validate their insistence that the biblical story, in Genesis, told the tale of Israel's coming salvation? Obviously, it is the merit of the ancestors that connects the living Israel to the lives of the patriarchs and matriarchs of old. The reciprocity of the process of interpreting Israel's history in light of the founders' lives and the founders' lives through the later history of Israel infuses the explanation of the debate over Sodom. Never far from sages' minds is the entire sweep and scope of Israel's long history. Never distant from the lips of the patriarchs and matriarchs is the message of Israel's destiny. Israel's history takes place in eternity, so considerations of what comes first and what happens later – that is, priority and order – do not apply.

III

For Scripture, history forms a chapter of eschatology, and eschatology encompasses the figure of the Messiah, and, for some heirs of Scripture, even the doctrine of the Messiah as the climax and end of history. But the Mishnaic system had come to full expression without an elaborated doctrine of the Messiah, or even an eschatological theory of the purpose and goal of matters. The Mishnah had put forth (in tractate Abot) a teleology without an eschatological dimension at all. By the closing of the Talmud of the Land of Israel, by contrast, the purpose and end of everything centered upon the coming of the Messiah, all within sages' terms and definition, to be sure. That is surprising in light of the character of the Mishnah's system, to which the Talmud of the Land of Israel attached itself as a commentary. In order to understand sages' development of the Messiah-theme in the Talmud of the Land of Israel, therefore, we have to backtrack and consider how the theme had made its appearance in the Mishnah. Only in comparison to its earlier expression and use therefore does the Talmud's formulation of the matter enter proper context for interpretation Critical issues of teleology had been worked out through messianic eschatology in other, earlier Judaic systems. Later ones as well would invoke the messiah-theme. These systems, including the Christian one of course, resorted to the myth of the Messiah as savior and redeemer of Israel, a supernatural figure engaged in political-historical tasks as king of the Jews, even a God-man facing the crucial historical questions of Israel's life and then resolving them – Christ as king of the world, of the ages, even of death itself.

In the Mishnah we look in vain for a doctrine of the Messiah. There "messiah" serves as a taxonomic indicator, e.g., distinguishing one type of priest or general from some other. There is no doctrine of the Messiah, coming at the end of time; in the Mishnah's system, matters focus on other issues entirely. Although the figure of a Messiah does appear, when the framers of the Mishnah spoke of "the Messiah," they meant a high priest designated and consecrated to office in a certain way, and not in some other way. The reference to "days of the Messiah" constitutes a conventional division of history at the end time but before the ultimate end. But that category of time plays no consequential role in the teleological framework established within the Mishnah. Accordingly, the Mishnah's framers constructed a system of Judaism in which the entire teleological dimension reached full exposure while hardly invoking the person or functions of a messianic figure of any kind. Perhaps in the aftermath of Bar Kokhba's debacle, silence on the subject served to express a clarion judgment. I am inclined to think so. But, for the purpose of our inquiry, the main thing is a simple fact, namely, that salvation comes through sanctification. The salvific figure, then becomes an instrument of consecration and so fits into an historical system quite different from the one built around the Messiah.

In the Talmud of the Land of Israel by contrast we find a fully exposed doctrine of not only a Messiah, but *the* Messiah: who he is, how we will know him, what we must do to bring him. It follows that the Talmud of the Land of Israel presents clear evidence that the Messiah myth had come that larger Torah myth that characterized Judaism in its later formative literature. A clear effort to identify the person of the Messiah and to confront the claim that a specific, named individual had been, or would be, the Messiah – these come to the fore. This means that the issue had reached the center of lively discourse at least in some rabbinic circles. Of course the disposition of the issue proves distinctive to sages: the Messiah will be a sage, the Messiah will come when Israel has attained that condition of sanctification, marked also by profound humility and complete acceptance of God's will, that signify sanctification.

In the Talmud of the Land of Israel two historical contexts framed discussion of the Messiah, the destruction of the Temple, as with Chrysostom's framing of the issue, and the messianic claim imputed to Bar Kokhba. Rome played a role in both, and the authors of the materials gathered in the Talmud made a place for Rome in the history of Israel. This they did in conformity to their larger theory of who is Israel, specifically by assigning to Rome a place in the family. As to the destruction of the Temple, we find a statement that the Messiah was born on the day that the Temple was destroyed. The

Talmud's doctrine of the Messiah therefore finds its place in its encompassing doctrine of history. What is fresh in the Talmud is the perception of Rome as an autonomous actor, as an entity with a point of origin (just as Israel has a point of origin) and a tradition of wisdom (just as Israel has such a tradition). So as Rome is Esau, so Esau is part of the family – a point to which we shall return – and therefore plays a role in history. And – yet another point of considerable importance – since Rome does play a role in history, Rome also finds a position in the eschatological drama. This sense of poised opposites, Israel and Rome, comes to expression in two ways. First, Israel's own history calls into being its counterpoint, the anti-history of Rome. Without Israel, there would be no Rome – a wonderful consolation to the defeated nation. For if Israel's sin created Rome's power, then Israel's repentance would bring Rome's downfall. Here is the way in which the Talmud presents the match:

IV E. Saturnalia means "hidden hatred" [*sina'ah temunah*]: The Lord hates, takes vengeance, and punishes.

F. This is in accord with the following verse: "Now Esau hated Jacob" [Gen. 27:41].

G. R. Isaac b. R. Eleazar said, "In Rome they call it Esau's Saturnalia."

H. Kratesis: It is on the day on which the Romans seized power.

K. Said R. Levi, "It is the day on which Solomon intermarried with the family of Pharaoh Neccho, King of Egypt. On that day Michael came down and thrust a reed into the sea, and pulled up muddy alluvium, and this was turned into a huge pot, and this was the great city of Rome. On the day on which Jeroboam set up the two golden calves, Remus and Romulus came and built two huts in the city of Rome. On the day on which Elijah disappeared, a king was appointed in Rome: "There was no king in Edom; a deputy was king" [1 Kings 22:47].

Yerushalmi Abodah Zarah 1:2.IV

The important point is that Solomon's sin provoked heaven's founding of Rome. The entire world and what happens in it enter into the framework of meaning established by Israel's Torah. So what the Romans do, their historical actions, can be explained in terms of Israel's conception of the world.

The concept of two histories, balanced opposite one another, comes to particular expression, within the Talmud of the Land of Israel, in the balance of Israelite sage and Roman emperor. Just as Israel and Rome, God and no-gods, compete (with a foreordained conclusion), so do sage and emperor. In this age, it appears that the emperor has the power. God's Temple, by contrast to the great Churches of the age, lies in ruins. But just as sages can overcome the emperor through their inherent supernatural power, so too will Israel and Israel's God in the coming age control the course of events. In the doctrine at hand, we see the true balance: sage as against emperor. In the age of the Christian emperors, the polemic acquires power. The sage, in his small claims court, weighs in the balance against the emperor in Constantinople – a rather considerable claim. So two innovations appear: first, the notion of emperor and sage in mortal struggle; second, the idea of an age of idolatry and an age beyond idolatry. The world had to move into a new orbit indeed for Rome to enter into the historical context formerly defined wholly by what happened to Israel. How does all this relate to the Messianic crisis at hand? The doctrine of sages, directly pertinent to the issue of the coming of the Messiah, holds that Israel can free itself of control by other nations only by humbly agreeing to accept God's rule. The nations – Rome, in the present instance – rest on one side of the balance, while God rests on the other. Israel must then choose between them. There is no such thing for Israel as freedom from both God and the nations, total autonomy and independence. There is only a choice of masters, a ruler on earth or a ruler in heaven.

Once the figure of the Messiah has come on stage, there arises discussion on who, among the living, the Messiah might be. The identification of the Messiah begins, of course, with the person of David himself: "If the Messiah-King comes from among the living, his name will be David. If he comes from among the dead, it will be King David himself" (Y. Ber. 2:3 V P). A variety of evidence announced the advent of the Messiah as a figure in the larger system of formative Judaism. The rabbinization of David constitutes one kind of evidence. Serious discussion, within the framework of the accepted document of Mishnaic exegesis and the law, concerning the identification and claim of diverse figures asserted to be messiahs, presents still more telling proof.

A. Once a Jew was plowing and his ox snorted once before him. An Arab who was passing and heard the sound said to him, "Jew, loosen your ox and loosen the plow and stop plowing. For today your Temple was destroyed."

B. The ox snorted again. He [the Arab] said to him, "Jew, bind your ox and bind your plow, for today the Messiah-King was born."

C. He said to him, "What is his name?"

D. "Menahem."

E. He said to him, "And what is his father's name?"

F. The Arab said to him, "Hezekiah."

G. He said to him, "Where is he from?"

H. He said to him, "From the royal capital of Bethlehem in Judea."

I. The Jew went and sold his ox and sold his plow. And he became a peddler of infant's felt-cloths [diapers]. And he went from place to place until he came to that very city. All of the women bought from him. But Menahem's mother did not buy from him.

J. He heard the women saying, "Menahem's mother, Menahem's mother, come buy for your child."

K. She said, "I want to bring him up to hate Israel. For on the day he was born, the Temple was destroyed."

L. They said to her, "We are sure that on this day it was destroyed, and on this day of the year it will be rebuilt."

M. She said to the peddler, "I have no money."

N. He said to her, "It is of no matter to me. Come and buy for him and pay me when I return."

O. A while later he returned to that city. He said to her, "How is the infant doing?"

P. She said to him, "Since the time you saw him a spirit came and carried him away from me."

Q. Said R. Bun, "Why do we learn this from [a story about] an Arab? Do we not have explicit scriptural evidence for it? 'Lebanon with its majestic trees will fall' [Isa. 10:34]. And what follows this? 'There shall come forth a shoot from the stump of Jesse' [Isa. 11:1]. [Right after an allusion to the destruction of the Temple the prophet speaks of the messianic age.]"

Y. Berakhot 2:4 (Translated by T. Zahavy)

This is a set-piece story, adduced to prove that the Messiah was born on the day the Temple was destroyed. The Messiah was born when the Temple was destroyed; hence, God prepared for Israel a better fate than had appeared.

A more concrete matter – the identification of the Messiah with a known historical personality – was associated with the name of Aqiba. He is said to have claimed that Bar Kokhba, leader of the second-century revolt, was the Messiah. The important aspect of the story, however, is the rejection of Aqiba's view. The discredited messiah figure (if Bar Kokhba actually was such in his own day) finds no apologists in the later rabbinical canon. What is striking in what follows, moreover, is that we really have two stories. At G Aqiba is said to have believed that Bar Kokhba was a disappointment. At H–I, he is said to have identified Bar Kokhba with the King-Messiah. Both cannot be true, so what we have is simply two separate opinions of Aqiba's judgment of Bar Kokhba/Bar Kozebah.

X.G. R. Simeon b. Yohai taught, "Aqiba, my master, would interpret the following verse: 'A star (*kokhab*) shall come forth out of Jacob' [Num. 24:17] "A disappointment (*Kozeba*) shall come forth out of Jacob.'"

H. R. Aqiba, when he saw Bar Kozeba, said, "This is the King Messiah."

I. R. Yohanan ben Toreta said to him, "Aqiba! Grass will grow on your cheeks before the Messiah will come!"

Y. Taanit 4:5

The important point is not only that Aqiba had been proved wrong. It is that the very verse of Scripture adduced in behalf of his viewpoint could be treated more generally and made to refer to righteous people in general, not to the Messiah in particular. And that leads us to the issue of the age, as sages' had to face it: what makes a messiah a false messiah? When we know the answer to that question, we also uncover the distinctively rabbinic version of the Messiah-theme that the Talmud of the Land of Israel contributes.

What matters is not the familiar doctrine of the Messiah's claim to save Israel, but the doctrine that Israel will be saved through total submission, under the Messiah's gentle rule, to God's yoke and service. In the model of the sage, the Messiah will teach Israel the power of submission. So God is not to be manipulated through Israel's humoring heaven in rite and cult. The notion of keeping the commandments so as to please heaven and get God to do what Israel wants is totally incongruent to the text at hand. Keeping the commandments as a mark of submission, loyalty, humility before God is the rabbinic system of salvation. So Israel does not save itself. Israel never controls its own destiny, either on earth or in heaven. The only choice is whether to cast one's fate into the hands of cruel, deceitful men, or to trust in the living God of mercy and love. We now understand the stress on the centrality of hope. Hope signifies patient acceptance of God's rule, and as an attitude of mind and heart, it is something that Israel can sustain on its own as well, the ideal action. We shall now see how this critical position that Israel's task is humble acceptance of God's rule is spelled out in the setting of discourse about the messiah in the Talmud of the Land of Israel. Bar Kokhba weighs in the balance against the sage, much as the Roman emperor weighs in the balance against the sage, and for the same reason. The one represents arrogance, the other, humility. Bar Kokhba, above all, exemplified arrogance against God. He lost the war because of that arrogance. In particular, he ignored the authority of sages – a point not to be missed, since it forms the point of critical tension of the tale:

X. J. Said R. Yohanan, "Upon orders of Caesar Hadrian, they killed eight hundred thousand in Betar."

K. Said R. Yohanan, "There were eighty thousand pairs of trumpeters surrounding Betar. Each one was in charge of a number of troops. Ben Kozeba was there and he had two hundred thousand troops who, as a sign of loyalty, had cut off their little fingers.

L. "Sages sent word to him, 'How long are you going to turn Israel into a maimed people?'

M. "He said to them, 'How otherwise is it possible to test them?'

N. "They replied to him, 'Whoever cannot uproot a cedar of Lebanon while riding on his horse will not be inscribed on your military rolls.'

O. "So there were two hundred thousand who qualified in one way, and another two hundred thousand who qualified in another way."

P. When he would go forth to battle, he would say, "Lord of the world! Do not help and do not hinder us! 'Hast thou not rejected us, O God? Thou dost not go forth, O God, with our armies'" [Ps. 60:10].

Q. Three and a half years did Hadrian besiege Betar.

R. R. Eleazar of Modiin would sit on sackcloth and ashes and pray every day, saying "Lord of the ages! Do not judge in accord with strict judgment this day! Do not judge in accord with strict judgment this day!"

S. Hadrian wanted to go to him. A Samaritan said to him, "Do not go to him until I see what he is doing, and so hand over the city [of Betar] to you. [Make peace ... for you.]"

T.   He got into the city through a drain pipe. He went and found R. Eleazar of Modiin standing and praying. He pretended to whisper something into his ear.

U.   The townspeople saw [the Samaritan] do this and brought him to Ben Kozeba. They told him, "We saw this man having dealings with your friend."

V.   [Bar Kokhba] said to him, "What did you say to him, and what did he say to you?"

W.   He said to [the Samaritan], "If I tell you, then the king will kill me, and if I do not tell you, then you will kill me. It is better that the king kill me, and not you."

X.   [Eleazar] said to me, 'I should hand over my city.' ['I shall make peace ....']"

Y.   He turned to R. Eleazar of Modiin. He said to him, "What did this Samaritan say to you?"

Z.   He replied, "Nothing."

AA. He said to him, "What did you say to him?"

BB. He said to him, "Nothing."

CC. [Ben Kozeba] gave [Eleazar] one good kick and killed him.

DD. Forthwith an echo came forth and proclaimed the following verse:

EE. "Woe to my worthless shepherd, who deserts the flock! May the sword smite his arm and his right eye! Let his arm be wholly withered, his right eye utterly blinded! [Zech. 11:17].

FF. "You have murdered R. Eleazar of Modiin, the right arm of all Israel, and their right eye. Therefore may the right arm of that man wither, may his right eye be utterly blinded!"

GG. Forthwith Betar was taken, and Ben Kozeba was killed.

Y. Taanit 4:5

We notice two complementary themes. First, Bar Kokhba treats heaven with arrogance, asking God merely to keep out of the way. Second he treats an especially revered sage with a parallel arrogance. The sage had the power to preserve Israel. Bar Kokhba destroyed Israel's one protection. The result was inevitable.

Now we may draw together the two related, but distinct themes, the doctrine of history and the theory of the Messiah. We turn first to history, the point which leads us to the matter of the Messiah. The convictions of Chrysostom and other Church fathers about how political events prove what God favors finds its counterpart in sages' view here. In the Talmud of the Land of Israel (as much as in Genesis Rabbah) Israel's history works out and expresses Israel's relationship with

God. The critical dimension of Israel's life, therefore, is salvation, the definitive trait, a movement in time from now to then. It follows that the paramount and organizing category is history and its lessons. As I suggested at the outset, in the Talmud of the Land of Israel we witness, among the Mishnah's heirs, a striking reversion to biblical convictions about the centrality of history in the definition of Israel's reality. The heavy weight of prophecy, apocalyptic, and biblical historiography, with their emphasis upon salvation and on history as the indicator of Israel's salvation, stood against the Mishnah's quite separate thesis of what truly mattered. What, from sages' viewpoint, demanded description and analysis and required interpretation? It was the category of sanctification, for eternity. The true issue framed by history and apocalypse was how to move toward the foreordained end of salvation, how to act in time to reach salvation at the end of the time. The Mishnah's teleology beyond time and its capacity to posit an eschatology without a place for an historical Messiah to take a position beyond that of the entire antecedent sacred literature of Israel. Only one strand, the priestly one, had ever taken so extreme a position on the centrality of sanctification and the peripheral nature of salvation. Wisdom had stood in between, with its own concerns, drawing attention both to what happened and to what endured. But to Wisdom what finally mattered was not nature or supernature, but rather abiding relationships in historical time.

But we should not conclude that the Talmud at hand has simply moved beyond the Mishnah's orbit. The opposite is the case. What the framers of the document have done is to assemble materials in which the eschatological, therefore Messianic, teleology is absorbed within the ahistorical, therefore sagacious one. The Messiah turned into a sage is no longer the Messiah embodied in the figure of the arrogant Bar Kokhba (in the Talmud's representation of the figure). The reversion to the prophetic notion of learning history's lessons carried in its wake a re-engagement with the Messiah myth. But the re-engagement does not represent a change in the unfolding system. Why not? Because the climax comes in an explicit statement that the conduct required by the Torah will bring the coming Messiah. That explanation of the holy way of life focuses upon the end of time and the advent of the Messiah – both of which therefore depend upon the sanctification of Israel. So sanctification takes priority, salvation depends on it. The framers of the Mishnah had found it possible to construct a complete and encompassing teleology for their system with scarcely a single word about the Messiah's coming at that time when the system would be perfectly achieved.

So with their interest in explaining events and accounting for history, the third- and fourth-century sages represented in these units of discourse invoked what their predecessors had at best found to be of peripheral consequence to their system. The following contains the most striking expression of this viewpoint.

X.J. "The oracle concerning Dumah. One is calling to me from Seir, 'Watchman, what of the night? Watchman, what of the night?' [Isa. 21:11]."

K. The Israelites said to Isaiah, "O our Rabbi, Isaiah, what will come for us out of this night?"

L. He said to them, "Wait for me, until I can present the question."

M. Once he had asked the question, he came back to them.

N. They said to him, "Watchman, what of the night? What did the Guardian of the ages tell you?"

O. He said to them, "The watchman says: 'Morning comes; and also the night. If you will inquire, inquire; come back again' [Isa. 21:12]."

P. They said to him, "Also the night?"

Q. He said to them, "It is not what you are thinking. But there will be morning for the righteous, and night for the wicked, morning for Israel, and night for idolaters."

R. They said to him, "When?"

S. He said to them, "Whenever you want, He too wants [it to be] – if you want it, he wants it."

T. They said to him, "What is standing in the way?"

U. He said to them, "Repentance: 'Come back again' [Isa. 21:12]."

V. R. Aha in the name of R. Tanhum b. R. Hiyya, "If Israel repents for one day, forthwith the son of David will come.

W. "What is the scriptural basis? 'O that today you would hearken to his voice!' [Ps. 95:7]."

X. Said R. Levi, :If Israel would keep a single Sabbath in the proper way, forthwith the son of David will come.

Y. "What is the scriptural basis for this view? 'Moses said, 'Eat it today, for today is a Sabbath to the Lord; today you will not find it in the field'" [Exod. 16:25].

Z. "And it said, 'For thus said the Lord God, the Holy One of Israel, "In returning and rest you shall be saved; in quietness and in trust shall be your strength." And you would not' [Isa. 30:15]."

Y. Taanit 1:1

A discussion of the power of repentance would hardly have surprised a Mishnah sage. What is new is the explicit linkage between bringing the end of time and the coming of the Messiah, on the one side, and, on the other keeping the law. That motif stands separate from the notions of righteousness and repentance, which surely did not require it. We must not lose sight of the importance of this passage, with its emphasis on repentance, on the one side, and the power of Israel to reform itself, on the other. The Messiah will come any day that Israel makes it possible. Let me underline the most important statement of this large conception: *If all Israel will keep a single Sabbath in the proper (rabbinic) way, the Messiah will come. If all Israel will repent for one day, the Messiah will come. "Whenever you want ...," the Messiah will come.*

Now, with the reappearance of the Sabbath and hence the restoration of Eden's perfection, two things are happening here. First, the system of religious observance, including study of Torah, is explicitly invoked as having salvific power. Second, the persistent hope of the people for the coming of the Messiah is linked to the system of rabbinic observance and belief. Restorationist theology reaches its climax. In this way, the austere program of the Mishnah develops in a different direction, with no trace of a promise that the Messiah will come if and when the system is fully realized. Here a teleology lacking all eschatological dimension gives way to an explicitly messianic statement that the purpose of the law is to attain Israel's salvation: "If you want it, God wants it too." The one thing Israel commands is its own heart; the power it yet exercises is the power to repent. These suffice. The entire history of humanity will respond to Israel's will, to what happens in Israel's heart and soul. With the Temple in ruins, repentance can take place only within the heart and mind.

We should note, also, a corollary to the doctrine at hand, which carries to the second point of interest, the Messiah. Israel may contribute to its own salvation, by the right attitude and the right deed. But Israel bears responsibility for its present condition. So what Israel does makes history. Any account of the Messiah-doctrine of the Talmud of the Land of Israel must lay appropriate stress on that conviction: Israel makes its own history, therefore shapes its own destiny. This lesson, sages maintained, derives from the very condition of Israel even then, its suffering and its despair. How so? History taught moral lessons. Historical events entered into the construction of a teleology for the Talmud of the Land of Israel's system of Judaism as a whole. What the law demanded reflected the consequences of wrongful action on the part of Israel. So, again, Israel's own deeds defined the events of history. Rome's role, like Assyria's and Babylonia's, depended upon Israel's provoking divine wrath as it was executed by the great empire. This mode of thought comes to simple expression in what follows. Israel had to learn the lesson of its history to also take command of its own destiny. But this notion of determining one's own destiny should not be misunderstood. The framers of the Talmud of the Land of Israel were not telling the Jews to please God by doing commandments in order that they should thereby gain control of their own destiny. God was not there to be humored and manipulated.

To the contrary, the paradox of the Talmud's system of history and Messiah lies in the fact that Israel can free itself of control by other nations only by humbly agreeing to accept God's rule. The nations – Rome, in the present instance – rest on one side of the balance, while God rests on the other. Israel must then choose between them. There is no such thing for Israel as freedom from both God and the nations, total autonomy and independence. There is only a choice of masters, a ruler on earth or a ruler in heaven. In the Talmud's theory of salvation, therefore, the framers provided Israel with an account of how to overcome the unsatisfactory circumstances of an unredeemed present, so as to accomplish the movement from here to the much-desired future. When the Talmud's authorities present statements on the promise of the law for those who keep it, therefore, they provide glimpses of the goal of the system as a whole. These invoked the primacy of the rabbi and the legitimating power of the Torah, and in those two components of the system we find the principles of the Messianic doctrine. And these bring us back to the argument with Christ triumphant, as the Christians perceived him.

The Mishnah's system, whole and complete, had remained reticent on the entire Messiah-theme. By contrast, this Talmud, followed in every detail by the second and definitive one, finds ample place for a rich collection of statements on the messianic theme. What this means is that, between the conclusion of the Mishnah and the closure of the Talmud, room had been found for the messianic hope, expressed in images not revised to conform to the definitive and distinctive traits of the Talmud itself. We do not have to argue that the stunning success of Christ (in the Christians' views) made the issue urgent for Jews. My judgment is that the issue had never lost its urgency, except in the tiny circle of philosophers who, in the system of the Mishnah, reduced the matter to a minor detail of taxonomy. And yet, in that exercise, the Mishnah's sages confronted a considerable social problem, one that faced the fourth century authorities as well.

What is most interesting in Talmuds' picture is that the hope for the Messiah's coming is further joined to the moral condition of each individual Israelite. Hence the messianic fulfillment was made to depend on the repentance of Israel. The entire drama, envisioned by others in earlier types of Judaism as a world-historical event, was reworked in context into a moment in the life of the individual and the people of Israel collectively. The coming of the Messiah depended not on historical action but on moral regeneration. So from a force that moved Israelites to take up weapons on the battlefield, the messianic hope and yearning were transformed into motives for spiritual regeneration and ethical behavior. The energies released in the messianic fervor were then linked to rabbinical government, through which Israel would form the godly society. When we reflect that the message, "If you want it, He too wants it to be," comes in a generation confronting a dreadful disappointment, its full weight and meaning become clear.

The advent of the Messiah will not be heralded by the actions of a pagan or of a Christian king. Whoever relies upon the salvation of a gentile is going to be disappointed. Israel's salvation depends wholly upon Israel itself. Two things follow. First, as we saw, the Jews were made to take up the burden of guilt for their own sorry situation. But, second, they also gained not only responsibility for, but also power over, their fate. They could do something about salvation, just as their sins had brought about their tragedy. This old, familiar message, in no way particular to the Talmud's bureaucrats, took on specificity and concreteness in the context of the Talmud, which offered a rather detailed program for reform and regeneration. The message to a disappointed generation, attracted to the kin-faith, with its now-triumphant messianic fulfillment, and fearful of its own fate in an age of violent attacks upon the synagogue buildings and faithful alike, was stern. But it also promised strength to the weak and hope to the despairing. No one could be asked to believe that the Messiah would come very soon. The events of the day testified otherwise. So the counsel of the Talmud's sages was patience and consequential deeds. People could not hasten things, but they could do something. The duty of Israel, in the meantime, was to accept the sovereignty of heavenly government. The heavenly government, revealed in the Torah, was embodied in this world by the figure of the sage. The meaning of the salvific doctrine just outlined becomes fully clear when we uncover the simple fact that the rule of Heaven and the learning and authority of the rabbi on earth turned out to be identified with one another. It follows that salvation for Israel depended upon adherence to the sage and acceptance of his discipline. God's will in Heaven and the sage's words on earth – both constituted Torah. And Israel would be saved through Torah, so the sage was the savior.

To conclude, let us ask Chrysostom and the framers of the Talmuds to take up the same issue.

Will there be a Messiah for Israel?

Sages: Yes.
Chrysostom: No.

Will the Messiah save the world, including Israel?

Sages: Yes, in the future.
Chrysostom: He already has.

And if we ask whether or not the parties to the dispute invoke the same facts, in the form of a shared corpus of texts, the answer is affirmative.

The messianic texts of Isaiah and other passages, important to Christians, gain a distinctive reading on the part of sages as well. So the issue is shared, the probative facts a point of agreement. True, Chrysostom and the authors and framers of the Yerushalmi in no way confront the viewpoints of one another. But they do argue about the same matter and invoke the same considerations: is the Messiah coming or has he come? Do we have now to keep the law or not? The linking of Messiah to the keeping of the torah then joins the two sides in a single debate. To be sure, Chrysostom's framing of the messianic issue responds to concerns of the Church and the young presbyter's worry for its future. That is why the matter of the keeping of the law forms the centerpiece of his framing of the messianic question. But the issue of keeping the laws of the Torah then joins his version of the messiah-theme with that of sages. Again, everything we hear from sages turns inward, upon Israel. There is no explicit confrontation with the outside world: with the Christian emperor, with the figure of Christ enthroned. It is as if nothing has happened to demand attention. Yet the stress for sages is on the centrality of the keeping of the laws of the Torah in the messianic process. Keep the law and the Messiah will come. This forms an exact reply to Chrysostom's doctrine: do not keep the law, for the Messiah has come.

Looking backward from the end of the fourth century to the end of the first, the framers of the Talmud surely perceived what two hundred years earlier, with the closure of the Mishnah, need not have appeared obvious and unavoidable, namely, the definitive end, for here and now at any rate, of the old order of cultic sanctification. After a hundred years there may have been some doubt. With the fiasco of Julian near at hand, there can have been little hope left. The Mishnah had designed a world in which the Temple stood at the center, a society in which the priests presided at the top, and a way of life in which the dominant issue was the sanctification of Israelite life. Whether the full realization of that world, society, and way of life was thought to come sooner or later, the system had been meant only initially as a utopia, but in the end, as a plan and constitution for a material society here in the Land of Israel.

Two hundred years now had passed from the closure of the Mishnah to the completion of the Talmud of the Land of Israel. Much had changed. Roman power had receded from part of the world. Pagan rule had given way to the sovereignty of Christian emperors. The old order was cracking; the new order not yet established. But, from the perspective of Israel, the waiting went on. The interim from Temple to Temple was not differentiated. Whether conditions were less favorable or more favorable hardly made a difference. History stretched backward, to a point of disaster, and forward, to an unseen and incalculable time beyond the near horizon. Short of supernatural events, salvation was not in sight. Israel for its part lived under its own government, framed within the rules of sanctification, and constituted a holy society. But when would salvation come, and how could people even now hasten its day? These issues, in the nature of things, proved more pressing as the decades rolled by, becoming first one century, then another, while none knew how many more, and how much more, must still be endured. So the unredeemed state of Israel and the world, the uncertain fate of the individual – these framed and defined the context in which all forms of Judaism necessarily took shape. The question of salvation presented each with a single ineluctable agendum. But it is not merely an axiom generated by our hindsight that makes it necessary to interpret all of a system's answers in the light of the single question of salvation. In the case of the Judaism to which the Talmud of the Land of Israel attests, the matter is explicitly stated.

For the important fact is that Talmud of the Land of Israel expressly links salvation to keeping the law. And, in the opposite way, so did Chrysostom. We recall that he held that not keeping the law showed that the Messiah had come and Israel's hope was finally defeated.

Sages maintained that keeping the law now signified keeping the faith: the act of hope. This means that the issues of the law were drawn upward into the highest realm of Israelite consciousness. Keeping the law in the right way is represented as not merely right or expedient. It is the way to bring the Messiah, the son of David. This is stated by Levi, as follows:

X. Said R. Levi, "If Israel would keep a single Sabbath in the proper way, forthwith the son of David would come.

Y. "What is the Scriptural basis for this view? 'Moses said, Eat it today, for today is a Sabbath to the Lord; today you will not find it in the field' (Ex. 16:25)."

Z. And it says, "For thus said the Lord God, the Holy One of Israel, 'In returning and rest you shall be saved; in quietness and in trust shall be your strength. And you would not' (Is. 30:15)."

Y. Taanit 1:1.IX

Here, in a single saying, we find the entire Talmudic doctrine set out. How like, yet how different from, the Mishnah's view!. Keeping the law of the Torah represented the visible form of love of God. Moses in the Pentateuch surely concurs, for that is precisely his message, as sages grasped it, start to finish. What began in the Garden of Eden would end there, in life eternal, for nearly all Israel – meaning, for all those who love God and aspire to live in his kingdom and by his revealed Torah. That is the position concerning the human condition that Judaism had reached at the end of the formative age – and would maintain, come what may, for centuries to follow.

NOTES

PREFACE

1 Not to be confused, in the study of religion, with the contemporary State of Israel, hence "holy Israel" refers to the community portrayed in Scripture and embodied, thereafter, by those who see their genealogy in Scripture: the Israel called into being at Sinai out of the family of Abraham, Isaac, and Jacob.

2 Ramsay MacMullen, *Christianity and Paganism in the Fourth to Eighth Centuries* (New Haven and London:Yale University Press) pp. 32–3.

3 Little in my reading of matters rests upon that particular date and the situation it represents, since I deal with the relationships between and among completed documents, not the comparison and contrast of the particular points in time at which those documents came to composition and closure, whether Moses at Sinai in 1200 BCE or Ezra in Jerusalem, out of Babylonia, in 450 BCE.

1 THE PENTATEUCHAL STAGE

1 I have noticed that integrationist-Orthodox scholars evince a special interest in dating as far back as possible into the centuries BCE the contents, if not the formulation, of various laws that surface in the Mishnah or in even later compilations. But the Judaism of the dual Torah finds its own origins at Sinai, not with Ezra, and no theological apologetics upon historical bases derives from the allegation (rarely then demonstrated) that such and such a law goes "way way back." If not to the historical Sinai (if that is what is at stake for the integrationist-Orthodox), then what good such an allegation accomplishes in the apologetic enterprise I cannot say.

2 *The Theology of the Oral Torah. Revealing the Justice of God* (Kingston and Montreal, 1998: McGill-Queens University Press) validates these statements.

3 If I were engaged here in constructive systematic theology, not just the historical kind represented by an account of the stages of Judaism, I should further claim that the sages' is the only possible system that the Hebrew Scriptures sustain. Whether or not other theologies built upon the Hebrew Scriptures may be deemed congruent with those Scriptures

is not at issue here, only the claim that the sages' is. But I think a powerful case can be made on behalf of the congruity with Scripture, in proportion, balance, and also detail, of the sages' re-telling of the Scriptural tale. How sages diverge from Scripture in their basic theological structure and system I simply cannot discern. In my view, transcending the promiscuous use of proof-texts is the evidence on the surface of matters. At no point can I find important differences between the sages' and Scripture's respective theological systems and structures.

4 That is with two exceptions, for, so far as that tradition can be naturalized into the framework established by sages' structure and system, sages do so, as in the case of Daniel. Second, they take over as fact and accept apocalyptic expectations, as with the war of Gog and Magog.

5 *Biblical Theology of the Old and New Testaments,* p. 720.

2 FROM SCRIPTURE TO THE MISHNAH

1 In my *History of the Mishnaic Law,* I systematically work my way back from the final stages of the halakhah of a given tractate to its earlier and finally its earliest layers. This I do by matching the order of the authorities, by generations, to whom sayings are attributed against the logical sequences of propositions, the one taking for granted the given of the other. Where what is earlier in attribution also forms the foundation of what is attributed to a later authority, I find in that correspondence of logic and order of attribution grounds for assigning to an earlier period the notion that is under discussion, if not the exact wording of it. When, therefore, I speak of generative premises of a tractate or the building blocks of all thought in a tractate, and when I identify what is primary and what is secondary and derivative, it is on the basis of complete and systematic analysis, with the results fully in print, see Neusner, *History.* The givens of what follows rest on very solid bases in the characterization of the several native-categories under discussion.

2 To elaborate: the governing consideration in this account of the stage from the Pentateuch to the Mishnah is the position of these generative premises within the articulation of the halakhic system that comes to expression in the Mishnah and the Tosefta. Specifically, these generative premises, everywhere taken for granted, turn out to define the organizing category itself, the entire category-formation representing the a priori that dictates the problematics of the law and its norms. Unarticulated and implicit, they form the necessary premise of all halakhic discourse.

3 I have completed the systematic account of the matter in *Scripture and the Generative Premises of the Halakhah* (in press) in four volumes.

4 Bold-face type signifies the origin of the designated, coherent composition in the Mishnah or the Tosefta, then its insertion whole into Sifra.

5 Mandelbaum, *Kilayim,* p. 3.

6 Mandelbaum, *Kilayim,* p. 4.

7 Obviously, the sages will not have used the language of contemporary science. But they certainly recognized when the leavening process

ceased and knew the conditions for bringing it about, as their discussion here and at Pesahim makes quite apparent.

8 Not necessarily grown in the Land of Israel, but possibly from the interstitial territory of Syria, which is neither part of the Land of Israel nor part of the land of the gentiles.

9 Samuel A. Matz, "Baking and Bakery Products," *Encyclopaedia Britannica* 2:597.

3 THE MISHNAH ON ITS OWN

1 Because scholarship on the Pentateuch analyzes and dissects, rather than examining the bases of synthesis and reconstruction, little has been done in recent times on the overall construction and coherence of the Pentateuchal laws viewed as a whole, as a code or set of codes that work together. From the viewpoint of the comparison of the Mishnah as a code to the Pentateuch as a code, each viewed whole, these remarks should be taken as preliminary observations, requiring much further work. They suffice for the present purpose, the differentiation of the Mishnah from Scripture on the foundation of inductive analysis of definitive traits of each.

2 I discussed the socio-linguistics of the document at some length in *A History of the Mishnaic Law of Purities*. Leiden, 1977: Brill. XXI. *The Redaction and Formulation of the Order of Purities in the Mishnah and Tosefta*.

3 G. E. R. Lloyd, *Early Greek Science. Thales to Aristotle*. New York, 1970: W. W. Norton & Co., pp. 11–12. See also Lloyd, *Greek Science after Aristotle*. New York, 1973: W. W. Norton Co., and his *Polarity and Analogy. Two Types of Argumentation in Early Greek Thought*. Cambridge, 1966: Cambridge University Press.

4 Lloyd, *op. cit.*, p. 12.

5 Lloyd, *op. cit.*, p. 15.

6 I do not concur in that allegation as to the "genre" of the Mishnah, but once more introduce it for the sake of argument. In fact a single document cannot define, or constitute, a genre at all. And the Mishnah's singularity is its indicative trait in Israelite context.

7 On the relationship of Qumran and Rabbinic Sabbath law, see Lawrence H. Schiffman, *The Halakhah at Qumran* (Leiden, 1975). In that work Schiffman does not undertake form-analytical comparisons.

8 If we further consider the literary ambition exhibited in the massive size of the Mishnah as compared with the paltry volume of laws preserved among other Judaisms, that point is reenforced.

9 We make provision for a possible exception in the case of Job, but supernatural debate and debate between men surely are to be classified differently.

10 Lloyd, *Early Greek Science*, p. 8.

11 That is not to argue for one minute that the Rabbinic sages studied philosophy before, during, or after their yeshiva-years (so to speak). Questions of origins, theories of influence and borrowing – these presuppose traits of culture and its formation and diffusion that require attention in their own terms. Why anyone should find

surprising in the age of Neo-Platonism that our sages should produce a work such as the Mishnah congruent in method and in intent to neo-Platonic writing (as I show in *Judaism as Philosophy*) seems to me also to require an explanation. There I argue that comparison and contrast by definition acknowledge no boundaries of culture or historical context. By rights and by simple logic we can compare and contrast anything that falls into the same classification with anything else in that same classification. Since people in widely separated places may and often do come to the same conclusions about the same things, we commit no act of violence against common sense by invoking in this context the names of Aristotle as to method and Plato and Middle Platonism and particularly the Neo-Platonism that came to full expression only later on in the writings of Plotinus as to proposition. What we seek, as a matter of fact, is nothing more than the *classification*, as philosophy, of the Mishnah's method and message. I maintain that that message and method exhibit congruence with philosophies of the same kind, that is, philosophies that, whole or in part, ask the same types of questions and pursue the same means for answering them.

6 THE TALMUDS IN PENTATEUCHAL CONTEXT

1 Wilken, p. 155–8.

BIBLIOGRAPHY

Avery-Peck, *Terumot* = Alan J. Avery-Peck, *The Priestly Gift in Mishnah. A Study of Tractate Terumot* (Chico, 1981: Scholars Press for Brown Judaic Studies.)

Avery-Peck, *Yerushalmi Terumot* = Alan J. Avery-Peck, *The Talmud of the Land of Israel. A preliminary Translation and Explanation. Volume 6. Terumot.*

Avery-Peck, *Yerushalmi Shebi'it* = Alan J. Avery-Peck, *The Talmud of the Land of Israel. A Preliminary Translation and Explanation. Volume 5. Shebiit.* Jacob Neusner, General Editor (Chicago, 1991: The University of Chicago Press.)

Brooks, *Mishnah* = Roger Brooks, *Support for the Poor in the Mishnaic Law of Agriculture: Tractate Peah* (Chico, 1983: Scholars Press), for the Mishnah and the Tosefta.

Brooks, *Yerushalmi* = *The Talmud of the Land of Israel. A Preliminary Translation and Explanation. Volume 2. Peah* (Chicago, 1990: The University of Chicago Press.)

Brooks, *Yerushalmi Maaser Sheni* = *The Talmud of the Land of Israel. A Preliminary Translation and Explanation. Volume 8. Maaser Sheni.* Translated by Roger Brooks (Chicago, 1993: The University of Chicago Press.)

Essner = Howard Essner, "The Mishnah Tractate 'Orlah: Translation and Commentary," in William Scott Green, ed., *Approaches to Ancient Judaism.* (Chico, 1983: Scholars Press for Brown Judaic Studies) 3:105–48.

Haas = Peter J. Haas, *A History of the Mishnaic Law of Agriculture. Tractate Maaser Sheni* (Chico, 1980: Scholars Press for Brown Judaic Studies.)

Havivi, *Mishnah* = Abraham Havivi, "Mishnah Hallah Chapter One: Translation and Commentary," *Approaches to Ancient Judaism III: Text as Context in Early Rabbinic Literature,* edited by William Scott Green (Chico, 1981: Scholars Press for Brown Judaic Studies), pp, 149–85.

Havivi, *Yerushalmi* = Jacob Neusner, *The Talmud of the Land of Israel. A Preliminary Translation and Explanation. Volume 9. Hallah.* With an

Introduction by Abraham Havivi. (Chicago, 1991: The University of Chicago Press.)

Hyman = Aharon Mordecai Hyman, *Torah hakketubah vehammesurah 'al torah, nebi'im, uketubim* (Tel Aviv, 1938: Debir) I-III.

Jaffee, *Mishnah* = Martin S. Jaffee, *Mishnah's Theology of Tithing: A Study of Tractate Maaserot.* (Chico, 1981: Scholars Press for Brown Judaic Studies.)

Jaffee, *Yerushalmi* = Martin S. Jaffee, *The Talmud of the Land of Israel. A Preliminary Translation and Explanation. Volume 7. Maaserot.* (Chicago, 1987: University of Chicago Press.)

Lloyd, G. E. R., *Early Greek Science. Thales to Aristotle.* (New York, 1970: W. W. Norton & Co.)

Lloyd, G. E. R. *Greek Science after Aristotle.* (New York, 1973: W. W. Norton & Co.)

Lloyd, G. E. R., *Polarity and Analogy. Two Types of Argumentation in Early Greek Thought.* (Cambridge, 1966: Cambridge University Press.)

Mandelbaum, *Kilayim* = Irving Mandelbaum, *A History of the Mishnaic Law of Agriculture: Kilayim.* (Chico, 1981: Scholars Press for Brown Judaic Studies.)

Neusner, J, *Bavli* = *The Talmud of Babylonia. An American Translation.* (Atlanta: 1984–1995: Scholars Press for Brown Judaic Studies.)

I	*Tractate Berakhot*
II.A.	*Tractate Shabbat. Chapters One and Two.*
II.B.	*Tractate Shabbat Chapters Three through Six*
II.C	*Tractate Shabbat Chapters Seven through Ten*
II.D	*Tractate Shabbat Chapters Eleven through Seventeen*
II.E	*Tractate Shabbat Chapters Eighteen through Twenty-Four*
III A.	*Tractate Erubin. Chapters One and Two*
III B.	*Tractate Erubin, Chapters Three and Four*
III.C.	*Tractate Erubin, Chapters Five and Six*
III D.	*Tractate Erubin, Chapters Seven through Ten*
IV.A	*Tractate Pesahim. Chapter One*
IV.B	*Tractate Pesahim. Chapters Two and Three*
IV.C	*Tractate Pesahim. Chapters Four through Six*
IV.D	*Tractate Pesahim. Chapters Seven and Eight*
IV.E	*Tractate Pesahim. Chapters Nine and Ten*
V.A	*Tractate Yoma. Chapters One and Two*
V.B	*Tractate Yoma. Chapters Three through Five*
V.C	*Tractate Yoma. Chapters Six through Eight*
VI.	*Tractate Sukkah*
XI.	*Tractate Moed Qatan*
XII	*Tractate Hagigah*
XIII.A.	*Tractate Yebamot. Chapters One through Three*
XIII.B.	*Tractate Yebamot. Chapters Four through Six*

XIII.C.   *Tractate Yebamot. Chapters Seven through Nine*
XIII.D   *Tractate Yebamot. Chapters Ten through Sixteen*
XIV.A.   *Tractate Ketubot. Chapters One through Three*
XIV.B.   *Tractate Ketubot. Chapters Four through Seven*
XIV.C.   *Tractate Ketubot. Chapters Eight through Thirteen*
XV. A.   *Tractate Nedarim. Chapters One through Four*
XV.B.   *Tractate Nedarim. Chapters Five through Eleven*
XVII   *Tractate Sotah*
XVIII.A.   *Tractate Gittin. Chapters One through Three*
XVIII.B.   *Tractate Gittin. Chapters Four and Five*
XVIII.C.   *Tractate Gittin. Chapters Six through Nine*
XIX.A.   *Tractate Qiddushin. Chapter One*
XIX.B.   *Tractate Qiddushin. Chapters Two through Four*
XX.A   *Tractate Baba Qamma. Chapters One through Three*
XX.B.   *Tractate Baba Qamma. Chapters Four through Seven*
XX.C   *Tractate Baba Qamma. Chapters Eight through Ten*
XXI.A.   *Tractate Baba Mesia. Introduction. Chapters One and Two*
XXI.B.   *Tractate Baba Mesia. Chapters Three and Four*
XXI.C.   *Tractate Baba Mesia. Chapters Five and Six*
XXI.D.   *Tractate Baba Mesia. Chapters Seven through Ten*
XXII. A.   *Tractate Baba Batra. Chapters One and Two*
XXII.B.   *Tractate Baba Batra. Chapter Three*
XXII.C.   *Tractate Baba Batra. Chapters Four through Six*
XXII.D.   *Tractate Baba Batra. Chapters Seven and Eight*
XXII.E.   *Tractate Baba Batra. Chapters Nine and Ten*
XXIII.A   *Tractate Sanhedrin. Chapters One through Three*
XXIII.B   *Tractate Sanhedrin. Chapters Four through Eight*
XXIII.C   *Tractate Sanhedrin. Chapters Nine through Eleven*
XXIV.   *Tractate Makkot*
XXV.A.   *Tractate Abodah Zarah. Chapters One and Two*
XXV.B.   *Tractate Abodah Zarah. Chapters Three, through Five*
XXVII.A   *Tractate Shebuot. Chapters One through Three*
XXVII.B   *Tractate Shebuot. Chapters Four through Eight*
XXVIII.A.   *Tractate Zebahim. Chapters One through Three*
XXVIII.B.   *Tractate Zebahim. Chapters Four through Eight*
XXVIII.   *Tractate Zebahim. Chapters Nine through Fourteen*
XXIX.A.   *Tractate Menahot. Chapters One through Three*
XXIX.B.   *Tractate Menahot. Chapters Four through Seven*
XXIX.C.   *Tractate Menahot. Chapters Eight through Thirteen*
XXXI.A.   *Tractate Bekhorot. Chapters One through Four*
XXXI.B.   *Tractate Bekhorot. Chapters Five through Nine*
XXXII.   *Tractate Arakhin*
XXXIII.   *Tractate Temurah*
XXXIV.   *Tractate Keritot*
XXXVI.A   *Tractate Niddah. Chapters One through Three*
XXXVI.B   *Tractate Niddah. Chapters Four through Ten*

Neusner, J, *Constantine = Judaism and Christianity in the Age of Constantine. Issues of the Initial Confrontation.* (Chicago, 1987: University of Chicago Press.)

Neusner, J, *Dialectics = Talmudic Dialectics: Types and Forms.* (Atlanta, 1995: Scholars Press for South Florida Studies in the History of Judaism. I-II.)

Neusner, J, *History = A History of the Mishnaic Law of Purities.* (Leiden, 1977: Brill. XXI.)

The Redaction and Formulation of the Order of Purities in the Mishnah and Tosefta.

A History of the Mishnaic Law of Purities. (Leiden, 1977: Brill. XXII.), *The Mishnaic System of Uncleanness. Its Context and History.*

The Mishnah before 70. (Atlanta, 1987: Scholars Press for Brown Judaic Studies.) [Reprise of pertinent results of *A History of the Mishnah Law of Purities* Vols. III, V, VIII, X, XII, XIV, XVI, XVII, and XVIII.]

A History of the Mishnaic Law of Holy Things. (Leiden, 1979: Brill. VI.) *The Mishnaic System of Sacrifice and Sanctuary.*

A History of the Mishnaic Law of Women. (Leiden, 1980: Brill. V.) *The Mishnaic System of Women.*

A History of the Mishnaic Law of Appointed Times. (Leiden, 1981: Brill. V.) *The Mishnaic System of Appointed Times.*

A History of the Mishnaic Law of Damages. (Leiden, 1985: Brill. V.) *The Mishnaic System of Damages.*

Neusner, J, *Judaism = The Judaism Behind the Texts. The Generative Premises of Rabbinic Literature.* I. *The Mishnah.* A. *The Division of Agriculture.* (Atlanta, 1993: Scholars Press for South Florida Studies in the History of Judaism.)

I. *The Mishnah.* B. *The Divisions of Appointed Times, Women, and Damages (through Sanhedrin.)* Atlanta, 1993: Scholars Press for South Florida Studies in the History of Judaism.

I. *The Mishnah.* C. *The Divisions of Damages (from Makkot), Holy Things and Purities.* (Atlanta, 1993: Scholars Press for South Florida Studies in the History of Judaism.)

II. *The Tosefta, Tractate Abot, and the Earlier Midrash-Compilations: Sifra, Sifré to Numbers, and Sifré to Deuteronomy.* (Atlanta, 1993: Scholars Press for South Florida Studies in the History of Judaism.)

III. *The Later Midrash-Compilations: Genesis Rabbah, Leviticus Rabbah and Pesiqta deRab Kahana.* (Atlanta, 1994: Scholars Press for South Florida Studies in the History of Judaism.)

IV. *The Latest Midrash-Compilations: Song of Songs Rabbah, Ruth Rabbah, Esther Rabbah I, and Lamentations Rabbati. And The Fathers According to Rabbi Nathan.* (Atlanta, 1994: Scholars Press for South Florida Studies in the History of Judaism.)

V.   *The Talmuds of the Land of Israel and Babylonia.* (Atlanta, 1994: Scholars Press for South Florida Studies in the History of Judaism.)
     The Judaism the Rabbis Take for Granted. (Atlanta, 1995: Scholars Press for South Florida Studies in the History of Judaism.)

Neusner, J, *Mishnah = A History of the Mishnaic Law of Purities.* (Leiden, 1974–77: Brill. I-XXII.)

I.   *Kelim. Chapters One through Eleven.* 1974.
II.   *Kelim. Chapters Twelve through Thirty.* 1974.
III.   *Kelim. Literary and Historical Problems.* 1974.
IV.   *Ohalot. Commentary.* 1975.
V.   *Ohalot. Literary and Historical Problems.* 1975.
VI.   *Negaim. Mishnah-Tosefta.* 1975.
VII.   *Negaim. Sifra.* 1975.
VIII.   *Negaim. Literary and Historical Problems.* 1975.
IX.   *Parah. Commentary.* 1976.
X.   *Parah. Literary and Historical Problems.* 1976.
XI.   *Tohorot. Commentary,* 1976.
XII.   *Tohorot. Literary and Historical Problems.* 1976.
XIII.   *Miqvaot. Commentary.* 1976.
XIV.   *Miqvaot. Literary and Historical Problems.* 1976.
XV.   *Niddah. Commentary.* 1976.
XVI.   *Niddah. Literary and Historical Problems.* 1976.
XVII.   *Makhshirin.* 1977.
XVIII   *Zabim.* 1977.
XIX.   *Tebul Yom. Yadayim.* 1977.
XX.   *Uqsin. Cumulative Index, Parts I–XX.* 1977.

A History of the Mishnaic Law of Holy Things. (Leiden, 1985: Brill. I–VI.)

I.   *Zebahim. Translation and Explanation.*
II.   *Menahot. Translation and Explanation.*
III.   *Hullin, Bekhorot. Translation and Explanation.*
IV.   *Arakhin, Temurah. Translation and Explanation.*
V.   *Keritot, Meilah, Tamid, Middot, Qinnim. Translation and Explanation.*

A History of the Mishnaic Law of Women. (Leiden, 1979–1980: Brill. I–V.)

I.   *Yebamot. Translation and Explanation.*
II.   *Ketubot. Translation and Explanation.*
III.   *Nedarim, Nazir. Translation and Explanation.*
IV.   *Sotah, Gittin, Qiddushin. Translation and Explanation.*

A History of the Mishnaic Law of Appointed Times. (Leiden, 1981–1983: Brill. I–V.)

I.   *Shabbat. Translation and Explanation.*

II.   *Erubin, Pesahim. Translation and Explanation.*
III. *Sheqalim, Yoma, Sukkah. Translation and Explanation.*
IV.   *Besah, Rosh Hashanah, Taanit, Megillah, Moed Qatan, Hagigah. Translation and Explanation.*

A History of the Mishnaic Law of Damages. (Leiden, 1983–1985: Brill. I–V.)

I.   *Baba Qamma. Translation and Explanation.*
II.   *Baba Mesia. Translation and Explanation.*
III. *Baba Batra, Sanhedrin, Makkot. Translation and Explanation.*
IV.   *Shebuot, Eduyyot, Abodah Zarah, Abot, Horayyot. Translation and Explanation.*

Neusner, J, *Jerusalem* = *Jerusalem and Athens: The Congruity of Talmudic and Classical Philosophy.* (Leiden, 1997: Brill.) *Supplements to the Journal for the Study of Judaism.*

Neusner, J, *Philosophy* = *Judaism as Philosophy. The Method and Message of the Mishnah.* (Columbia, 1991: University of South Carolina Press. Paperback edition: Baltimore, 1999: The Johns Hopkins University Press.)

Neusner, J, *Presence* = *Presence of the Past, the Pastness of the Present. History, Time, and Paradigm in Rabbinic Judaism.* (Bethesda, 1996: CDL Press.)

Neusner, J, *Religious Commentary* + Volume and Part Number = Jacob Neusner, *The Halakhah of the Oral Torah. A Religious Commentary*, Introduction and Volume I. *Between Israel and God. Part One. Thanksgiving: Tractate Berakhot. Enlandisement: Tractates Kilayim, Shebi'it, and 'Orlah.* (Atlanta, 1997: Scholars Press for South Florida Studies in the History of Judaism.)

Volume I.   *Between Israel and God. Part Two. Possession and Partnership. Tractates Ma'aserot and Terumot.* (Atlanta, 1999: Scholars Press for South Florida Studies in the History of Judaism.)

Volume I.   *Between Israel and God. Part Three. Possession and Partnership: Tractates Hallah, Ma'aser Sheni, and Bikkurim.* (Atlanta, 1999: Scholars Press for South Florida Studies in the History of Judaism.)

Volume I.   *Between Israel and God. Part Four. Possession and Partnership: Tractates Pe'ah and Dema'i.* (Atlanta, 1999: Scholars Press for South Florida Studies in the History of Judaism.)

Volume I.   *Between Israel and God. Part Five. Transcendent Transactions: Meeting God without the Land. Tractates Sheqalim, Arakhin, and Ta'anit.* (Atlanta, 1999: Scholars Press for South Florida Studies in the History of Judaism.)

Volume I.   *Between Israel and God. Part Six. Transcendent Transactions: Where Heaven and Earth Intersect. Tractate Zebahim.* (Atlanta,

1999: Scholars Press for South Florida Studies in the History of Judaism.)

Volume I.   *Between Israel and God.* Part Seven. *Transcendent Transactions: Where Heaven and Earth Intersect. Tractate Menahot.* (Atlanta, 1999: Scholars Press for South Florida Studies in the History of Judaism.)

Volume I.   *Between Israel and God.* Part Eight. *Transcendent Transactions: Where Heaven and Earth Intersect. Tractates Tamid and Yoma.* (Atlanta, 1999: Scholars Press for South Florida Studies in the History of Judaism.)

Volume I.   *Between Israel and God.* Part Nine. *Transcendent Transactions: Where Heaven and Earth Intersect. Tractates Hagigah, Bekhorot and Me'ilah.* (Atlanta, 1999: Scholars Press for South Florida Studies in the History of Judaism.)

Volume I.   *Between Israel and God.* Part Ten. *Transcendent Transactions: Where Heaven and Earth Intersect. Tractates Temurah, Megillah, and Rosh Hashanah.* (Atlanta, 1999: Scholars Press for South Florida Studies in the History of Judaism.)

Volume II.   *Within Israel's Social Order.* Part One. *Civil Society. Repairing Damage to, Preserving the Perfection of, the Social Order. Tractates Baba Qamma, Baba Mesia, and Baba Batra.* (Atlanta, 1999: Scholars Press for South Florida Studies in the History of Judaism.)

Volume II.   *Within Israel's Social Order.* Part Two. *Protecting the Commonwealth: Idolators, Sinners and Criminals and the Courts. Tractates Sanhedrin-Makkot and Shebuot.* (Atlanta, 1999: Scholars Press for South Florida Studies in the History of Judaism.)

Volume II.   *Within Israel's Social Order.* Part Three. *Protecting the Commonwealth: Idolators, Sinners and Criminals and the Courts Tractates Keritot and Horayot. The Outsider. Tractate Abodah Zarah.* (Atlanta, 1999: Scholars Press for South Florida Studies in the History of Judaism.)

Volume III.   *Inside the Walls of the Israelite Household.* Part One. *At the Meeting of Time and Space. Tractates Shabbat and Erubin.* (Atlanta, 1999: Scholars Press for South Florida Studies in the History of Judaism.)

Volume III.   *Inside the Walls of the Israelite Household.* Part Two. *At the Meeting of Time and Space. Tractates Pesahim, Sukkah, Mo'ed Qatan, and Besah.* (Atlanta, 1999: Scholars Press for South Florida Studies in the History of Judaism.)

Volume III. *Inside the Walls of the Israelite Household.* Part Three. *Sanctification in the Here and Now. The Table and the Bed. Tractates Hullin, Qiddushin, and Ketubot.* (Atlanta, 1999: Scholars Press for South Florida Studies in the History of Judaism.)

Volume III. *Inside the Walls of the Israelite Household. Part Four. Sanctification and the Marital Bond. Tractates Nedarim, Nazir and Sotah.* (Atlanta, 1999: Scholars Press for South Florida Studies in the History of Judaism.)

Volume III. *Inside the Walls of the Israelite Household. Part Five. The Desacralization of the Household. The Bed. Tractates Gittin and Yebamot.* (Atlanta, 1999: Scholars Press for South Florida Studies in the History of Judaism.)

Volume III. *Inside the Walls of the Israelite Household. Part Six. The Desacralization of the Household.. Foci of Uncleanness. The Table. Tractate Kelim.* (Atlanta, 1999: Scholars Press for South Florida Studies in the History of Judaism.)

Volume III. *Inside the Walls of the Israelite Household. Part Seven. The Desacralization of the Household. Foci of Uncleanness. The Table. Tractates Uqsin and Tohorot.* (Atlanta, 1999: Scholars Press for South Florida Studies in the History of Judaism.)

Volume III. *Inside the Walls of the Israelite Household. Part Eight. The Desacralization of the Household. Sources of Uncleanness, Dissemination of Uncleanness. Tractates Ohalot and Makhshirin.* (Atlanta, 1999: Scholars Press for South Florida Studies in the History of Judaism.)

Volume III. *Inside the Walls of the Israelite Household. Part Nine. The Desacralization of the Household. Animate Sources of Uncleanness. Tractates Zabim and Niddah.* (Atlanta, 1999: Scholars Press for South Florida Studies in the History of Judaism.)

Volume III. *Inside the Walls of the Israelite Household. Part Ten. Animate Sources of Uncleanness. Tractates Negaim, Tebul Yom, and Yadayim.* (Atlanta, 1999: Scholars Press for South Florida Studies in the History of Judaism.)

Volume III. *Inside the Walls of the Israelite Household. Part Eleven. Purification from the Pollution of Death. Tractates Parah and Miqvaot.* (Atlanta, 1999: Scholars Press for South Florida Studies in the History of Judaism.)

Neusner, J, *Scripture = Scripture and the Generative Premises of the Halakhah. A Systematic Inquiry. I. Halakhah Based Principally on Scripture and Halakhic Categories Autonomous of Scripture.*

Scripture and the Generative Premises of the Halakhah. A Systematic Inquiry. II. *Scripture's Topics Derivatively Amplified in the Halakhah.*
Scripture and the Generative Premises of the Halakhah. A Systematic Inquiry. III. *Scripture's Topics Independently Developed in the Halakhah. From the Babas through Miqvaot.*
Scripture and the Generative Premises of the Halakhah. A Systematic Inquiry. IV. *Scripture's Topics Independently Developed in the Halakhah. From Moed Qatan through Zebahim.*

Neusner, J, *Theology/Halakhah = The Theology of the Halakhah.* (Forthcoming from the University of Chicago Press.)
Neusner, J, *Theology/Oral Torah= The Theology of the Oral Torah: Revealing the Justice of God.* (Kingston and Montreal, 1999: McGill and Queens University Press.)
Neusner, J, *Tosefta = The Tosefta. Translated from the Hebrew.* (New York, 1977–80: Ktav. II–VI.)

II. *The Tosefta. Translated from the Hebrew. Second Division. Moed.*
III. *The Tosefta. Translated from the Hebrew. Third Division. Nashim.*
IV. *The Tosefta. Translated from the Hebrew. Fourth Division. Neziqin.*
V. *The Tosefta. Translated from the Hebrew. Fifth Division. Qodoshim.* Second printing: Atlanta, 1997: Scholars Press for USF Academic Commentary Series.
VI *The Tosefta. Translated from the Hebrew. Sixth Division. Tohorot.* Second printing: Atlanta, 1990: Scholars Press for *South Florida Studies in the History of Judaism.* With a new preface.

Neusner, J, *Transformation = Transformation of Judaism. From Philosophy to Religion.* (Champaign, 1992: University of Illinois Press.)
Neusner, J, *Yerushalmi = The Talmud of the Land of Israel. A Preliminary Translation and Explanation.* (Chicago: The University of Chicago Press: 1982–93. IX–XII, XIV–XV, XVII–XXXV.)

IX. *Hallah.* 1991
X. *Orlah. Bikkurim.* 1991.
XI. *Shabbat.* 1991.
XII. *Erubin.* 1990.
XIV. *Yoma.* 1990.
XV. *Sheqalim.* 1990.
XVII. *Sukkah.* 1988.
XVIII. *Besah. Taanit.* 1987.
XIX. *Megillah.* 1987.
XX. *Hagigah. Moed Qatan.* 1986.
XXI. *Yebamot.* 1986.
XXII. *Ketubot.* 1985.

XXIII.   *Nedarim.* 1985.
XXIV.   *Nazir.* 1985.
XXV.   *Gittin.* 1985
XXVI.   *Qiddushin.* 1984.
XXVII. *Sotah.* 1984.
XXVIII *Baba Qamma.* 1984.
XXIX.   *Baba Mesia.* 1984.
XXX.   *Baba Batra.* 1984.
XXXI.   *Sanhedrin. Makkot.* 1984.
XXXII. *Shebuot.* 1983.
XXXIII *Abodah Zarah.* 1982.
XXXIV *Horayot. Niddah.* 1982.

Neusner, J, *Zoroastrianism* = *Judaism and Zoroastrianism at the Dusk of Late Antiquity. How Two Ancient Faiths Wrote Down Their Great Traditions.* (Atlanta, 1993: Scholars Press for South Florida Studies in the History of Judaism.)

Newman, *Shebi'it* = Louis E. Newman, *The Sanctity of the Seventh Year: A Study of Mishnah Tractate Shebiit* (Chico, 1983: Scholars Press for Brown Judaic Studies.)

Rubenstein, Margaret Wenig, "A Commentary on Mishnah-Tosefta Bikkurim Chapters One and Two," in William Scott Green, ed., *Approaches to Ancient Judaism.* III. *Text as Context in Early Rabbinic Literature* (Chico, 1981: Scholars Press for Brown Judaic Studies, pp. 47–88.)

Sarason, *Mishnah* = Richard S. Sarason, *A History of the Mishnaic Law of Agriculture. Section Three. A Study of Tractate Demai. Part One. Commentary* (Leiden, 1979: E. J. Brill. Studies in Judaism in Late Antiquity, Volume XXVII. Edited by Jacob Neusner.)

Sarason, *Yerushalmi* = Richard S. Sarason, *The Talmud of the Land of Israel. A Preliminary Translation and Explanation. Volume 3. Demai,* translated by Richard S. Sarason (Chicago, 1993: The University of Chicago Press.)

Weiner, David, "A Study of Mishnah Tractate Bikkurim Chapter Three," in William Scott Green, ed., *Approaches to Ancient Judaism.* III. *Text as Context in Early Rabbinic Literature* (Chico, 1981: Scholars Press for Brown Judaic Studies, pp. 89–104.)

Wilken = Robert L. Wilken, *John Chrysostom and the Jews: Rhetoric and Reality in the Late Fourth Century* (Berkeley and Los Angeles, 1983: University of California Press.)

INDEX

Abba Yose b. Hanan: topics in the Torah constituting law 31

agriculture: Mishnaic laws of 79, 83; Peah, corner of the field 79; sabbatical year for the land of Israel; tithing 79

Appointed times: Mishnaic laws of 79–80, 83; revision of laws about rite and cult after destruction of the Temple 109–19

Aqiba and sayings of Moses at Sinai 2–3, 24, 26

Avery-Peck, Alan J.: God sharing man's production from the Land of Israel 56; Sabbath day of rest for mankind Sabbatical year for the land of Israel 33–37

Childs, Brevard 27

City of God: promise of citizenship in 19–20; sages writing law in 15

cleanness and uncleanness, Mishnaic law of 89–90

cultic cleanness: Mishnaic law 80–81; of offerings from the Land of Israel 63–78; red heifer and purification water 65–78

damages, Mishnaic law 86–89

debts, freedom from responsibility for 33, 38

dough-offering 79; God sharing man's produce from the Land of Israel 59–65; man sharing with priestly cult 54–59

Eden: classification for orderly arrangement of species of animal and vegetable life 46–50

Edenic narrative translated into a system for governance 39–46; forgiveness of sin 20; Rabbinic Judaism's response to the Pentateuch within a Holy social order 13–16; requirements for restoration 13–16, 20; restoration with orderly classification of animal and vegetable life 46–50; sanctified place in Sabbath repose 31–39

eschatology: atonement and redemption of the individual and Israel 21; Pentateuchal Stage of Rabbinic Judaism 1–27

Halakhah: absolution of vows 30–31; Edenic narrative translated into a system for governance 38–40; intentional and inadvertent violation of 122–36; Mishnah and Pentateuch organizing construction of the law of Judaism 28–78; Oral Torah providing for its formation 15; remission of debts 33, 38; written by sages in *City of God* 15

Hallah *see* dough-offering

224